MW01169328

A VICTORIAN READER

A VICTORIAN READER

Edited by
Peter Faulkner

B. T. Batsford Ltd · London

Selection and editorial matter
© Peter Faulkner 1989

First published 1989

All rights reserved. No part of this publication
may be reproduced, in any form or by any means,
without permission from the Publisher

Typeset by J&L Composition Ltd, Filey, North Yorkshire
and printed in Great Britain by
Billings, Worcester

Published by B. T. Batsford Ltd
4 Fitzhardinge Street, London W1H OAH

A CIP catalogue for this book is
available from the British Library

ISBN 0 7134 5804 6 (cased)
0 7134 5805 4 (limp)

CONTENTS

8   *Contents*

ACKNOWLEDGEMENT

The author and publisher would like to thank Manchester University Press for permission to print extracts from *The Letters of Mrs Gaskell*, ed. J.A.V. Chapple and Arthur Pollard, 1966.

A CHRONOLOGY OF PUBLICATIONS 1830–70

* indicates texts included in this volume

CREATIVE	CRITICAL
1830 Bulwer Lytton, *Paul Clifford* Tennyson, *Peoms, Chiefly Lyrical*	
1831 Peacock, *Crotchet Castle*	* Hallam on Tennyson
1832 Bulwer Lytton, *Eugene Aram* Tennyson, *Poems*	
1833 Browning, *Pauline* Carlyle, *Sartor Resartus*	* Mill, 'The Two Kinds of Poetry'
1834 Bulwer Lytton, *Last Days of Pompeii* Taylor, *Philip van Artevelde*	* Taylor, Preface
1835 Browning, *Paracelsus*	
1836 Dickens, *Pickwick Papers* (to 1837)	
1837 Carlyle, *The French Revolution* Dickens, *Oliver Twist* (to 1839)	

CREATIVE

CRITICAL

1838
Dickens, *Nicholas Nickleby*
 (to 1839)

* Bulwer Lytton, 'On Art in
 Fiction'

1839
Thackeray, *Catherine* (to 1840)

1840
Browning, *Sordello*
Dickens, *Old Curiosity Shop*
 (to 1841)

1841
Browning, *Pippa Passes*
Carlyle, *On Heroes, Hero-
 Worship, and the Heroic in
 History*
Dickens, *Barnaby Rudge*

* Carlyle, 'The Hero as Man
 of Letters'

* Dickens, Introduction to
 the Third Edition of
 Oliver Twist

1842
Tennyson, *Poems*

1843
Carlyle, *Past and Present*
Dickens, *Martin Chuzzlewit*
 (to 1844)

Ruskin, *Modern Painters I*

1844
Elizabeth Barrett, *Poems*
Disraeli, *Coningsby*
Thackeray, *Barry Lyndon*

Horne, *The New Spirit of the
 Age*

1845
Carlyle, *Oliver Cromwell*
Disraeli, *Sybil*

CREATIVE   **CRITICAL**

1846
Dickens, *Dombey and Son*
  (to 1848)

1847
Currer Bell (Charlotte Brontë),
  Jane Eyre
Acton Bell (Emily Brontë),
  Wuthering Heights
Thackeray, *Vanity Fair*
  (to 1848)

1848
Acton Bell (Anne Brontë),
  The Tenant of Wildfell Hall
Gaskell, *Mary Barton*   * Gaskell, Preface to *Mary
Kingsley, *Yeast*   *Barton*
Thackeray, *Pendennis* (to
  1850)

1849
Arnold, *The Strayed Reveller* Ruskin, *Seven Lamps of
Currer Bell (Charlotte   Architecture*
  Brontë), *Shirley*
Dickens, *David Copperfield*
  (to 1850)

1850
Carlyle, *Latter-Day Pamphlets* * Thackeray, Preface to
Kingsley, *Alton Locke*   *Pendennis*
W.M. Rossetti (Editor), *The*   * C. Brontë, Preface to the
  Germ   Second Edition of
Tennyson, *In Memoriam*   *Wuthering Heights*

1851
Gaskell, *Cranford*   Ruskin, *Stones of Venice I*
Meredith, *Poems*   (to *III*, 1853)

CREATIVE   CRITICAL

1852

Arnold, *Empedocles on Etrea*   * Browning, *Essay on Shelley*
Dickens, *Bleak House*   Dallas, *Poetics: an Essay on*
  (to 1853)   *Poetry*
Thackeray, *Henry Esmond*

1853

Arnold, *Poems*   * Arnold, Preface to *Poems*
Currer Bell (Charlotte Brontë)* Clough, review of recent
  Villette   poems
Gaskell, *Ruth*   Thackeray, *English*
Thackeray, *The Newcomes*   *Humourists of the*
                                    Eighteenth Century

1854

Dickens, *Hard Times*   * Arnold, Preface to Second
Gaskell, *North and South*   Edition of *Poems*

1855

Browning, *Men and Women*
Dickens, *Little Dorrit* (to 1857)
Tennyson, *Maud*
Trollope, *The Warden*

1856

Reade, *It is Never Too Late*   * Eliot 'German Life' and
to Mend   'Silly Novels'
                                  Ruskin, *Modern Painters III*

1857

Elizabeth Barrett Browning,   * Arnold, 'On the Modern
  Aurora Leigh   Element in Literature'
Eliot, *Scenes of Clerical Life*
Trollope, *Barchester Towers*

1858

Carlyle, *Frederick the Great* * Lewes, 'Realism in Art'
  I & II (to 1865)
Clough, *Amours de Voyage*

CREATIVE   CRITICAL

1859

Collins, *The Woman in White* Masson, *British Novelists*
(to 1860)   *since Scott*
Dickens, *A Tale of Two Cities*
Eliot, *Adam Bede*
Meredith, *The Ordeal of*
Richard Feverel
Tennyson, *Idylls of the King*
(to 1885)

1860

Dickens, *Great Expectations* Thackeray, *Roundabout*
(to 1861)   *Papers* (to 1862)
Eliot, *The Mill on the Floss*
Trollope, *Framley Parsonage*
(to 1861)

1861

Eliot, *Silas Marner*   Arnold, *On Translating*
Palgrave (Editor), *The*   *Homer*
Golden Treasury   * Collins, Preface to *The*
Trollope, *Orley Farm* (to 1862) *Woman in White*

1862

Collins, *No Name*   * Swinburne, review of
Eliot, *Romola* (to 1863)   Baudelaire
Meredith, *Modern Love*
Christina Rossetti, *Goblin*
Market

1863

Gaskell, *Sylvia's Lovers*

1864

Browning, *Dramatis Personae* * Bagehot, 'Sterne and
Dickens, *Our Mutual Friend*   Thackeray' and 'Pure,
(to 1865)   Ornate and Grotesque
Gaskell, *Wives and Daughters* Poetry'
(to 1866)

CREATIVE

CRITICAL

Tennyson, *Enoch Arden*

1865

Trollope, *The Belton Estate*
Swinburne, *Atalanta in Calydon*

* Arnold, *Essays in Criticism*
Lewes, *Principles of Success in Literature*
Ruskin, *Sesame and Lilies*

1866

Eliot, *Felix Holt the Radical*
Swinburne, *Poems and Ballads*

Dallas, *The Gay Science*
* Morley, 'Mr Swinburne's New Poems'
* Swinburne, *Notes on Poems and Reviews*

1867

Arnold, *New Poems*
Morris, *The Life and Death of Jason*
Trollope, *Phineas Finn* (to 1869)

Arnold, *On the Study of Celtic Literature*
Carlyle, 'Shooting Niagara: and After?'

1868

Browning, *The Ring and the Book*
Collins, *The Moonstone*
Morris, *The Earthly Paradise* I (to IV, 1870)
Trollope, *He Knew He was Right*

* Pater, 'Poems by William Morris'

1869

Tennyson, *The Holy Grail*

Arnold, *Culture and Anarchy*
Mill, *On the Subjection of Women*

1870

Dickens, *Edwin Drood* (unfinished)

Austin, *The Poetry of the Period*

INTRODUCTION

The purpose of this volume is to bring together in convenient form passages from Victorian writers which provide a basis for understanding the principles on which Victorian literature was written, to the extent that its practitioners were conscious of these. A feature of the period, however, which makes a strong contrast with the Romantic writers immediately beforehand and the Modernists afterwards, was that Victorian writers were on the whole less concerned to put forward their ideas in this area with the polemical vigour of, say, Wordsworth and Shelley, or Eliot and Woolf. Victorian writers did not characteristically define themselves by polemics against their predecessors. They seem to have been involved in the more contained process of working out their principles in practice, modifying but not often directly attacking the approaches of their predecessors, though Arnold was not alone in his critique of Romanticism. But if the Victorian period produced no Preface to *The Lyrical Ballads* or 'Mr Bennett and Mrs Brown', it did produce a number of expressions of literary principle, attention to which can help us to understand better the creative work of the Victorian poets and novelists.

During this period a major change was occurring, in the displacement of poetry by the novel as the most significant literary form. (Drama remained less important than either, despite the vitality of many types of theatre.) Whereas the great Romantics were poets, with the novelists Scott and Austen in the critical background at the time, the great Victorian novelists gained a popularity and authority not equalled by contemporary poets, despite the achievements of Tennyson and Browning. Thus in 1849, when R. H. Horne published *The New Spirit of the Age* – a work, written in conjunction with Elizabeth Barrett, modelled on Hazlitt's *The Spirit of the Age* (1825) – he registered the change of attitude in his chapter on G. P. R. James[1] and other historical novelists:

Prose fiction has acquired a more respectable status within the last half-century than it held at any previous period in English literature. Very grave people, who set up to be thought wiser than their neighbours, are no longer ashamed to be caught reading a novel. The reason is plain enough. It is not that your conventional reader has abated a jot of his dignity, or relaxed a single prejudice in favour of 'light reading', but that the novel itself has undergone a complete revolution. It is no longer a mere fantasy of the imagination, a dreamy pageant of unintelligible sentiments and impossible incidents; but a sensible book, insinuating in an exceedingly agreeable form ... a great deal of useful knowledge, historical, social and moral.[2]

Not everyone shared Horne's belief in the improved qualities of contemporary fiction, but there was no denying its popularity, greatly extended by the achievement of Dickens from the 1837 publication of *Pickwick Papers* onwards. By 1866, when E. S. Dallas published his work on criticism, *The Gay Science*, he noted the enormous bulk of fiction. 'There has never been anything like it before',[3] he wrote. The difference between the fortunes of fiction and poetry in the period can be clearly felt in the two essays of 1864 by Walter Bagehot of which parts are included here (Nos. 30 and 31). In 'Sterne and Thackeray', Bagehot has no hesitation in claiming that although the eighteenth-century novelist Sterne has some admirable qualities, his fiction falls well below the standard required in a Victorian novelist. Sterne may excel in 'mere simple description of common sensitive human actions', but he has several defects, of which the worst is 'the fantastic disorder of the form'. Bagehot has no doubt that Sterne's lack of orderly narrative sequence (which has attracted so much admiration from more recent critics like

Virginia Woolf and Victor Shklovsky) is a defect, and that George Eliot's manner in *Adam Bede* is superior: 'she has no loose lumps of beauty; she puts in nothing at random'. Sterne is criticized also for 'indecency'. Here Bagehot has some interesting observations on the changes of taste since the eighteenth century which meant that the acceptable subject-matter of fiction had become more restricted. He sees some problems in modern reticence, but also regards it as inevitable: 'as soon as works of fiction are addressed to boys and girls, they must be fit for boys and girls. . . .' Bagehot does not explain how this change of audience has occurred, and despite his reservations about it – 'the habitual formation of a scheme of thought and a code of morality upon incomplete materials is a very serious evil' – he can see no alternative to accepting the resultant restrictions. He is giving classic expression to what seems now to be a highly debatable point of view, and one which will be considered further later on. Here it is only necessary to stress that he sees Sterne's 'indecency' as making him unsuitable for modern reading. Another factor which he argues would by itself make Sterne unacceptable to a Victorian reader is his characterization: *Tristram Shandy* 'contains eccentric characters only'. However entertaining these may be, the reader requires something more normal: in the 'best works' of the 'great masters . . . a constant atmosphere of half commonplace personages surrounds, and shades off, illustrates and explains, every central goup of singular persons'. All in all, Sterne's work is '*provincial*' in its method, its tone, and its characterization. We can see that Bagehot is contrasting Sterne's work with that of contemporary novelists, particularly George Eliot, who had developed the mode that was coming to be recognized as Realism with its orderly sequence and solid characterization. In Bagehot's article, as in writings by Eliot and Lewes included here, the confidence of belief in the quality of the new mode is quite clear, the assumption that its methods can lead the reader to a true insight into 'the world in which we live'.

But if Bagehot feels confidence in the realist mode of

contemporary fiction, when it comes to poetry he is aware mainly of difficulties and problems. His article on Wordsworth, Tennyson and Browning (No. 31) also appeared in 1864. The main thrust of its argument is that contemporary poetry is no longer capable of the 'purity' attributed to Wordsworth, Milton and Shelly. Instead there is the 'ornate' mode of Tennyson, characterized not by 'choice and selection, but by accumulation and aggregation'. In *Enoch Arden* the story is a simple one, but Tennyson enlarges and decorates it by 'giving to every incident in the volume an accompanying commentary'. Bagehot goes on to refer to Arnold's criticism of the complexities of Shakespeare's style (see No. 20), but finds 'an infinity of pure art in Shakespeare, although there is a great deal else too'. He argues that some kinds of subject-matter need to be dealt with in the ornate manner, namely 'Illusion, half-belief, unpleasant types, imperfect types', but it is hard to feel that he really believes, as he here asserts, that a 'romantic art' of this kind is really as valuable as 'pure' art. When he comes to his next category, 'grotesque art', which is represented for him by Browning's *Dramatis Personae*, Bagehot is still more evidently divided: he is impressed by Browning's 'great mind' – 'He has applied a hard strong intellect to real life. . . . He has striven to know what *is* . . .' – but uneasy about his tendency to deal with 'abnormal specimens'. Thus the ending of the essay gives a negative view of the reading public quite unlike that assumed in relation to the novel: 'We live in the realm of the *half* educated. The number of readers grows daily, but the quality of readers does not improve rapidly.' In such conditions, 'ornate' and 'grotesque' writing will have a stronger appeal than pure art: showiness is all. Bagehot partly blames this state of affairs on the influence of women as readers: 'women . . . ever prefer a delicate unreality to a true or firm art'. The patriachal assumptions here, and in other material included, will be discussed later. But what is obvious is that while Bagehot was sure that nineteenth-century fiction was a marked improvement on that of the eighteenth century because of its embodiment of the new critical principles, he was puzzled as well as impressed by the poetry of the age, and felt that the principles on which it was based were open to serious objections.

The contrast pointed out by this consideration of Bagehot's two essays is typical, as other material included here shows. Though there might be signs of an emerging consensus about the desirable qualities of a novel, there was far less agreement in relation to poetry, and the two best-known poets of the age, Tennyson and Browning, were regularly contrasted with each other. Even at the beginning of the period, before these poets were established, there was a marked tendency for criticism to operate in terms of a clear-cut contrast. Thus in the earliest passage included (No. 1), Hallam is arguing in 1831 that there are two main types of poetry, 'poetry of reflection', represented by Wordsworth, and 'poetry of sensation', represented by Keats, Shelley and the young Tennyson. Hallam is dismissive of Wordsworth's use of poetry to convey moral and social ideas, preferring a 'pure' poetry which is non-didactic and concerned only with its own beauty. Readers, it is suggested, prefer 'impure' art because it is easier, less demanding. Two years later, in 1833, the young philosopher John Stuart Mill employed a similar contrast in two articles in *The Monthly Repository*. The second, reprinted here (No. 2), is entitled 'The Two Kinds of Poetry' and is based on a contrast similar to Hallam's, referring again to Wordsworth as against Shelley. Wordsworth is seen as an example of 'a cultivated but not naturally poetic mind' in whose poems 'the thought itself is still the conspicuous object', so that he resembles 'any other didactic author' who wants to convey his ideas and uses what he considers the most appropriate language to do so. Shelley, by contrast, is simply a poet; he 'mostly pours forth the overflowing of his feelings; and all the thoughts which these feelings suggest are floated promiscuously along the stream'. Mill's argument depends on assumptions about the relation of language to thought and feelings which seem questionable today. But we can clearly see the way Victorian ideas about poetry were based on what appears at first to be a very simple antithesis, between the didactic and the 'pure' poet.

However, it is important to see that this did not necessarily involve a value judgement in favour of the latter. Mill refers to Wordsworth and Shelley as 'the two authors of our own day who have produced the greatest quantity of true and enduring poetry'. Mill the philosopher, unlike Hallam the defender of Tennyson, is simply establishing categories. Thus there is no inconsistency in the fact that the essay ends with the argument that the writer whom Mill terms 'the logician poet' – such as Milton or Coleridge – in whom a 'poetic nature has been united with a logical and scientific culture' should be superior to 'the mere poet', because 'it would be absurd to doubt that two endowments are better than one' (though the situation is complicated for Mill by what he regards as the disastrous imperfections of contemporary education). And so it is no contradiction, though it is at first a surprise, to find Mill two years later in 1835 (No. 3) advising Tennyson to 'cultivate, and with no half devotion, philosophy as well as poetry', on the grounds that 'every poet who has extensively or permanently influenced mankind, has been a great thinker'. By now Mill has moved a long way from Hallam's position. Tennyson's development as a poet shows his own concern *not* to remain merely a 'poet of sensation'. Although Tennyson made no full-length exposition of his view of poetry, he did respond to the advice often given him by critics[4] to concern himself with social issues. The early poem 'The Palace of Art' is usually seen as Tennyson's response to the assertion of his friend R. C. Trench: 'Tennyson, we cannot live in art.'[5] It tells how the poet's soul builds a beautiful palace in which she is tempted to seclude herself from the problems and sufferings of the world outside, but comes to notice that the 'riddle of the painful earth' must not be ignored. After four years purgation she flings away her royal robes:

> "Make me a cottage in the vale," she said,
>   "Where I may mourn and pray

> Yet pull not down my palace towers, that are
>   So lightly, beautifully built;
> Perchance I may return with others there
>   When I have purged my guilt."

The poet recognizes the need for social responsibility, but he also wishes to preserve the beautiful palace that he has created. The tension between these two aspirations, between what we may call the moral and the aesthetic elements, remains central to Tennyson and to other Victorian poets.[6] It was a question susceptible of no simple solution.

A version of the reflection/sensation contrast may be found in Browning's 1852 *Essay on Shelley* (No. 17), his most sustained piece of literary criticism.[7] The distinction Browning makes employs the terms objective and subjective. The objective poet, like Shakespeare, is a 'fashioner', whose effort is 'to reproduce things external (whether the phenomena of the scenic unive se, or the manifested actions of the human heart and brain)'. The subjective poet, like Shelley, is a 'seer', who struggles to convey 'not what man sees, but what God sees – the *Ideas* of Plato, seeds of creation lying burningly on the Divine Hand'. He works by introspection, and what he produces is described as 'an effluence', the flowing and showing forth of his personality. With such poets, therefore, biography assumes a peculiar interest. It is important again to see that the argument here is not simply evaluative: it is unlikely that Browning considered Shelley a greater writer than Shakespeare. Indeed, the essay goes on to assert that both types are valuable to humanity, and that the same poet might employ the two modes in different poems. The passage ends with a suggestion of a kind of historical dialectic between the two modes. We may feel here that Browning is not only giving a clear description of two different kinds of poetry, but also thinking about his own allegiance. He clearly felt the attraction of Shelley's subjectivism, but just as clearly respects the achievement of Shakespeare. The mode of the dramatic monologue which Browning went on to develop in volumes like *Men and Women* (1855) in which a variety of characters express their own views of life, and that of his most ambitious poem *The Ring and the Book* (1868–9) which tells a dramatic story from several points of view, combines both subjective and objective elements.

A simple contrast forms the central argument of Henry Taylor's Preface to his dramatic poem *Philip van Artevelde* (1834). Here Taylor delivers a forthright attack on the poets of the previous generation, Byron and Shelley in particular. They have been very popular, but Taylor suggests that there has been 'an unbounded indulgence in the mere luxuries of poetry' – exciting language and imagery, and melodious versification – at the expense of 'adequate appreciation for its intellectual and immortal part'. Taylor writes in a tone of somewhat pompous indignation, taking up a position diametrically opposed to that of Hallam, though resembling that of Mill when Byron's achievement is said to be limited because 'no man can be a very great poet who is not also a great philosopher'. Byron is also condemned on the moral grounds that his heroes 'are creatures essentially abandoned to their passions'. Shelley is said to have possessed 'a more powerful and expansive imagination' but to have lacked 'a sound understanding and a just judgement'. His followers are dismissed as 'the phantastic school'. Taylor therefore stands for a kind of poetry which will avoid the extravagances he sees in the younger Romantics, and achieve clarity and dignity.

This approach is developed much more subtly and persuasively in the central document of Victorian poetics, Matthew Arnold's Preface to his *Poems* (1853) (No. 20). In the previous year he had published the poem *Empedocles on Etna*, which told of the suicide of the Sicilian philosopher who had become disillusioned with human life. In 1853 Arnold decided not to reissue the poem because it lacked what he now considered essential to a literary work, a significant underlying action. Arnold – whose letters to his friend Arthur Hugh Clough show his concern for a poetry that will achieve a coherence he cannot find in the Romantics (No. 19) – sees the Greek classics as the best models for the modern writer because of their commitment to significant actions as the bases of their works. Arnold goes on to argue that what matters about the action to be chosen for a work of literature is that it should be one that appeals to 'the great primary human affections, to those elementary feelings which subsist permanently in the race, as well as independent of time'. As examples of such actions he gives the stories of Achilles in *The Iliad*, of Clytemnestra in *The Oresteia* of Aeschylus, and of Dido in *The Aeneid*. Because of their innate interest, as Arnold sees it, these actions are better than those of many modern works – though Arnold is not claiming, as his Preface to the Second Edition (No. 21) emphasizes, that only Greek and Roman themes should be written about: what matters is the quality of an action, not its period. Indeed, Arnold went on later to criticize the English Romantics by contrast with the German poet Heine (No. 22) for not having manifested 'the modern spirit', to which it appears English culture was peculiarly recalcitrant.

Arnold's criticism provided an authoritative exposition of what may reasonably be termed a Classical or Aristotelian point of view, emphasizing the importance of dramatic action rather than verbal felicity. Nevertheless there is something restrictive about the position he is taking up: he seems much clearer in criticizing the development of recent English poetry than in opening up an alternative approach, as Clough was attempting to do. Clough's review of the same year (No. 18) remarks on the fact that readers prefer novels like *Vanity Fair* and *Bleak House* to the poetry being written, and suggests that this is because 'to be widely popular ... poetry should deal, more than at present it usually does, with general wants, ordinary feelings, the obvious rather than the rare facts of human nature'. Here he is engaged with a very important Victorian issue, the choice of subject-matter. If writers were often attracted to history, whether Classical or medieval, critics were often insistent on the claims of the present. The short-lived Pre-Raphaelite magazine *The Germ* of 1850 contained a discussion by John Tupper entitled 'The Subject in Art' which attacked 'the many ... attracted to the poetry of things past, yet impervious to the poetry of things present'. The case was put in a series of rhetorical questions:

If, as every poet, every painter, every sculptor will acknowledge, his best and most original ideas are derived from his own time; if his great lessonings to piety, truth, charity, love, honour, honesty, gallantry, generosity, courage, are derived from the same source; why transfer them to distant periods, and make them *not things of today*? Why teach us to revere the saints of old, and not our own family-worshippers? Why admire the lance-armed knight and not the patience-armed hero of misfortune?[8]

But Dante Gabriel Rossetti had contributed the 'medieval' poem 'The Blessed Damozel' to the previous number, and Pre-Raphaelite art was often drawn to medieval subjects. Its poetry, especially, showed that emphasis. William Morris's first volume was called *The Defence of Guenevere and Other Poems* (1856), and Christina Rossetti began with *Goblin Market and Other Poems* (1862). Tennyson meditated on the issue in 'The Epic (Morte d'Arthur)' (1833), and eventually decided to commit himself to the Arthurian subject-matter of *The Idylls of the King* (1859; completed 1885). Ruskin's response (No. 24) was to question the choice of such subject-matter.

Ruskin had also, in *Modern Painters III* (1856) (No. 23) drawn attention to the tendency of contemporary poets, particularly Tennyson, to employ what he termed the 'Pathetic Fallacy', that is, to allow their own or their characters' feelings to colour the accounts given of the external world. Ruskin's objection to Romantic subjectivism led him to admire the Pre-Raphaelites' attempts at Truth to Nature, and brought him close to the Classicism of Arnold, and Bagehot's idea of a pure poetry which is neither ornate nor grotesque.

Of the issues raised by Elizabeth Barrett Browning in *Aurora Leigh* (1856), that of the poet's subject-matter is thus familiar (No. 27). She is on the side of the modern. The poem is articulated by a woman poet, and in Book V she directly challenges the assumption that the past provides suitable material for poetry; the poet's business is with:

> this live, throbbing age,
> That brawls, cheats, maddens, calculates, aspires,
> And spends more passion, more heroic heat
> Betwixt the mirrors of its drawing-rooms,
> Than Roland with his knights at Roncesvalles.
>
> (Lines 203–7)

She also gives a striking account of the relation between life and art for the poet:

> The artist's part is both to be and do,
> Transfixing with a special, central power
> The flat experience of the common man,
> And turning outward, with a sudden wrench,
> Half agony, half ecstasy, the thing
> He feels the inmost, – never felt the less
> Because he sings it.
>
> (Lines 366–73)

Robert Brownings's subjective and objective poets seem to combine here in an art that gives vividness and shape to the 'flat experience of the common man' through his own articulated feelings.

The question of how far poetry should relate to the experience of the common man (taken by many to be the province of the novel) was becoming more controversial. The subversive young Swinburne found in Baudelaire's *Les Fleurs du Mal* in 1862 (No. 33) a poetry which refused social purpose and was the better for it: the 'just and sane view' is that 'the art of poetry has absolutely nothing to do with didactic matter at all'. Critics like John Morley (No. 35) saw this as merely an excuse for immorality and salaciousness. Swinburne in *Poems and Ballads* (1866) often celebrated rapturously the sensuality of characters like Messalina and Faustine, and this provoked Morley to eloquent denunciation of the 'mixed vileness and childishness of depicting the spurious passions of putrescent imagination, the un-named lusts of sated wantons, as if they were the crown of character and their enjoyment the great glory of human life'. Swinburne's reply in *Notes on Poems and Reviews* (No. 34) raises the serious question of the implied censorship of Victorian literature by the claimed necessity to be inoffensive to young readers, particularly girls, so frequently invoked, then and now, by those who wish to limit the range of the permissible. Thackeray had made a similar point in the Preface to *Pendennis* (1850) (No. 13), while Bagehot accepted the situation (No. 30) as a necessary aspect of his society. Swinburne acutely points out that exaggerated claims to morality often accompany prurience: 'Literature, to be worthy of man, must be large, liberal, sincere; and cannot be chaste if it is prudish. Purity and prudery cannot keep house together.'

The argument is of course one that constantly recurs between the exponents of artistic freedom and the defenders of public morals. In the last passage included here, from Walter Pater's 1868 review of Morris's poetry (No. 35), there is a sense of the historical development of romanticism culminating in a poetry whose passion challenges religion itself. But the conclusion relates the poetry to 'the tendency of modern thought' which is seen to be 'to regard all things or principles of things as inconstant modes or fashions'. This extreme relativism leads Pater at the end to suggest that human beings should try to live as vividly as possible, and that this can best be done by developing 'the poetic passion, the desire of beauty, the love of art for art's sake'. In this aestheticism, it would seem, a kind of serenity may be achieved.

The 'love of art for art's sake': if this was the ethos to which poetry might be seen to aspire in 1868 – though it is not one that any of its major practitioners would have accepted – it was certainly not that of the novel. We have seen that by 1864 Bagehot had a confident view of the qualities needed in a good novel (No. 31), namely clarity of structure, acceptable morality, and some sense of human character. These assumptions had been growing throughout this period. The earliest convincing account of the basic requisites is Bulwer Lytton's 'On Art in Fiction' of 1838 (No. 5). He notes that fiction is 'a class of literature now so widely cultivated, and hitherto almost wholly unexamined by the critic'. He was obviously aware of the reviews of fiction that were widely published at the time, but is referring to the absence of discussion of critical principles. His own essay makes sensible remarks on the need for careful thought about the basic conception of a novel and considers some methods of organization. His criticism of Scott as concerned with externals by contrast with Shakespeare's insight into character is based on the assumption that what literature should seek to convey is 'the development of the secret man', that is to say, the inner life. But what is brought out in the discussion of the contrast between drama and fiction which runs throughout the essay is that 'in prose fiction we require more of the Real than we do in the drama (which belongs, of right, to the region of pure poetry)'. That concern with 'the Real' is central to Victorian thinking about fiction, though Lytton is careful to stress that 'We must let the heart be a student as well as the head'. The novelist must observe life *and* respond to what is seen with imaginative sympathy.

We will find concern for 'the Real' in all Victorian critical discussions of fiction, though it will not always be defined in the same way. Dickens, in his Introduction to the Third Edition of *Oliver Twist* (1841) (No. 7), while emphasizing his moral intentions – 'to shew, in little Oliver, the principle of Good surviving through very adverse circumstance, and triumphing at last' – insists that when he came to describe Oliver's criminal associates he had aimed 'to shew them as they really are', depicting the 'miserable reality' which only Hogarth's pictorial art had previously conveyed. Dickens contrasts this with Gay's *The Beggar's Opera*, which presents what he suggests is a glamourized and misleading picture of criminal life. Dickens defends his presentation of Nancy on the same grounds: 'It is true'. Since Dickens is noted for the elements of simplification and exaggeration in his presentation of character, it is all the more striking that he makes the claim in this way. It was a claim made for him also by Horne in *The New Spirit of the Age* in 1844:

As a general summary of the result of Mr Dickens's works, it might be said that they contain a larger number of faithful pictures and records of the middle and lower classes of England of the present period than can be found in any other modern works.[9]

Sometimes Dickens laid greater stress on the element of entertainment in his work, in line with his insistence in *Hard Times* (1854) on the need for Fancy (or imagination) to be allowed a full part in human life. This was an important part of the aim of *Household Words*, the monthly journal Dickens initiated in 1850. In 'A Preliminary Word', he wrote:

No mere utilitarian spirit, no iron binding of the mind to grim realities, will give a harsh tone to our Household Words. In the bosoms of the young and old, of the well-to-do and of the poor, we would tenderly cherish the light of Fancy which is inherent in the human breast. . . . To show to all, that in all familiar things, even in those which are repellent on the surface, there is Romance enough, if we will find it out . . . is the main object of Household Words.[10]

Dickens was no tidy theoretical thinker, and for him the claims to represent the real and to bring out the romance of familiar things were equally valid. He consistently ridiculed, as in the Prefaces to *Martin Chuzzlewit* (1844) and *Little Dorrit* (1857), those who defended themselves against his satirical accounts of society by asserting that he exaggerated. He saw himself as working from a basis of observation. The Preface to *Bleak House* (1853) puts it neatly: 'I have purposely dwelt upon the romantic side of familiar things.'

This could never have been said by Thackeray, Dickens's great contemporary and rival, who aimed deliberately to awaken his readers to the realities of the age. In the Preface to *Pendennis* in 1850 (No. 13) he based his claim to attention on the grounds that 'this person writing strives to tell the truth', and states that a modern novelist cannot be as explicit as Fielding was in the eighteenth century. 'Since the author of *Tom Jones* was buried, no writer of fiction among us has been permitted to depict to his utmost power a MAN. We must drape him, and give him a certain conventional simper. Society will not tolerate the Natural in our Art.' But although Thackeray evidently regrets this state of affairs, he seems to have accepted it is inevitable. What he did was to seek ways round it by challenging the reader to compare the works he was reading with other works of fiction (No. 12) or the ending provided by the novelist with that which the reader who prefers 'fable-land' may provide for himself (No. 14). Thackeray took his vocation seriously, as his 1847 letter to Mark Lemmon (No. 12) shows, but he defined it as that of a satirical–moralist rather than a novelist. We may see this as having given him scope to make the reader approach reality without himself straightforwardly describing 'the Real'.

The problem of defining the reality in which a novelist might be expected to be interested comes out clearly in relation to Thackeray's great admirer, Charlotte Brontë, who described him as 'the first social regenerator of the day' (No. 8). Brontë's well-known comments on Jane Austen (No. 9) show the point at issue: Austen's 'business is not half so much with the human heart as with the human eyes, mouth, hands and feet'. For Brontë, the writer should be concerned with something more than 'the surface of the lives of genteel English people'; she should be concerned with the Passions and the Feelings. This Romantic emphasis is everywhere felt in *Jane Eyre*, which the Preface defends against 'the timorous or carping few' who found the book's power offensive. When it comes to her sister Emily's *Wuthering Heights* (No. 10), however – a novel at the opposite extreme from Austen's – Charlotte Brontë herself feels uneasy. She sees Heathcliff as 'unredeemed; never once swerving from his arrow-straight course to perdition', and doubts whether 'it is right or advisable to create beings like Heathcliff'. But finally she defends his creation on the Romantic grounds that 'the writer who possesses the creative gift owns something of which he is not always master – something that at times strangely wills and works for itself'.

No other Victorian went so far in claiming that the writer was to such a degree the vehicle of inspiration.

Elizabeth Gaskell's remarks in the Preface to her first novel, *Mary Barton* (1848) (No. 15), take us back to the spirit of Dickens: 'I bethought me how deep might be the romance in the lives of some of those who elbowed me daily in the busy streets of the town in which I resided.' Living in Manchester she has become aware of the strength of class feelings, and she wants 'to give some utterance to the agony which, from time to time, convulses this dumb people'. She is careful to plead ignorance of political economy, but asserts, 'I have tried to write truthfully' – a typical claim, as we have seen. Elizabeth Gaskell's Manchester novels are rightly seen as related to others directly concerned with social issues published at the time, including Disraeli's *Coningsby* (1844) and *Sybil* (1845), and Kingsley's *Yeast* (1848) and *Alton Locke* (1850), which all bear witness to the increased popularity and assumed social influence of fiction. In his 1849 Preface to the Fifth Edition of *Coningsby*, Disraeli noted:

It was not originally the intention of the writer to adopt the form of fiction as the instrument to scatter his suggestions, but, after reflection, he resolved to avail himself of a method which, in the temper of the times, offered the best chance of influencing opinion.[11]

Mrs Gaskell's 1859 letter (No. 16) gives practical advice on novel-writing which emphasizes the importance of plot and the necessity for clarity: the imagined scene must become 'a reality' to the writer. The advice indicates the norms accepted for novels at the time.

These were indeed the years in which these novels were finding their most authoritative expression, in the writings of George Eliot and, to a lesser extent, Anthony Trollope. Eliot is now known as the great Victorian realist because of the sequence of novels from *Adam Bede* (1859) to *Middlemarch* (1872). These novels contain reflections on the art of fiction, especially in Chapter 17 of the former, 'In

which the Story pauses a little' to allow the novelist to
comment on the value of Dutch art, with its attention to
everyday human life. But before starting – with Lewes's
encouragement – to write fiction, Eliot had already published a number of discussions of it, of which the two most
important are included in part here. Both were published in
The Westminster Review in 1856. The earlier, which discusses two books by a German sociologist (No. 25), gives us
the clearest statement in English of the desirability of
Realism. The central argument is that 'the real characteristics of the working classes' are hardly known, and that
English critics consistently misinterpret and sentimentalize
them. Even 'our social novels' fail to represent 'the people
as they are'. The artist's or writer's greatest power is 'the
extension of our sympathies', but this can only be brought
about by accurate representation. Even Dickens is said to
fail here. He 'is gifted with the utmost power of rendering
the external traits of our town population', but when he
deals with 'the emotional and the tragic', he becomes
'transcendent in his unreality'. This severe criticism is based
on the belief that accurate knowledge of the habits, ideas
and motives of the people is what is needed, and what might
be provided by the novelist. This was indeed the task to
which 'George Eliot' was to devote all her splendid powers.

The second, well-known article 'Silly Novels by Lady
Novelists' (No. 26) is far more witty and savage, but it is
powered by the same sense that a realistic literature would
be of great social benefit. Indignation is aroused by the
various kinds of unreality and extravagance found in the six
novels under discussion, and their like. The basic objection
is the belief that women who publish such self-indulgent fantasies do a disservice to the cause of women's advancement.
Fortunately there is plenty of evidence that 'women can
produce work not only fine, but among the finest', but they
will not do so without cultivating 'those moral qualities that
contribute to literary excellence – patient diligence, and an
appreciation of the sacredness of the writer's art'. George
Eliot's sense of her responsibility as a novelist was deeply

enmeshed with her view of the novel as a genre able to give a full account of human reality. A similar belief is to be found in the criticism of G. H. Lewes, represented here in an article of 1858 (No. 28) which argues that 'Realism is . . . the base of all Art' because 'Art always aims at the representation of Reality'. But Lewes makes it clear that he is not suggesting that art can deal only with ordinary life. It may seek the Ideal, as in Raphael's picture of the Madonna: but it must keep within the bounds of truth, it must not so far transcend the human as to become unbelievable.

In 1858 the critic David Masson published an account of *British Novelists and their Styles* in which he distinguished the practice of Thackeray from that of Dickens:

> Thackeray is a novelist of what is called the Real school; Dickens is a novelist of the Ideal or Romantic school. (The terms Real and Ideal have been so run upon of late, that their repetition begins to nauseate; but they must be kept, for all that, till better equivalents are provided.) It is Thackeray's aim to represent life as it is actually and historically . . . . He will have no faultless characters, no demigods. . . . Dickens, on the other hand . . . has characters of ideal perfection and beauty, as well as of ideal ugliness and brutality. . . . [12]

But he modifies the contrast along lines similar to those of Lewes when he goes on to say that the 'Ideal or Romantic artist must be true to nature as well as the Real artist, but he may be true in a different fashion'.[13] The antithesis is more directly repudiated by the young George Meredith when he wrote to his friend the Rev. Augustus Jessopp in 1864:

> Between realism and idealism there is no natural conflict. This completes that. Realism is the basis of good composition: it implies study, observation, artistic power, and (in those who can do more) humility. Little writers should be realistic. They would then at least do solid work. They afflict the world because they will attempt that it is given to none but noble workmen to achieve. A great genius must necessarily employ ideal means, for a vast conception cannot be placed bodily before the eye, and remains to be suggested. Idealism is as an atmosphere whose effects of grandeur are wrought out through a series of illusions, that are

illusions to the sense within us only when divorced from the
groundwork of the real. Need there be exclusion, the one of the
other? The artist is incomplete who does this. Men to whom I bow
my head (Shakespeare, Goethe; and in their way, Molière,
Cervantes) are Realists *au fond*. But they have the broad arms of
Idealism at command. They give us Earth; but it is earth with an
atmosphere. One may find as much amusement in a Kaleidoscope
as in a merely idealistic writer: and, just as sound prose is of more
worth than pretentious poetry, I hold the man who gives a plain
wall of fact higher in esteem than one who is constantly shuffling
the clouds and dealing with airy, delicate sentimentalities, headless and tailless imaginings, despising our good, plain strength.[14]

The common-sense vigour of this, like Wilkie Collins's
insistence in his Preface to the 1861 edition of *The Woman in
White* (No. 29) that story and character are mutually inter-
dependent, may be seen as feeding into the confident assumptions of the article by Bagehot in 'Sterne and Thackeray'
discussed earlier. They are also explored fully and clearly by
Anthony Trollope, one of the most successful practitioners
of the realist mode, especially in his Barsetshire novels, in a
chapter[15] from *An Autobiography* (1883) which deserves to
be better known than it is. His statement 'In all things
human nature must be the novel-writer's guide'[16] may be
seen as central to the Victorian discussions of fiction that
have been considered here.

It will have been observed that the material in this volume
is concerned with both poetry and fiction, and sometimes
with literature in a general sense, but seldom with drama.
This is no accident. However popular the theatre may have
been in the Victorian period as a place of spectacle and
entertainment, it produced no new drama of the highest
quality, though plays like Dion Boucicault's *The Colleen
Bawn* (1860) are still enjoyable. No Dickens emerged to
reconcile entertainment and high achievement. Henry Taylor
states explicitly (No. 4) that his *Philip van Artevelde* is not
intended for the stage, and the heroine argues in Book V of
Aurora Leigh that the theatre is too dominated by poor
public taste for her to attempt to write for it. Most comments

on drama during these years support this view. Horne included a chapter on 'Sheridan Knowles and William Macready' in *The New Spirit of the Age* in 1844: Knowles was a playwright (*The Wife*, 1823; *The Love Chase*, 1837) and Macready a great actor (manager of Covent Garden Theatre 1837-9, and of Drury Lane 1841-3). But Horne admits that the 'acted drama of our age is at the best but of a poor kind',[17] and claims that 'There has never been in our own times one successful acted dramatist of the higher class'.[18] Until such a dramatist appears, 'the most profuse and admirable external aids can only foster mediocrity'.[19] Six years later, in 1850, G. H. Lewes wrote in *The Leader* explaining the weakness of contemporary English drama in terms of the over-estimation of Elizabethan drama (an argument parallel in some respects to what we find in Arnold's view of poetry): 'if they had never known the Old Drama, they must perforce have created a new form, and instead of the hundred-and-one imitators of the old dramatists, which these last twenty years have produced, we might have had some sterling plays'.[20] Lewes ends with a rousing appeal for the creation of 'a nineteenth-century drama: something that will appeal to a wider audience than that of a few critics and black-letter students'. When he came to edit *Selections from the Modern British Dramatists* in 1867 Lewes was still as concerned about the standard of the drama available. He noted that there was no obvious link between the quality of the actors and the drama of any period: 'at the time when our stage was in its most flourishing condition, the drama was pitiably poor. The greatest actors we have ever had – Garrick and Kean – failed to produce one single play of permanent worth.'[21] No recovery seems to have occurred in a society where a narrow-minded 'religious world' is overtly hostile to the theatre: 'One gloomy section bitterly declaims against it because it is an Amusement (and all amusement beyond the control of the priest is sinful); the other section turns away from it because it is no longer amusing.'[22] Drama may once have been morally questionable, but now it has been 'purified of these causes of offence – and the drama is rapidly decaying'.[23]

E. S. Dallas was no more positive in *The Gay Science* in
1866: 'The decline of the drama is a by-word'.[24] Dallas attempted to explain this as an 'inevitable result of civilisation'.[25]
He argued that as people find their work becoming more
mentally demanding, they require their entertainments to be
more frivolous:

In our enlightened age the really successful amusements are not of
the intellectual sort. On the stage it is the pantomime and
extravaganza, the farce and the ballet, that succeed.[26]

The contemporary audience is imagined calling out for 'the
fantasies of pantomime and the pageantry of a Shakespearian
revival', for 'farce and frivolity, bubble and ballet'.[27] Whatever we may feel about Dallas's attempted explanation,
there is no doubt that serious critics believed the drama to be
in decline, and that no significant critical statement of
dramatic principle was to emerge before Bernard Shaw's
Prefaces, and *The Quintessence of Ibsenism* in 1891.

The material in this volume has been chosen to represent
underlying assumptions about literary forms in the mid-
nineteenth century. It is not surprising therefore that it
should cast light on an issue that has become prominent in
our own time – that of the woman writer. Of the 22 writers
included here, four are women. Not surprisingly it is they
who are most directly concerned with this question. Their
views must be set against the assertion of Horne in 1844, in
an enthusiastic essay on 'Miss E. B. Barrett and Mrs Norton'
that 'The period when a strong prejudice existed against
learned ladies and 'blues' had gone by, some time since'.[28]
Charlotte Brontë (whose contrasting views of Jane Austen
and Thackeray show that she did not take a simplistically
feminist position) explained in the 'Biographical Notice' to
Wuthering Heights why she and her sisters used the am-
biguous names Currer, Ellis and Acton Bell when publishing
their works: the choice was 'dictated by a sort of conscientious scruple at assuming Christian names positively masculine, while we did not like to declare ourselves women
because – without at that time suspecting that our mode of

writing and thinking was not what is called 'feminine' – we had a vague impression that authoresses are liable to be looked on with prejudice; we had noticed how critics sometimes use for their chastisement the weapon of personality, and for their reward, a flattery, which is not true praise'.[29] Similarly Romney teases Aurora Leigh (No. 27) by quoting imaginary condescending male reviews of women's writing:

"What grace, what facile turns, what fluent sweeps,
What delicate discernment – almost thought!"

Women's claim to 'thought' as well as feeling was central to the arguments. Mary Ann Evans's 'Silly Novels by Lady Novelists' – written before 'George Eliot' was brought into existence (for reasons similar to those given for 'Currer Bell' by Charlotte Brontë) – is written in a spirit of exasperation with women writers who were happy to accept their 'lady' status. However, she had no doubt that 'women can produce work not only fine but among the finest – novels, too, that have a precious speciality, lying apart from masculine aptitudes and experience'. The last part of the sentence raises another important question for feminist criticism and suggests Evans's great capacity for opening up major avenues of thought.

Elizabeth Gaskell is less polemical in stance than the other women writers, and offers her advice to the author of *The Three Paths* (No. 16) simply as a fellow-writer. But her correspondence shows her to have been particularly supportive to other women who wanted to write, and very much aware of their particular problems. In a letter to Eliza Fox in 1850 she wrote:

One thing is pretty clear, *women* must give up living an artist's life, if home duties are to be paramount. It is different with men, whose home duties are so small a part of their lives. However, we are talking of women. I am sure it is healthy for them to have the refuge of the hidden world of Art – to shelter themselves in when too much pressed upon by daily small Lilliputian arrows of peddling cares; it keeps them from being morbid as you say; and takes them into a land where King Arthur lies hidden, and soothes them with its peace. I have felt this in writing, I see others feel it in music, you in painting, so assuredly a blending of the two is desirable. (Home duties and the development of the Individual I mean). . . .[30]

In a moving letter to a young woman who had sent her the manuscript of a novel in 1862, Mrs Gaskell gives practical advice about domestic life, and suggests that she should rear her children before trying to become a writer:

When I had *little* children I do not think I could have written stories, because I should have become too much absorbed in my *fictitious* people to attend to my *real* ones. . . . Besides viewing the subject from a solely artistic point of view a good writer of fiction must have *lived* an active and sympathetic life if she wants her books to have strength and vitality in them.[31]

Here we are made aware of the practical constraints on women as writers which were to be articulated by Virginia Woolf in *A Room of One's Own* in 1929. But we also see a Victorian belief in the writer's 'active and sympathetic life' feeding into her literary work. These discussions, and the achievements of these and other women writers, need to be put in the context of the patriarchal assumptions which lie behind male critical positions in the period, and occasionally become overt. Perhaps the most striking case is in Bagehot, who praises the logical style of *Adam Bede* as 'the most logical, probably, which a woman ever wrote', but considers the current preference for showiness in poetry as in part a result of the tastes of women readers: 'women, such as we know them, such as they are likely to be, ever prefer a delicate unreality to a true or firm art'. The remark contrasts uneasily with his admiration for George Eliot, whose status in Bagehot's eyes may be felt to be that of an honorary male, but it brings out well the context in which these women writers worked.

It would be misleading to try to make too tidy a pattern out of the critical discussions of the period: there are plenty of varieties of emphasis to be observed within the overall concern for 'the Real' which is evident in them. But a reading of these is helpful in enabling us to see the central preoccupations of those concerned with contemporary writing. For a more speculative suggestion, we may end with Dallas in 1866:

The development of literature in our day ... has led and is leading to many interesting changes, but to none more important than the withering of the individual as hero, the elevation and reinforcement of the individual as private man.... Private life, private character, all the whisperings of privacy, are the peculiar property of modern art.[32]

References

1 G. R. P. James (1790–1860) was a popular historical novelist, author of *Richelieu* (1829) and *Philip Augustus* (1831).
2 R. H. Horne, *The New Spirit of the Age* (1844); ed. W. Jerrold (1907), p. 153.
3 E. S. Dallas, *The Gay Science*, 2 vols. (1866), II, 285.
4 See J. D. Jump (ed.), *Tennyson, The Critical Heritage* (1967), *passim*.
5 Hallam Tennyson, *Alfred Lord Tennyson*, 2 vols (1897), I, 118; Charles Tennyson, *Alfred Tennyson* (1949), p. 131 gives the remark in the form, 'Alfred, we cannot live by Art.'
6 It is thoughtfully discussed by Isobel Armstrong in *Victorian Scrutinies* (1972), together with many other issues raised here.
7 Browning also published an 'Essay on Chatterton' in the *Foreign Quarterly Review* in July 1842; it is available in a modern edition, edited by D. Smalley (1948).
8 John Tupper, 'The Subject in Art; No.II' in *The Germ: Thoughts towards Nature in Poetry, Literature and Art*, No. 3, March 1850, p. 121. There is a facsimile of the 1901 edition of *The Germ* edited by Andrea Rose (1984).
9 Horne, *New Spirit*, p. 48.
10 Dickens, *Household Words*, No.1, 30 March 1850, p. 1.
11 Disraeli, *Coningsby* (1844).
12 David Masson, *British Novelists and their Styles* (1859), pp. 248–9.
13 ibid., p. 250.
14 *The Letters of George Meredith*, collected and edited by his son, 2 vols. (1912), I, 156–7.
15 Ch.XII 'On Novels and the Art of Writing Them' in Anthony Trollope, *An Autobiography*, edited by P. D. Edwards (1980), pp. 215–42. Ch.XII 'On English Novelists of the Present Day' (pp. 243–60) is also of interest.

16 ibid., p. 240.

17 Horne, *New Spirit*, p. 312.

18 ibid., p. 329.

19 ibid., p. 330.

20 G. H. Lewes, *The Leader*, 3 August 1850, p. 451.

21 Lewes, *Selections from the Modern British Dramatists* (Leipzig, 1867), I, 6–12.

22 ibid.

23 ibid.

24 Dallas, *Gay Science*, p. 318.

25 ibid., p. 319.

26 ibid., p. 320.

27 ibid., p. 322.

28 Horne, *New Spirit*, p. 339. It is also relevant that although Elizabeth Barrett contributed substantially to the book, Horne's name alone appears on the title-page; see W. Jerrold, Introduction, pp. xii–xiii.

29 'Biographical Notice' to *Wuthering Heights* (1850); ed. D. Daiches (1964), p. 31. As the Routledge Critical Heritage volume on the Brontës shows, they were often criticized as 'unfeminine'.

30 Letter to Eliza Fox, February 1850; in J. A. V. Chapple and Arthur Pollard (eds.), *The Letters of Mrs Gaskell* (1966), p. 106.

31 Letter of 25 September ? 1862; ibid., pp. 694–5.

32 Dallas, *Gay Science*, pp. 323, 325.

ARTHUR HENRY HALLAM

Hallam (1811–33) was Tennyson's closest friend at Cambridge, whose early death led to the writing of *In Memoriam* (1850); his *Remains*, in prose and verse, were published in 1834.

The unsigned review, of which extracts are given here, appeared in the *Englishman's Magazine* I, August 1831, 616–28, and was entitled 'On Some of the Characteristics of Modern Poetry and on the Lyrical Poems of Alfred Tennyson'.

1 From 'On Some of the Characteristics of Modern Poetry', 1831

It is not true, as his [Wordsworth's] exclusive admirers would have it, that the highest species of poetry is the reflective: it is a gross fallacy, that, because certain opinions are acute or profound, the expression of them by the imagination must be eminently beautiful. Whenever the mind of the artist suffers itself to be occupied, during its periods of creation, by any other predominant motive than the desire of beauty, the result is false in art. Now there is undoubtedly no reason, why he may not find beauty in those moods of emotion, which arise from the combinations of reflective thought, and it is possible that he may delineate these with fidelity, and not be led astray by any suggestions of an unpoetical mood. But, though possible, it is hardly probable: for a man, whose reveries take a reasoning turn, and who is accustomed to measure his ideas by their logical relations rather than the congruity of the sentiments to which they refer, will be apt to mistake the pleasure he has in knowing a thing to be true, for the pleasure he would have in knowing it to be beautiful, and so will pile his thoughts in a rhetorical battery, that they may convince, instead of letting them glow in the natural course of contemplation, that they may enrapture. It would not be difficult to shew, by reference to the most admired poems of Wordsworth, that he is frequently chargeable with this error, and that much has been said by him which is good as philosophy, powerful as rhetoric, but false as poetry. Perhaps this very distortion of the truth did more in the peculiar juncture of our literary affairs to enlarge and liberalize the genius of our age, than could have been effected by a less sectarian temper. However this may be, a new school of reformers soon began to attract attention, who, professing the same independence of immediate favour, took their stand on a different region of Parnassus from that occupied by the Lakers,[1] and one, in our opinion, much less liable to perturbing currents of air from ungenial climates. We shall not hesitate to express our conviction, that the Cockney school[2] (as it was termed in derision, from a cursory view of its accidental circumstances) contained more genuine inspiration, and adhered more speedily to that portion of truth which it embraced, than any *form* of art that has existed in this country since the day of Milton. Their *caposetta*[3] was Mr. Leigh Hunt,[4] who did little more than point the way, and was diverted from his aim by a thousand personal predilections and political habits of thought. But he was followed by two men of a very superior make; men who were born poets, lived poets, and went poets to their untimely graves. Shelley and Keats were, indeed, of opposite genius; that of the one was vast, impetuous, and sublime: the other seemed to be 'fed with honey-dew', and to have 'drunk the milk of Paradise'.[5] Even the softness of Shelley comes out in bold, rapid, comprehensive strokes; he has no patience for minute beauties, unless they can be massed into a general effect of grandeur. On the other hand, the tenderness of Keats cannot sustain a lofty flight; he does not generalize or allegorize Nature; his imagination works with few symbols, and reposes willingly on what is given freely. Yet in this formal opposition of character there is, it seems to us, a ground-work of similarity sufficient for the purposes of classification, and constituting a remarkable point in the progress of literature. They are both poets of sensation rather than reflection. Susceptible of the slightest impulse from external nature, their fine organs trembled into emotion at colours, and sounds, and movements, unperceived or unregarded by duller temperaments. Rich and clear were their perceptions of visible forms; full and deep their feelings of music. So vivid was the delight attending the simple exertions of eye and ear, that it became mingled more and more with their trains of active thought, and tended to absorb their whole being into the energy of sense. Other poets *seek* for images to illustrate their conceptions; these men had no need to seek; they lived in a world of images; for the most important and extensive portion of their life consisted in those emotions, which are immediately conversant with sensation. Like the hero of Goethe's novel,[6] they would hardly have been affected by what are called the pathetic parts of a book; but the *merely beautiful* passages, 'those from which the spirit of the author looks clearly and mildly forth', would have melted them to tears. Hence they are not descriptive; they are picturesque. They are not smooth and *negatively* harmonious; they are full of deep and varied melodies. This powerful tendency of imagination to a life of immediate sympathy with the external universe, is not nearly so liable to false views of art as the opposite disposition of purely intellectual contemplation. For where beauty is constantly passing before 'that inward eye, which is the bliss of solitude';[7] where the soul seeks it as a perpetual and necessary refreshment to the sources of activity and intuition; where all the other sacred ideas of our nature, the idea of good, the idea of perfection, the idea of truth, are habitually contemplated through the medium of this predominant mood, so that they assume its colour, and are subject to its peculiar laws – there is little danger that the

ruling passion of the whole mind will cease to direct its
creative operations, or the energetic principle of love for the
beautiful sink, even for a brief period, to the level of a mere
notion in the understanding. We do not deny that it is, on
other accounts, dangerous for frail humanity to linger with
fond attachment in the vicinity of sense.[8] Minds of this
description are especially liable to moral temptations, and
upon them, more than any, it is incumbent to remember that
their mission as men, which they share with all their fellow-
beings, is of infinitely higher interest than their mission as
artists, which they possess by rare and exclusive privilege.
But it is obvious that, critically speaking, such temptations
are of slight moment. Not the gross and evident passions of
our nature, but the elevated and less separable desires are
the dangerous enemies which misguide the poetic spirit in its
attempts at self-cultivation. That delicate sense of fitness,
which grows with the growth of artist feelings, and strengthens
with their strength, until it acquires a celerity and weight of
decision hardly inferior to the correspondent judgments of
conscience, is weakened by every indulgence of hetero-
geneous aspirations, however pure they may be, however
lofty, however suitable to human nature. We are therefore
decidedly of opinion that the heights and depths of art are
most within the reach of those who have received from
Nature the 'fearful and wonderful' constitution we have
described, whose poetry is a sort of magic, producing a
number of impressions too multiplied, too minute, and too
diversified to allow of our tracing them to their causes,
because just such was the effect, even so boundless, and so
bewildering, produced on their imaginations by the real
appearance of Nature. These things being so, our friends of
the new school had evidently much reason to recur to the
maxim laid down by Mr. Wordsworth, and to appeal from
the immediate judgments of lettered or unlettered contemporaries to the decision of a more equitable posterity.[9] How
should they be popular, whose senses told them a richer and
ampler tale than most men could understand, and who
constantly expressed, because they constantly felt, sentiments

of exquisite pleasure or pain, which most men were not permitted to experience? The public very naturally derided them as visionaries, and gibbeted *in terrorem*[10] those inaccuracies of diction, occasioned sometimes by the speed of their conceptions, sometimes by the inadequacy of language to their peculiar conditions of thought. But, it may be asked, does not this line of argument prove too much? Does it not prove that there is a barrier between these poets and all other persons, so strong and immoveable, that, as has been said of the Supreme Essence, we must be themselves before we can understand them in the least? Not only are they not liable to sudden and vulgar estimation, but the lapse of ages, it seems, will not consolidate their fame, nor the suffrages of the wise few produce any impression, however remote or slowly matured, on the judgments of the incapacitated many. We answer, this is not the import of our argument. Undoubtedly the true poet addresses himself, in all his conceptions, to the common nature of us all. Art is a lofty tree, and may shoot up far beyond our grasp, but its roots are in daily life and experience. Every bosom contains the elements of those complex emotions which the artist feels, and every head can, to a certain extent, go over in itself the process of their combination, so as to understand his expressions and sympathize with his state. But this requires exertion; more or less, indeed, according to the difference of occasion, but always some degree of exertion. For since the emotions of the poet, during composition, follow a regular law of association, it follows that to accompany their progress up to the harmonious prospect of the whole, and to perceive the proper dependence of every step on that which preceded, it is absolutely necessary *to start from the same point*, i.e., clearly to apprehend that leading sentiment in the poet's mind, by their conformity to which the host of suggestions are arranged. Now this requisite exertion is not willingly made by the large majority of readers. It is so easy to judge capriciously, and according to indolent impulse! For very many, therefore, it has become *morally* impossible to attain the author's point of vision, on account of their

habits, or their prejudices, or their circumstances; but it is
never *physically* impossible, because nature has placed
in every man the simple elements, of which art is the
sublimation. Since then this demand on the reader for
activity, when he wants to peruse his author in a luxurious
passiveness, is the very thing that moves his bile, it is
obvious that those writers will always be most popular, who
require the least degree of exertion. Hence, whatever is
mixed up with art, and appears under its semblance, is
always more favourably regarded than art free and unalloyed.
Hence, half the fashionable poems in the world are mere
rhetoric, and half the remainder are perhaps not liked by the
generality for their substantial merits. Hence, likewise, of
the really pure compositions those are most universally
agreeable, which take for their primary subject the *usual*
passions of the heart, and deal with them in a simple state,
without applying the transforming powers of high imagination.
Love, friendship, ambition, religion, &c., are matters of
daily experience, even amongst unimaginative tempers. The
forces of association, therefore, are ready to work in these
directions, and little effort of will is necessary to follow the
artist. For the same reason such subjects often excite a
partial power of composition, which is no sign of a truly
poetic organization. We are very far from wishing to depreciate this class of poems, whose influence is so extensive, and
communicates so refined a pleasure. We contend only that
the facility with which its impressions are communicated, is
no proof of its elevation as a form of art, but rather the
contrary. What then, some may be ready to exclaim, is the
pleasure derived by most men from Shakespeare, or Dante,
or Homer, entirely false and factitious? If these are really
masters of their art, must not the energy required of the ordinary intelligences, that come in contact with their mighty
genius, be the greatest possible? How comes it then that
they are popular? Shall we not say, after all, that the
difference is in the power of the author, not in the tenor of
his meditations? Those eminent spirits find no difficulty in
conveying to common apprehension their lofty sense, and

profound observation of Nature. They keep no aristocratic state, apart from the sentiments of society at large; they speak to the hearts of all, and by the magnetic force of their conceptions elevate inferior intellects into a higher and purer atmosphere. The truth contained in this objection is undoubtedly important; geniuses of the most universal order, and assigned by destiny to the most propitious eras of a nation's literary development, have a clearer and larger access to the minds of their compatriots, than can ever be open to those who are circumscribed by less fortunate circumstances. In the youthful periods of any literature there is an expansive and communicative tendency in mind, which produces unreservedness of communion, and reciprocity of vigour between different orders of intelligence. Without abandoning the ground which has always been defended by the partizans of Mr. Wordsworth, who declare with perfect truth that the number of real admirers of what is really admirable in Shakespeare and Milton are much fewer than the number of apparent admirers might lead one to imagine, we may safely assert that the intense thoughts set in circulation by those 'orbs of song', and their noble satellites, 'in great Eliza's golden time', did not fail to awaken a proportionable intensity in the natures of numberless auditors. Some might feel feebly, some strongly; the effect would vary according to the character of the recipient; but upon none was the stirring influence entirely unimpressive. The knowledge and power this imbibed, became a part of national existence; it was ours as Englishmen; and amid the flux of generations and customs we retain unimpaired this privilege of intercourse with greatness. But the age in which we live comes late in our national progress. That first raciness, and juvenile vigour of literature, when nature 'wantoned as in her prime, and played at will her virgin fancies', is gone, never to return. Since that day we have undergone a period of degradation. 'Every handicraftsman has worn the mark of Poesy.' It would be tedious to repeat the tale, so often related, of French contagion, and the heresies of the Popian school.[11] With the close of the last century came an era of reaction, an era of painful struggle, to bring our overcivilised condition of thought into union with the fresh productive spirit that brightened the morning of our literature. But repentance is unlike innocence: the laborious endeavour to restore has more complicated methods of action, than the freedom of untainted nature. Those different powers of poetic disposition, the energies of Sensitive,[12] of Reflective, of Passionate Emotion, which in former times were intermingled, and derived from mutual support an extensive empire over the feelings of men, were now restrained within separate spheres of agency. The whole system no longer worked harmoniously, and by intrinsic harmony acquired external freedom; but there arose a violent and unusual action in the several component functions, each for itself, all striving to reproduce the regular power which the whole had once enjoyed. Hence the melancholy, which so evidently characterises the spirit of modern poetry; hence that return of the mind upon itself, and the habit of seeking relief in idiosyncrasies rather than community of interest. In the old times the poetic impulse went along with the general impulse of the nation; in these, it is a reaction against it, a check acting for conservation against a propulsion towards change. We have indeed seen it urged in some of our fashionable publications, that the diffusion of poetry must necessarily be in the direct ratio of the diffusion of machinery, because a highly civilised people must have new objects of interest, and thus a new field will be opened to description. But this notable argument forgets that against this *objective* amelioration may be set the decrease of *subjective* power, arising from a prevalance of social activity, and a continual absorption of the higher feelings into the palpable interests of ordinary life. The French Revolution may be a finer theme than the war of Troy; but it does not so evidently follow that Homer is to find his superior. Our inference, therefore, from this change in the relative position of artists to the rest of the community is, that modern poetry, in proportion to its depth and truth, is likely to have little immediate authority over public opinion. Admirers it will have; sects consequently it will form; and these strong under-currents will in time sensibly affect the principal stream. Those writers, whose genius, though great, is not strictly and essentially poetic, become mediators between the votaries of art and the careless cravers for excitement. Art herself, less manifestly glorious than in her periods of undisputed supremacy, retains her essential prerogatives, and forgets not to raise up chosen spirits, who may minister to her state, and vindicate her title.

One of this faithful Islam, a poet in the truest and highest sense, we are anxious to present to our readers. He has yet written little, and published less; but in these 'preludes of a loftier strain', we recognise the inspiring god. Mr. Tennyson belongs decidedly to the class we have already described as Poets of Sensation.

1 The colloquial term used to describe Wordsworth, Coleridge and Southey because of their connection with the Lake District. Hallam notes: 'This cant term was justly ridiculed by Mr Wordsworth's supporters; but it was not so easy to substitute an inoffensive denomination.'
2 The colloquial term used to describe Hunt, Keats and Shelley, poets associated with London, as Hallam explains.
3 Leader of a sect.
4 James Henry Leigh Hunt (1784–1859) was a minor poet and essayist, who published Keats and Shelley in *The Examiner*.
5 From Coleridge's account of the poet in 'Kubla Khan'.
6 Johann Wolfgang von Goethe (1749–1832), the great German writer, published the novel *Wilhelm Meister* in 1829.
7 From Wordsworth's 'Daffodils', line 21.
8 i.e. the world of the senses.
9 Wordsworth, 'Preface' to *Poems* (1815), para 21.
10 To discourage through fear.
11 i.e. of what the Romantics took to be the decline of poetry through excessive cultivation of artifice on the French model, by Augustan writers like Alexander Pope (1688–1744).
12 Hallam notes that 'this is not the right word', and suggests 'sensuous' as an alternative; the reference is evidently to the senses.

JOHN STUART MILL

Mill (1806–73) at this time was at the beginning of the career that was to make him the leading philosophical exponent of Liberalism in the period. The two passages show interestingly different emphases in their accounts of the relationship between poetry and philosophy.

2 'The Two Kinds of Poetry', 1833

[In January 1833 Mill contributed an article entitled 'What is Poetry?' to the *Monthly Repository*, in which he argued that poetry aims to work exclusively on the emotions and to delineate states of feeling. He developed the implications of this view further in 'The Two Kinds of Poetry' in the *Monthly Repository* N.S. VII, October 1833, 714–24, which is represented here complete.

The two articles were later published in a slightly revised form in Mill's *Dissertations and Discussions* (1859). There is a modern edition of Mill's work edited by J. M. Robson and others, published by Routledge.]

NASCITUR POËTA[1] is a maxim of classical antiquity, which has passed to these latter days with less questioning than most of the doctrines of that early age. When it originated, the human faculties were occupied, fortunately for posterity, less in examining how the works of genius are created, than in creating them: and the adage, probably, had no higher source than the tendency common among mankind to consider all power which is not visibly the effect of practice, all skill which is not capable of being reduced to mechanical rules, as the result of a peculiar gift. Yet this aphorism, born in the infancy of psychology, will perhaps be found, now when that science is in its adolescence, to be as true as an epigram ever is, that is, to contain some truth: truth, however, which has been so compressed and bent out of shape, in order to tie up into so small a knot of only two words, that it requires an almost infinite amount of unrolling and laying straight, before it will resume its just proportions.

We are not now intending to remark upon the grosser misapplications of this ancient maxim, which have engendered so many races of poetasters. The days are gone by, when every raw youth whose borrowed phantasies have set themselves to a borrowed tune, mistaking, as Coleridge says, an ardent desire of poetic reputation for poetic genius,[2] while unable to disguise from himself that he had taken no means whereby he might *become* a poet, could fancy himself a born one. Those who would reap without sowing, and gain the victory without fighting the battle, are ambitious now of another sort of distinction, and are born novelists, or public speakers, not poets. And the wiser thinkers begin to understand and acknowledge that poetic excellence is subject to the same necessary conditions with any other mental endowment; and that to no one of the spiritual benefactors of mankind is a higher or a more assiduous intellectual culture needful than to the poet. It is true, he possesses this advantage over others who use the 'instruments of words,' that, of the truths which he utters, a larger proportion are derived from personal consciousness, and a smaller from philosophic investigation. But the power itself of discriminating between what really is consciousness, and what is only a process of inference completed in a single instant – and the capacity of distinguishing whether that of which the mind is conscious be an eternal truth, or but a dream – are among the last results of the most matured and perfected intellect. Not to mention that the poet, no more than any other person who writes, confines himself altogether to intuitive truths, nor has any means of communicating even these but by words, every one of which derives all its power of conveying a meaning, from a whole host of acquired notions, and facts learnt by study and experience.

Nevertheless, it seems undeniable in point of fact, and consistent with the principles of a sound metaphysics, that there are poetic *natures*. There is a mental and physical constitution or temperament, peculiarly fitted for poetry. This temperament will not of itself make a poet, no more than the soil will the fruit; and as good fruit may be raised by culture from indifferent soils, so may good poetry from naturally unpoetical minds. But the poetry of one who is a poet by nature, will be clearly and broadly distinguishable from the poetry of mere culture. It may not be truer, it may not be more useful; but it will be different: fewer will appreciate it, even though many should affect to do so; but in those few it will find a keener sympathy, and will yield them a deeper enjoyment.

One may write genuine poetry, and not be a poet; for whosoever writes out truly any one human feeling, writes poetry. All persons, even the most unimaginative, in moments of strong emotion, speak poetry; and hence the drama is poetry, which else were always prose, except when a poet is one of the characters. What *is* poetry, but the thoughts and words in which emotion spontaneously embodies itself? As there are few who are not, at least for *some* moments and in *some* situations, capable of *some* strong feeling, poetry is natural to most persons at some period of their lives. And any one whose feelings are genuine, though but of the average strength, – if he be not diverted by uncongenial thoughts or occupations from the indulgence of them, and if he acquire by culture, as all persons may, the faculty of delineating them correctly, – has it in his power to be a poet, so far as a life passed in writing unquestionable poetry may be considered to confer that title. But *ought* it to do so? Yes perhaps, in the table of contents of a collection of 'British Poets.' But 'poet' is the name also of a variety of *man*, not solely of the author of a particular variety of *book*: now, to have written whole volumes of real poetry, is possible to almost all kinds of characters, and implies no greater peculiarity of mental construction than to be the author of a history or a novel.

Whom, then, shall we call poets? Those who are so constituted, that emotions are the links of association by which their ideas, both sensuous and spiritual, are connected together. This constitution belongs (within certain limits) to all in whom poetry is a pervading principle. In all others, poetry is something extraneous and superinduced: something out of themselves, foreign to the habitual course of their every-day lives and characters; a quite other world to which they may make occasional visits, but where they are sojourners, not dwellers, and which, when out of it, or even when in it, they think of, peradventure, but as a phantom-world, a place of *ignes fatui*[3] and spectral illusions. Those only who have the peculiarity of association which we have mentioned, and which is one of the natural consequences of intense sensibility, instead of seeming not themselves when they are uttering poetry, scarcely seem themselves when uttering anything to which poetry is foreign. Whatever be the thing which they are contemplating ... the aspect under which it first and most naturally paints itself to them, is its poetic aspect. The poet of culture sees his object in prose, and describes it in poetry; the poet of nature actually sees it in poetry.

This point is perhaps worth some little illustration; the rather, as metaphysicians (the ultimate arbiters of all philosophical criticism), while they have busied themselves for two thousand years, more or less, about the few *universal* laws of human nature, have strangely neglected the analysis of its *diversities*. Of these, none lie deeper or reach further than the varieties which difference of nature and of education makes in what may be termed the habitual bond of association. In a mind entirely uncultivated, which is also without any strong feelings, objects, whether of sense or of intellect, arrange themselves in the mere casual order in which they have been seen, heard, or otherwise perceived. Persons of this sort may be said to think chronologically. If they remember a fact, it is by reason of a fortuitous coincidence with some trifling incident or circumstance which took place at the very time. If they have a story to tell, or testimony to deliver in a witness-box, their narrative must follow the exact order in which the events took place: *dodge* them, and the thread of association is broken, they cannot go on. Their associations, to use the language of philosophers, are chiefly of the successive, not the synchronous kind, and whether successive or synchronous, are mostly *casual*.

To the man of science, again, or of business, objects group themselves according to the artificial classifications which the understanding has voluntarily made for the convenience of thought or of practice. But where any of the impressions are vivid and intense, the associations into which these enter are the ruling ones; it being a well-known law of association, that the stronger a feeling is, the more rapidly and strongly it associates itself with any other object or feeling. Where, therefore, nature has given strong feelings, and education has not created factitious tendencies stronger than the natural ones, the prevailing associations will be those which connect objects and ideas with emotions, and with each other through the intervention of emotions. Thoughts and images will be linked together, according to the similarity of the feelings which cling to them. A thought will introduce a thought by first introducing a feeling which is allied with it. At the centre of each group of thoughts or images will be found a feeling; and the thoughts or images are only there because the feeling was there. All the combinations which the mind puts together, all the pictures which it paints, all the wholes which imagination constructs out of the materials supplied by fancy, will be indebted to some dominant *feeling*, not as in other natures to a dominant *thought*, for their unity and consistency of character – for what distinguishes them from incoherencies.

The difference, then, between the poetry of a poet, and the poetry of a cultivated but not naturally poetical mind, is, that in the latter, with however bright a halo of feeling the thought may be surrounded and glorified, the thought itself is still the conspicuous object; while the poetry of a poet is feeling itself, employing thought only as the medium of its utterance. In the one, feeling waits upon thought; in the other, thought upon feeling. The one writer has a distinct aim, common to him with any other didactic author; he desires to convey the thought, and he conveys it clothed in the feeling which it excites in himself, or which he deems most appropriate to it. The other merely pours forth the overflowing of his feelings; and all the thoughts which those feelings suggest are floated promiscuously along the stream.

It may assist in rendering our meaning intelligible, if we illustrate it by a parallel between the two English authors of our own day who have produced the greatest quantity of true and enduring poetry, Wordsworth and Shelley. Apter instances could not be wished for; the one might be cited as the type, the *exemplar*, of what the poetry of culture may accomplish; the other as perhaps the most striking example ever known of the poetic temperament. How different, accordingly, is the poetry of these two great writers! In Wordsworth, the poetry is almost always the mere setting of a thought. The thought may be more valuable than the setting, or it may be less valuable, but there can be no question as to which was first in his mind; what he is impressed with, and what he is anxious to impress, is some proposition, more or less distinctly conceived; some truth, or something which he deems such. He lets the thought dwell in his mind, till it excites, as is the nature of thought, other thoughts, and also such feelings as the measure of his sensibility is adequate to supply. Among these thoughts and feelings, had he chosen a different walk of authorship (and there are many in which he might equally have excelled), he would probably have made a different selection of media for enforcing the parent thought: his habits, however, being those of poetic composition, he selects in preference the strongest feelings, and the thoughts with which most of feeling is naturally or habitually connected. His poetry, therefore, may be defined to be, his thoughts, coloured by, and impressing themselves by means of, emotions. Such poetry, Wordsworth has occupied a long life in producing. And well and wisely has he so done. Criticisms, no doubt, may be made occasionally both upon the thoughts them-selves, and upon the skill he has demonstrated in the choice of his *media*: for, an affair of skill and study, in the most rigorous sense, it evidently was. But he has not laboured in vain: he has exercised, and continues to exercise, a power-ful, and mostly a highly beneficial influence over the forma-tion and growth of not a few of the most cultivated and vigorous of the youthful minds of our time, over whose heads poetry of the opposite description would have flown, for want of an original organization, physical and mental, in sympathy with it.

On the other hand, Wordsworth's poetry is never bound-ing, never ebullient; has little even of the appearance of spontaneousness: the well is never so full that it overflows. There is an air of calm deliberateness about all he writes, which is not characteristic of the poetic temperament: his poetry seems one thing, himself another; he seems to be poetical because he wills to be so, not because he cannot help it: did he will to dismiss poetry, he need never again, it might almost seem, have a poetical thought. He never seems *possessed* by a feeling; no emotion seems ever so strong as to have entire sway, for the time being, over the current of his thoughts. He never, even for the space of a few stanzas, appears entirely *given up* to exultation, or grief, or pity, or love, or admiration, or devotion, or even animal spirits. He now and then, though seldom, *attempts* to write as if he were; and never, we think, without leaving an impression of poverty: as the brook which on nearly level ground quite fills its banks, appears but a thread when running rapidly down a precipitous declivity. He has feeling enough to form a decent, graceful, even beautiful decoration to a thought which is in itself interesting and moving; but not so much as suffices to stir up the soul by mere sympathy with itself in its simplest manifestation, nor enough to summon up that array of 'thoughts of power' which in a richly stored mind always attends the call of really intense feeling. It is for this reason, doubtless, that the genius of Wordsworth is essentially unlyrical. Lyric poetry, as it was the earliest kind, is also, if the view we are now taking of poetry be correct, more eminently and peculiarly poetry than any other: it is the poetry most natural to a really poetic temperament, and least capable of being successfully imitated by one not so endowed by nature. All Wordsworth's attempts in that strain, if we may venture to say so much of a man whom we so exceedingly admire, appear to us cold and spiritless.

Shelley is the very reverse of all this. Where Wordsworth is strong, he is weak; where Wordsworth is weak, he is strong. Culture, that culture by which Wordsworth has reared from his own inward nature the richest harvest ever bought forth by a soil of so little depth, is precisely what was wanting to Shelley: or let us rather say, he had not, at the period of his deplorably early death, reached sufficiently far in that intellectual progression of which he was capable, and which, if it has done so much for far inferior natures, might have made of him the greatest of our poets. For him, intentional mental discipline had done little: the vividness of his emotions and of his sensations had done all. He seldom follows up an idea; it starts into life, summons from the fairy-land of his inexhaustible fancy some three or four bold images, then vanishes, and straight he is off on the wings of some casual association into quite another sphere. He had not yet acquired the consecutiveness of thought necessary for a long poem; his more ambitious compositions too often resemble the scattered fragments of a mirror; colours brilliant as life, single images without end, but no picture. It is only when under the overruling influence of some one state of feeling, either actually experienced, or summoned up in almost the vividness of reality by a fervid imagination, that he writes as a great poet; unity of feeling being to him the harmonizing principle which a central idea is to minds of another class, and supplying the coherency and consistency which would else have been wanting. Thus it is in many of his smaller, and especially his lyrical poems. They are obviously written to exhale, perhaps to relieve, a state of feeling, or of conception of feeling, almost oppressive from its vividness. The thoughts and imagery are suggested by the feeling, and are such as it finds unsought. The state of feeling may be either of soul or of sense, or oftener (might we not say invariably?) of both: for the poetic temperament is usually, perhaps always, accompanied by exquisite senses. The exciting cause may be either an object or an idea. But whatever of sensation enters into the feeling, must not be local, or consciously bodily; it is a state of the whole frame, not of a part only; like the state of sensation produced by a fine climate, or indeed like all strongly pleasurable or painful sensations in an impassioned nature, it pervades the entire nervous system. States of feeling, whether sensuous or spiritual, which thus possess the whole being, are the fountains of poetry which we have called the poetry of poets; and which is little else than the utterance of the thoughts and images that pass across the mind while some permanent state of feeling is occupying it.

To the same original fineness of organization, Shelley was doubtless indebted for another of his rarest gifts, that exuberance of imagery, which when unrepressed, as in many of his poems it is, amounts even to a vice. The susceptibility of his nervous system, which made his emotions intense, made also the impressions of his external senses deep and clear: and agreeably to the law of association by which, as already remarked, the strongest impressions are those which associate themselves the most easily and strongly, these vivid sensations were readily recalled to mind by all objects or thoughts which had coexisted with them, by all feelings which in any degree resembled them. Never did a fancy so teem with sensuous imagery as Shelley's. Wordsworth economizes an image, and detains it until he had distilled all the poetry out of it, and it will not yield a drop more: Shelley lavishes his with a profusion which is unconscious because it is inexhaustible. The one, like a thrifty housewife, uses all his materials and wastes none: the other scatters them with a reckless prodigality of wealth of which there is perhaps no similar instance.

If, then, the maxim *Nascitur poëta*, means, either that the power of producing poetical compositions is a peculiar faculty which the poet brings into the world with him, which grows with his growth like any of his bodily powers, and is as independent of culture as his height, and his complexion: or that *any* natural peculiarity *whatever* is implied in producing poetry, real poetry and in any quantity – such poetry too, as, to the majority of educated and intelligent readers, shall appear quite as good as, or even better than, any other; in either sense the doctrine is false. And nevertheless, there *is* poetry which could not emanate but from a mental and physical constitution peculiar, not in the *kind*, but in the *degree* of its susceptibility: a constitution which makes its possessor capable of greater happiness than mankind in general, and also of greater unhappiness; and because greater, so also more various. And such poetry, to all who know enough of nature to own it as being *in* nature, is much *more* poetry, is poetry in a far higher sense, than any other, since the common element of all poetry, that which constitutes poetry, human feeling, enters far more largely into this than into the poetry of culture. Not only because the natures which we have called poetical, really feel more, and consequently have more feeling to express; but because, the capacity of feeling being so great, feeling, when excited and not voluntarily resisted, seizes the helm of their thoughts, and the succession of ideas and images becomes the mere utterance of an emotion; not, as in other natures, the emotion a mere ornamental colouring of the thought.

Ordinary education and the ordinary course of life are constantly at work counteracting this quality of mind, and substituting habits more suitable to their own ends: if instead of *substituting*, they were content to *superadd*, then there were nothing to complain of. But when will education consist, not in repressing any mental faculty or power, from the uncontrolled action of which danger is apprehended, but in training up to its proper strength the corrective and antagonist power?

In whomsoever the quality which we have described

exists, and is not stifled, that person is a poet. Doubtless he is a *greater* poet in proportion as the fineness of his perceptions, whether of sense or of internal consciousness, furnishes him with an ampler supply of lovely images – the vigour and richness of his intellect with a greater abundance of moving thoughts. For it is through these thoughts and images that the feeling speaks, and through their impressiveness that it impresses itself, and finds response in other hearts; and from these media of transmitting it (contrary to the laws of physical nature) increase of intensity is reflected back upon the feeling itself. But all these it is possible to have, and not be a poet; they are mere materials, which the poet shares in common with other people. What constitutes the poet is not the imagery nor the thoughts, nor even the feelings, but the law according to which they are called up. He is a poet, not because he has ideas of any particular kind, but because the succession of his ideas is subordinate to the course of his emotions.

Many who have never acknowledged this in theory, bear testimony to it in their particular judgments. In listening to an oration, or reading a written discourse not professedly poetical, when do we begin to feel that the speaker or author is putting off the character of the orator or the prose writer, and is passing into the poet? Not when he begins to show strong feeling; *then* we merely say, he seems to feel what he says; still less when he expresses himself in imagery; *then*, unless illustration be manifestly his sole object, we are apt to say, This is affectation. It is when the feeling (instead of passing away, or, if it continue, letting the train of thoughts run on exactly as they would have done if there were no influence at work but the mere intellect) becomes itself the originator of another train of association, which expels, or blends, with the former; as when (to take a simple example) the ideas or objects generally, of which the person has occasion to speak for the purposes of his discourse, are spoken of in words which we spontaneously use only when in a state of excitement, and which prove that the mind is at least as much occupied by a passive state of its own feelings, as by the desire of attaining the premeditated end which the discourse has in view.[4]

Our judgments of authors who lay actual claim to the title of poets, follow the same principle. We believe that whenever, after a writer's meaning is fully understood, it is still a matter of reasoning and discussion whether he is a poet or not, he will be found to be wanting in the characteristic peculiarity of association which we have so often adverted to. When, on the contrary, after reading or hearing one or two passages, the mind instinctively and without hesitation cries out, This is a poet, the probability is, that the passages are strongly marked with this peculiar quality. And we may add that in such case, a critic who, not having sufficient feeling to respond to the poetry, is also without sufficient philosophy to understand it though he feel it not, will be apt to pronounce, not 'this is prose', but 'this is exaggeration', 'this is mysticism', or, 'this is nonsense'.

Although a philosopher cannot, by culture, make himself, in the peculiar sense in which we now use the term, a poet, unless at least he have that peculiarity of nature which would probably have made poetry his earliest pursuit; a poet may always, by culture, make himself a philosopher. The poetic laws of association are by no means incompatible with the more ordinary laws; are by no means such as *must* have their course, even though a deliberate purpose require their suspension. If the peculiarities of the poetic temperament were uncontrollable in any poet, they might be supposed so in Shelley: yet how powerfully, in *The Cenci*,[5] does he coerce and restrain all the characteristic qualities of his genius! what severe simplicity, in place of his usual barbaric splendour! how rigidly does he keep the feelings and the imagery in subordination to the thought!

The investigation of nature requires no habits or qualities of mind, but such as may always be acquired by industry and mental activity. Because at one time the mind may be so given up to a state of feeling, that the succession of its ideas is determined by the present enjoyment or suffering which pervades it, this is no reason but that in the calm retirement of study, when under no peculiar excitement either of the outward or of the inward sense, it may form any combinations, or pursue any trains of ideas, which are most conducive to the purposes of philosophic inquiry; and may, while in that state, form deliberate convictions, from which no excitement will afterwards make it swerve. Might we not go even further than this? We shall not pause to ask whether it be not a misunderstanding of the nature of passionate feeling to imagine that it is inconsistent with calmness, and whether they who so deem of it, do not confound the state of *desire* which unfortunately is possible to all, with the state of *fruition* which is granted only to the few. But without entering into this deeper investigation; that capacity of strong feeling, which is supposed necessarily to disturb the judgement, is also the material out of which all *motives* are made; the motives, consequently, which lead human beings to the pursuit of truth. The greater the individual's capability of happiness and of misery, the stronger interest has that individual in arriving at truth; and when once that interest is felt, an impassionate nature is sure to pursue this, as to pursue any other object, with greater ardour, for energy of character is the offspring of strong feeling. If therefore, the most impassioned natures do not ripen into the most powerful intellects, it is always from defect of culture, or something wrong in the circumstances by which the being has originally or successively been surrounded. Undoubtedly strong feelings *require* a strong intellect to carry them, as more sail requires more ballast; and when, from neglect, or bad education, that strength is wanting, no wonder if the grandest and swiftest vessels make the most utter wreck.

Where, as in Milton, or, to descend to our own times, in Coleridge, a poetic nature had been united with logical and scientific culture, the peculiarity of association arising from the finer nature so perpetually alternates with the associations attainable by commoner natures trained to high perfection, that its own particular law is not so conspicuously characteristic of the result produced, as in a poet like Shelley, to whom systematic intellectual culture, in a measure proportioned to the intensity of his own nature, has been wanting. Whether the superiority will naturally be on the side of the logician-poet or of the mere poet – whether the writings of the one ought as a whole, to be truer, and their influence more beneficent, than those of the other – is too obvious in principle to need statement: it would be absurd to doubt whether two endowments are better than one; whether truth is more certainly arrived at by two processes, verifying and correcting each other, than by one alone. Unfortunately, in practice the matter is not quite so simple; there the question often is, which is least prejudicial to the intellect, uncultivation or malcultivation. For, as long as so much of education is made up of artificialities and conventionalisms, and the so-called training of the intellect consists chiefly of the mere inculcation of traditional opinions, many of which, from the mere fact that the human intellect has not yet reached perfection, must necessarily be false, it is not always clear that the poet of acquired ideas has the advantage over him whose feeling has been his sole teacher. For, the depth and durability of wrong as well as of right impressions, is proportional to the fineness of the material; and they who have the greatest capacity of natural feeling are generally those whose artificial feelings are the strongest. Hence, doubtless, among other reasons, it is, that in an age of revolutions in opinion, the contemporary poets, those at least who deserve the name, those who have any individuality of character, if they are not before their age, are almost sure to be behind it. An observation curiously verified all over Europe in the present century. Nor let it be thought disparaging. However urgent may be the necessity for a breaking up of old modes of belief, the most strong-minded and discerning, next to those who head the movement, are generally those who bring up the rear of it. A text on which to dilate would lead us too far from the present subject.

1   A poet is born (not made).
2   Coleridge, *Biographia Literaria* Vol. I (Ch. ii) and Vol. II (Ch. xv).

3 Wandering fires; will-o'-the-wisps.
4 Mill added a note:

> "And this, we may remark by the way, seems to point to the true
> theory of poetic diction; and to suggest that true answer to as much as
> is erroneous of Mr. Wordsworth's celebrated doctrine on that subject.
> [In the 'Preface' to *Lyrical Ballads*] For on the one hand, *all* language
> which is the natural expression of feeling, is really poetical, and will
> always be felt as such, apart from conventional associations; but on the
> other, whenever intellectual culture has afforded a choice between
> several modes of expressing the same emotion, the stronger the feeling
> is, the more naturally and certainly will it prefer that language which is
> most peculiarly appropriated to itself, and kept sacred from the
> contact of all more vulgar and familiar objects of contemplation."

5 Shelley's tragedy *The Cenci* was published in 1819.

3 From a review of Tennyson's poems, 1835

[Mill's review of Tennyson's *Poems, Chiefly Lyrical* (1830)
and *Poems* (1833) appeared in the *London Review* I, July,
1835, 402–24. Here Mill emphasized the importance of
philosophy to a poet's overall achievements.]

Every great poet, every poet who has extensively or
permanently influenced mankind, has been a great thinker;
– has had a philosophy, though perhaps he did not call it by
that name; – has had his mind full of thoughts, derived not
merely from passive sensibility, but from trains of reflection,
from observation, analysis, and generalization; however
remote the sphere of his observation and meditation may
have lain from the studies of the schools. Where the poetic
temperament exists in its greatest degree, while the systematic culture of the intellect has been neglected, we may expect
to find, what we do find in the best poems of Shelley – vivid
representations of states of passive and dreamy emotion, fitted to give extreme pleasure to persons of similar organization to the poet, but not likely to be sympathized in, because
not understood, by any other persons; and scarcely conducting at all to the noblest end of poetry as an intellectual
pursuit, that of acting upon the desires and characters of

mankind through their emotions, to raise them towards the perfection of their nature. This, like every other adaptation of means to ends, is the work of cultivated reason; and the poet's success in it will be in proportion to the intrinsic value of his thoughts, and to the command which he has acquired over the materials of his imagination, for placing those thoughts in a strong light before the intellect, and impressing them on the feelings.

The poems which we have quoted from Mr. Tennyson prove incontestably that he possesses, in an eminent degree, the natural endowment of a poet – the poetic temperament. And it appears clearly, not only from a comparison of the two volumes, but of different poems in the same volume, that, with him, the other element of poetic excellence – intellectual culture – is advancing both steadily and rapidly; that he is not destined, like so many others, to be remembered for what he might have done, rather than for what he did; that he will not remain a poet of mere temperament, but is ripening into a true artist. Mr. Tennyson may not be conscious of the wide difference in maturity of intellect, which is apparent in his various poems. Though he now writes from greater fulness and clearness of thought, it by no means follows that he has learnt to detect the absence of those qualities in some of his earlier effusions. Indeed, he himself, in one of the most beautiful poems of his first volume (though, as a work of art, very imperfect), the 'Ode to Memory', confesses a parental predilection for the 'first-born' of his genius. But to us it is evident, not only that his second volume differs from his first as early manhood from youth, but that the various poems in the first volume belong to different, and even distant stages of intellectual development; – distant, not perhaps in years – for a mind like Mr. Tennyson's advances rapidly – but corresponding to very different states of the intellectual powers, both in respect of their strength and of their proportions. . . .

We predict, that, as Mr. Tennyson advances in general spiritual culture, these higher aims will become more and more predominant in his writings; that he will strive more

and more diligently, and, even without striving, will be more
and more impelled by the natural tendencies of an expanding character, towards what has been described as the
highest object of poetry, 'to incorporate the everlasting
reason of man in forms visible to his sense, and suitable to
it'. For the fulfilment of this exalted purpose, what we have
already seen of him authorizes us to foretell with confidence,
that powers of execution will not fail him; it rests with
himself to see that his powers of thought may keep pace with
them. To render his poetic endowment the means of giving
impressiveness to important truths, he must, by continual
study and meditation, strengthen his intellect for the dis-
crimination of such truths; he must see that his theory of life
and the world be no chimera of the brain, but the well-
grounded result of solid and mature thinking; – he must
cultivate, and with no half devotion, philosophy as well as
poetry.

It may not be superfluous to add, that he should guard
himself against an error, to which the philosophical specula-
tions of poets are peculiarly liable – that of embracing as
truth, not the conclusions which are recommended by the
strongest evidence, but those which have the most poetical
appearance; – not those which arise from the deductions of
impartial reason, but those which are most captivating to an
imagination, biassed perhaps by education and conventional
associations. That whatever philosophy he adopts will leave
ample materials for poetry, he may be well assured. Whatever is comprehensive, whatever is commanding, whatever
is on a great scale, is poetical. Let our philosophical system
be what it may, human feelings exist: human nature, with all
its enjoyments and sufferings, its strugglings, its victories
and defeats, still remain to us; and these are the materials
of all poetry. Whoever, in the greatest concerns of human
life, pursues truth with unbiassed feelings, and an intellect
adequate to discern it, will not find that the resources of
poetry are lost to him because he has learnt to use, and not
abuse them. They are as open to him as they are to the

sentimental weakling, who has no test of the true but the ornamental. And when he once has them under his command, he can wield them for purposes, and with a power, of which neither the dilettante nor the visionary have the slightest conception. . . .

HENRY TAYLOR

Taylor (1800–1886) held an appointment in the Colonial Office from 1824 to 1872, and also published a number of plays in verse, of which *Philip van Artevelde* is generally considered the best. His Preface, printed complete here, argues for clarity and cogency, foreshadowing some of Arnold's arguments. Taylor's *Autobiography* was published in 1886.

4 Preface to *Philip van Artevelde*, 1834

As this work, consisting of two Plays and an Interlude, is equal in length to about six such plays as are adapted to representation, it is almost unnecessary to say that it was not intended for the stage. It is properly an Historical Romance, cast in a dramatic and rhythmical form. Historic truth is preserved in it, as far as the material events are concerned – of course with the usual exception of such occasional dilatations and compressions of time as are required in dramatic composition.

This is, perhaps, all the explanation which is absolutely required in this place: but as there may be readers who feel an inclination to learn something of an author's taste in poetry before they proceed to the perusal of what he has written, I will take the opportunity which a preface affords me of expressing my opinions upon two or three of the most prominent features in the present state of poetical literature; and I shall do so the more gladly because I am apprehensive that without some previous intimations of the kind, my work

might occasion disappointment to the admirers of that
highly-coloured poetry which has been popular in these later
years. If in the strictures which, with this object, I may be
led to make upon authors of great reputation, I should
appear to be wanting in the respect due to prevalent
opinions, – opinions which, from the very circumstance of
their prevalence, must be assumed to be partaken by many
to whom deference is owing, I trust that it will be attributed,
not to any spirit of dogmatism, far less to a love of
disparagement, but simply to the desire of exercising, with a
discreet freedom, that humble independence of judgement
in matters of taste which it is for the advantage of literature
that every man of letters should maintain.

My views have not, in truth, been founded upon any
predisposition to depreciate the popular poetry of the times.
It will always produce a powerful impression upon very
young readers, and I scarcely think that it can have been
more admired by any than by myself when I was included in
that category. I have not ceased to admire this poetry in its
degree; and the interlude which I have inserted between
these plays will show that, to a limited extent, I have been
desirous even to cultivate and employ it; but I am unable to
concur in opinion with those who would place it in the
foremost ranks of the art; nor does it seem to have been
capable of sustaining itself quite firmly in the very high
degree of public estimation in which it was held at its first
appearance and for some years afterwards. The poetical
taste to which some of the popular poets of this century gave
birth, appears at present to maintain a more unshaken
dominion over the writers of poetry than over its readers.

These poets were characterized by great sensibility and
fervour, by a profusion of imagery, by force and beauty of
language, and by a versification peculiarly easy and adroit
and abounding in that sort of melody which, by its very
obvious cadences, makes itself most pleasing to an un-
practised ear. They exhibit, therefore, many of the most
attractive graces and charms of poetry – its vital warmth not
less than its external embellishments – and had not the

admiration which they excited tended to produce an in-
difference to higher, graver, and more various endowments,
no one would have said that it was, in any evil sense,
excessive. But from this unbounded indulgence in the mere
luxuries of poetry, has there not ensued a want of adequate
appreciation for its intellectual and immortal part? I confess
that such seems to me to have been both the actual and the
natural result; and I can hardly believe the public taste to
have been in a healthy state whilst the most approved poetry
of past times was almost unread. We may now perhaps be
turning back to it; but it was not, as far as I can judge, till
more than a quarter of a century had expired, that any signs
of reaction could be discerned. Till then, the elder luminaries
of our poetical literature were obscured or little regarded;
and we sate with dazzled eyes at a high festival of poetry,
where, as at the funeral of Arvalan, the torch-light put out
the star-light.

So keen was the sense of what the new poets possessed,
that it never seemed to be felt that anything was deficient in
them. Yet their deficiencies were not unimportant. They
wanted, in the first place, subject-matter. A feeling came
more easily to them than a reflection, and an image was
always at hand when a thought was not forthcoming. Either
they did not look upon mankind with observant eyes, or they
did not feel it to be any part of their vocation to turn what
they saw to account. It did not belong to poetry, in their
apprehension, to thread the mazes of life in all its classes and
under all its circumstances, common as well as romantic,
and, seeing all things, to infer and to instruct: on the
contrary, it was to stand aloof from everything that is plain
and true; to have little concern with what is rational or wise;
it was to be, like music, a moving and enchanting art, acting
upon the fancy, the affections, the passions, but scarcely
connected with the exercise of the intellectual faculties.
These writers had, indeed, adopted a tone of language which
is hardly consistent with the state of mind in which a man
makes much use of his understanding. The realities of
nature, and the truths which they suggest, would have

seemed cold and incongruous if suffered to mix with the strains of impassioned sentiment and glowing imagery in which they poured themselves forth. Spirit was not to be debased by any union with matter in their effusions, dwelling, as they did, in a region of poetical sentiment which did not permit them to walk upon the common earth or to breathe the common air.

Writers, however, whose appeal is made so exclusively to the excitabilities of mankind, will not find it possible to work upon them continuously without a diminishing effect. Poetry of which sense is not the basis, – sense rapt or inspired by passion, not bewildered or subverted, – poetry over which the passionate reason of Man does not preside in all its strength as well as all its ardours, – though it may be excellent of its kind, will not long be reputed to be poetry of the highest order. It may move the feelings and charm the fancy; but failing to satisfy the understanding, it will not take permanent possession of the strongholds of fame. Lord Byron, in giving the most admirable examples of this species of poetry, undoubtedly gave the strongest impulse to the appetite for it. Yet this impulse is losing its force; and even Lord Byron himself repudiated in the latter years of his life the poetical taste which he had espoused and propagated. The constitution of this writer's mind is not difficult to understand, and sufficiently explains the growth of his taste.

Had he united a cultivated and capacious intellect with his peculiarly poetical temperament, he would probably have been the greatest poet of his age. But no man can be a very great poet who is not also a great philosopher. Whatever Lord Byron's natural powers may have been, idleness and light reading, an early acquisition of popularity by the exercise of a single talent, and an absorbing and contracting self-love, confined the field of his operations within narrow limits. He was in knowledge merely a man of *belles-lettres*; nor does he appear at any time to have betaken himself to such studies as would have tended to the cultivation and discipline of his reasoning powers or the enlargement of his mind. He had, however, not only an ardent and brilliant

imagination, but a clear understanding; and the signs both of
what he had and of what he wanted are apparent in his
poetry. There is apparent in it a working and moulding
spirit, with a want of material to work up, – a great
command of language, with a want of any views or reflections which, if unembellished by imagery or unassociated
with passionate feelings, it would be very much worth while
to express. Page after page throughout his earlier poems,
there is the same uninformed energy at work upon the same
old feelings; and when at last he became conscious that a
theme was wanting, it was at a period of life when no man
will consent to put himself to school: he could change his
style and manner, but he could not change his moral and
intellectual being, nor extend the sphere of his contempla-
tions to subjects which were alien in *spirit* from those with
which he had been hitherto, whether in life or in literature,
exclusively conversant; in short, his mind was past the
period of growth; there was (to use a phrase of Ben
Jonson's) an *ingenistitium* or wit-stand: he felt, apparently,
that the food on which he had fed his mind had not been
invigorating; but he could no longer bear a stronger diet,
and he turned his genius loose to rove over the surface of
society, content with such slight observations upon life and
manners as any acute man of the world might collect upon
his travels, and conscious that he could recommend them to
attention by such wit, brilliancy, dexterity of phrase and
versatility of fancy, as no one but himself could command.

His misanthropy was probably, like his tenderness, not
practical, but merely matter of imagination, assumed for
purposes of effect. But whilst his ignorance of the better
elements of human nature may be believed to have been in a
great measure affected, it is not to be supposed that he knew
of them with a large and appreciating knowledge. Yet that
knowledge of human nature which is exclusive of what is
good in it, is to say the least, as shallow and imperfect as that
which is exclusive of what is evil. There is no such thing as
philosophical misanthropy; and if a misanthropical spirit, be
it genuine or affected, be found to pervade a man's writings,

that spirit may be poetical as far as it goes, but, being at fault in its philosophy, it will never, in the long run of time, approve itself equal to the institution of a poetical fame of the highest and most durable order.

These imperfections are especially observable in the portraitures of human character (if such it can be called) which are most prominent in Lord Byron's works. There is nothing in them of the mixture and modification, – nothing of the composite fabric which Nature has assigned to Man. They exhibit rather passions personified than persons impassioned. But there is yet a worse defect in them. Lord Byron's conception of a hero is an evidence, not only of scanty materials of knowledge from which to construct the ideal of a human being, but also of a want of perception of what is great or noble in our nature. His heroes are creatures abandoned to their passions, and essentially, therefore, weak of mind. Strip them of the veil of mystery and the trappings of poetry, resolve them into their plain realities, and they are such beings as, in the eyes of a reader of masculine judgement, would certainly excite no sentiment of admiration, even if they did not provoke contempt. When the conduct and feelings attributed to them are reduced into prose and brought to the test of a rational consideration, they must be perceived to be beings in whom there is no strength except that of their intensely selfish passions, – in whom all is vanity, their exertions being for vanity under the name of love or revenge, and their sufferings for vanity under the name of pride. If such beings as these are to be regarded as heroical, where in human nature are we to look for what is low in sentiment or infirm in character?

How nobly opposite to Lord Byron's ideal was that conception of an heroical character which took life and immortality from the hand of Shakspeare:–

> Give me that man
> That is not passion's slave, and I will wear him
> In my heart's core; aye, in my heart of heart.[1]

Lord Byron's genius, however, was powerful enough to cast a highly romantic colouring over these puerile creations, and to impart the charms of forcible expression, fervid feeling, and beautiful imagery, to thoughts in themselves not more remarkable for novelty than for soundness. The public required nothing more; and if he himself was bought latterly to a sense of his deficiencies of knowledge and general intellectual cultivation, it must have been more by the effect of time in so far maturing his very vigorous understanding than by any correction from without. No writer of his age has had less of the benefits of adverse criticism. His own judgement and that of his readers have been left equally without check or guidance; and the decline in popular estimation which he has suffered for these last few years may be rather attributed to a satiated appetite on the part of the public than to a rectified taste; for those who have ceased to admire his poetry so ardently as they did, do not appear in general to have transformed their admiration to any worthier object.

Nor can it be said that anything better, or indeed anything half so good, has been subsequently produced. The poetry of the day, whilst it is greatly inferior in quality, continues to be like his in kind. It consists of little more than a poetical diction, an arrangement of words implying a sensitive state of mind and therefore more or less calculated to excite corresponding associations, though, for the most part, not pertinently to any matter in hand; a diction which addresses itself to the sentient, not the percipient properties of the mind, and displays merely symbols or types of feelings which might exist with equal force in a being the most barren of understanding.

It may be proper, however, to make a distinction between the ordinary Byronian poetry, and that which may be considered as the offspring, either in the first or second generation, of the genius of Mr. Shelley. Mr. Shelley was a person of a more powerful and expansive imagination than Lord Byron, but he was inferior to him in those practical abilities which (unacceptable as such an opinion may be to those who believe themselves to be writing under the guidance of inspiration) are essential to the production of consummate poetry. The editor of Mr. Shelley's posthumous poems[2] apologizes for the publication of some fragments in a very incomplete state by remarking how much 'more than every other poet of the present day, every line and word he wrote is instinct with peculiar beauty'. Let no man sit down to write with the purpose of making every line and word beautiful and peculiar. The only effect of such an endeavour will be to corrupt his judgement and confound his understanding. In Mr. Shelley's case, besides an endeavour of this kind, there seems to have been an attempt to unrealize every object in nature, presenting them under forms and combinations in which they are never to be seen through the mere medium of our eyesight. Mr. Shelley seems to have written under the notion that no phenomena can be perfectly poetical until they shall have been so decomposed from their natural order and coherency as to be bought before the reader in the likeness of a phantasma or a vision. A poet is, in his estimation (if I may venture to infer his principles from his practice), purely and pre-eminently a visionary. Much beauty, exceeding splendour of diction and imagery, cannot but be perceived in his poetry, as well as exquisite charms of versification; and a reader of an apprehensive fancy will doubtless be entranced whilst he reads; but when he shall have closed the volume and considered within himself what it has added to his stock of permanent impressions, of recurring thoughts, of pregnant recollections, he will probably find his stores in this kind no more enriched by having read Mr. Shelley's poems, than by having gazed on so many gorgeously-coloured clouds in an evening sky. Surpassingly beautiful they were whilst before his eyes; but forasmuch as they had no relevancy to his life, past or future, the impression upon the memory barely survived that upon the senses.

I would by no means wish to be understod as saying that a poet can be too imaginative, provided that his other faculties be exercised in due proportion to his imagination. I would have no man depress his imagination, but I would have him raise his reason to be its equipoise. What I would be understood to oppugn is the strange opinion which seems to prevail amongst certain of our writers and readers of poetry, that reason stands in a species of antagonism to poetical genius, instead of being one of its most essential constituents. The maxim that a poet should be 'of imagination all compact,'[3] is not, I think, to be adopted thus literally. That predominance of the imaginative faculty, or of impassioned temperament, which is incompatible with the attributes of a sound understanding and a just judgement, may make a rhapsodist, a melodist, or a visionary, each of whom may produce what may be admired for the particular talent and beauty belonging to it: but imagination and passion thus unsupported will never make a poet in the largest and highest sense of the appellation:–

> For Poetry is Reason's self sublimed;
> 'Tis Reason's sovereignty, whereunto
> All properties of sense, all dues of wit,
> All fancies, images, perceptions, passions,
> All intellectual ordinance grown up
> From accident, necessity, or custom,
> Seen to be good, and after made authentic;
> All ordinance aforethought that from science
> Doth prescience take, and from experience law;
> All lights and institutes of digested knowledge,
> Gifts and endowments of intelligence,
> From sources living, from the dead bequests,–
> Subserve and minister.

Mr. Shelley and his disciples, however, – the followers (if I may so call them) of the phantastic school, labour to effect a revolution in this order of things. They would transfer the domicile of poetry to regions where reason, far from having any supremacy or rule, is all but unknown, an alien and an outcast; to seats of anarchy and abstraction, where imagination exercises the shadow of an authority, over a people of phantoms, in a land of dreams.

In bringing these cursory criticisms to an end, I must beg leave to warn the reader against any expectation that he will find my work free either from the faults which I attribute to others, or from faults which may be worse and more peculiarly my own. The actual works of men will not bear to be measured by their ideal standard in any case; and I may observe, in reference to my own, that my critical views have rather resulted from composition than directed it. If, however, I have been unable to avoid the errors which I condemn, or errors not less censurable, I trust that, on the other hand, I shall not be found to have deprived myself, by any narrowness or perversity of judgement, of the advantage which the study of these writers, exceptionable though they be, may undoubtedly afford to one who, whilst duly taking note of their general defects, shall not have closed his mind to a perception of their particular excellences. I feel and have already expressed, a most genuine and I hope not an inadequate admiration for the powers which they respectively possess; and wherever it might occur to me that the exercise of those powers would be appropriate and consistent, I should not fail to benefit by their example to the extent of my capabilities. To say, indeed, that I admire them, is to admit that I owe them much; for admiration is never thrown away upon the mind of him who feels it, except when it is misdirected or blindly indulged. There is perhaps nothing which more enlarges or enriches the mind than the disposition to lay it genially open to impressions of pleasure from the exercise of every species of power; nothing by which it is more impoverished than the habit of undue depreciation. What is puerile, pusillanimous, or wicked, it can do us no good to admire; but let us admire all that can be admired without debasing the disposition or stultifying the understanding.

1 *Hamlet*, III, ii, 76–8.
2 Mrs Shelley brought out an edition in 1824.
3 *A Midsummer Night's Dream*, V, i, 8.

EDWARD BULWER LYTTON

Bulwer Lytton (1803–73) was a very active writer in many literary forms, as well as a politician. His novels include *Eugene Aram* (1832), *The Last Days of Pompeii* (1834), *The Caxtons* (1849) and *The Coming Race* (1871). 'On Art in Fiction' was first published in two parts in the *Monthly Chronicle* for March and April 1838; the second part, reprinted here, constitutes the most thorough early Victorian account of the potentialities of the novel form.

5 From 'On Art in Fiction', 1838

THE CONCEPTION

A story may be well constructed, yet devoid of interest; on the other hand, the construction may be faulty and the interest vivid. This is the case even with the drama. Hamlet is not so well constructed a story as the Don Carlos of Alfieri,[1] but there is no comparison in the degree of interest excited in either tragedy. Still, though we ought not to consider that excellence in the technical arrangement of incidents as a certain proof of the highest order of art, it is a merit capable of the most brilliant effects, when possessed by a master. An exquisite mechanism in the construction of the mere story, not only gives pleasure in itself, but it displays other and loftier beauties to the best advantage. It is the setting of the jewels.

It is common to many novelists to commence a work

without any distinct chart of the country which they intend
to traverse – to suffer one chapter to grow out of another,
and invention to warm as the creation grows. Scott has
confessed to this mode of novel-writing but Scott, with all his
genius, was rather a great mechanist than a great artist. His
execution was infinitely superior to his conception. It may be
observed, indeed, that his conceptions are often singularly
poor and barren, compared with the vigour with which they
are worked out. He conceives a story with the design of
telling it as well as he can, but is wholly insensible to the high
and true aim of art, which is rather to consider for what
objects the story should be told. Scott never appears to say
to himself, 'Such a tale will throw a new light upon human
passions, or add fresh stores to human wisdom: for that
reason I select it.' He seems rather to consider what picturesque effects it will produce, what striking scenes, what
illustrations of mere manners. He regards the story with the
eye of the *property man*, though he tells it with the fervour
of the poet. It is not thus that the greatest authorities, in
fiction have composed. It is clear to us that Shakspeare,
when he selected the tale which he proposed to render
Χτημά ἐς ἀεὶ,[2] – the everlasting possession of mankind –
made it his first and paramount object to work out certain
passions, or affections of the mind, in the most complete and
profound form. He did not so much consider how the
incidents might be made most striking, as how the truths of
the human heart might be made most clear. And it is a
remarkable proof of his consummate art, that though in his
best plays we may find instances in which the mere incidents
might be made more probable, and the theatrical effects
more vivid, we can never see one instance in such plays
where the passion he desired to represent, could have been
placed in a broader light, or the character he designed
to investigate, could have been submitted to a minuter
analysis. We are quite sure that Othello and Macbeth were
not written without the clear and deep and premeditated
CONCEPTION of the story to be told us. For with Shakspeare
the conception itself is visible and gigantic from the first to

the last. So in the greatest works of Fielding a very obtuse critic may perceive that the author sat down to write in order to embody a design previously formed. The perception of moral truths urged him to the composition of his fictions. In Jonathan Wild,[3] the finest prose satire in the English language, Fielding, before he set pen to paper, had resolved to tear the mask from False Greatness. In his conception of the characters and histories of Blifil and Jones,[4] he was bent on dethroning that popular idol – False Virtue. The scorn of hypocrisy in all grades, all places, was the intellectual passion of Fielding; and his masterpieces are the results of intense convictions. That many incidents never contemplated would suggest themselves as he proceeded – that the technical plan of events might deviate and vary, according as he saw new modes of enforcing his aims, is unquestionable. But still Fielding always commenced *with* a plan – with a conception – with a moral end, to be achieved by definitive agencies, and through the medium of certain characters preformed in his mind. If Scott had no preconcerted story when he commenced Chapter the First of one of his delightful tales, it was because he was deficient in the highest attributes of art, viz., its philosophy and its ethics. He never seems to have imagined that the loftiest merit of a tale rests upon the effect it produces, not on the fancy, but on the intellect and the passions. He had no grandeur of conception, for he had no strong desire to render palpable and immortal some definite and abstract truth.

It is a sign of the low state of criticism in this country that Scott has been compared to Shakspeare. No two writers can be more entirely opposed to each other in the qualities of their genius, or the sources to which they applied. Shakspeare ever aiming at the development of the secret man, and half disdaining the mechanism of external incidents; Scott painting the ruffles and the dress, and the features and the gestures – avoiding the movements of the heart, elaborate in the progress of the incident. Scott never caught the mantle of Shakspeare, but he improved on the dresses of his wardrobe, and threw artificial effects into the scenes of his theatres.

Let us take an example; we will select one of the finest passages in Sir Walter Scott: a passage unsurpassed for its mastery over the PICTURESQUE. It is that chapter in 'Kenilworth', where Elizabeth has discovered Amy, and formed her first suspicions of Leicester.

Leicester was at this moment the centre of a splendid group of lords and ladies, assembled together under an arcade or portico, which closed the alley. The company had drawn together in that place, to attend the commands of her majesty when the hunting party should go forward, and their astonishment may be imagined, when instead of seeing Elizabeth advance towards them with her usual measured dignity of motion, they beheld her walking so rapidly, that she was in the midst of them ere they were aware; and then observed with fear and surprise, that her features were flushed betwixt anger and agitation, that her hair was loosened by her haste of motion, and that her eyes sparkled as they were wont when the spirit of Henry VIII mounted highest in his daughter. Nor were they less astonished at the appearance of the pale, extenuated, half-dead, yet still lovely female, whom the queen upheld by main strength with one hand, while with the other she waved aside the ladies and nobles, who pressed towards her, under the idea that she was taken suddenly ill. 'Where is my Lord of Leicester?' she said, in a tone that thrilled with astonishment all the courtiers who stood around – 'Stand forth, my Lord of Leicester!'

If, in the midst of the most serene day of summer, when all is light and laughing around, a thunderbolt were to fall from the clear blue vault of heaven, and rend the earth at the very feet of some careless traveller, he could not gaze upon the smouldering chasm which so unexpectedly yawned before him, with half the astonishment and fear which Leicester felt at the sight that so suddenly presented itself. He had that instant been receiving, with a political affectation of disavowing and misunderstanding their meaning, the half-uttered, half-intimated congratulations of the courtiers upon the favour of the queen, carried apparently to its highest pitch during the interview of that morning; from which most of them seemed to augur, that he might soon arise from their equal in rank to become their master. And now, while the subdued yet proud smile with which he disclaimed those inferences was yet curling his cheek, the queen shot into the circle, her passions excited to the uttermost; and, supporting with one hand, and apparently without an effort, the pale and sinking form of his almost expiring wife, and pointing with the finger of the other to her half-dead features, demanded in a voice that sounded to the ears of the astounded statesman like the last dread trumpet-call, that is to summon body and spirit to the judgement seat, 'Knowest thou this woman?'[5]

The reader will observe that the whole of this splendid passage is devoted to external effects: the loosened hair and sparkling eyes of Elizabeth – the grouping of the courtiers – the proud smile yet on the cheek of Leicester – the pale and sinking form of the wife. Only by external effects do we guess at the emotions of the agents. Scott is thinking of the costume and postures of the actors, not the passions they represent. Let us take a parallel passage in Shakspeare; parallel, for, in each, a mind disturbed with jealousy is the real object placed before the leader. It is thus that Iago describes Othello, after the latter has conceived *his* first suspicions:

> Look where he comes! Not poppy, nor mandragora,
> Nor all the drowsy syrups of the world,
> Shall ever medicine thee to that sweet sleep
> Which thou ow'dst yesterday.
> *Othello.*   Ha! ha! false to me?[6]

Here the reader will observe that there is no attempt at the Picturesque – no sketch of the outward man. It is only by a reference to the woe that kills sleep that we can form any notion of the haggard aspect of the Moor. So, if we compare the ensuing dialogue in the romance with that in the tragedy, we shall remark that Elizabeth utters only bursts of shallow passion, which convey none of the deep effects of the philosophy of jealousy; none of the sentiments that 'inform us what we are'. But every sentence uttered by Othello penetrates to the very root of the passion described: the farewell to fame and pomp, which comes from a heart that, finding falsehood in the prop it leaned on, sees the world itself, and all its quality and circumstance, crumbled away, the burst of vehement incredulity; the sudden return to doubt; the intense revenge proportioned to the intense love; the human weakness that must seek faith somewhere, and, with the loss of Desdemona, casts itself upon her denouncer, the mighty knowledge of the heart exhibited in those simple words to Iago, 'I greet *thy* love';[7] – compare all this with the mere words of Elizabeth, which have no force in themselves, but are made effective by the picturesque grouping of the scene, and you will detect at once the astonishing distinction between Shakspeare and Scott. Shakspeare could have composed the most wonderful plays from the stories in Scott; Scott could have written the most excellent stage directions to the plays of Shakspeare.

If the novelist be contented with the secondary order of Art in Fiction, and satisfied if his incidents be varied, animating, and striking, he may write from chapter to chapter, and grope his way to a catastrophe in the dark; but if he aim at loftier and more permanent effects, he will remember that to execute grandly we must conceive nobly. He will suffer the subject he selects to lie long in his mind, to be revolved, meditated, brooded over, until from the chaos breaks the light, and he sees distinctly the highest end for which his materials can be used, and the best process by which they can be reduced to harmony and order.

If, for instance, he found his tale upon some legend, the author, inspired with a great ambition, will consider what will be, not the most vivid interest, but the loftiest and most durable *order* of interest he can extract from the incidents. Sometimes it will be in a great truth elicited by the catastrophe; sometimes by the delineation of one or more characters; sometimes by the mastery over, and development of, some complicated passion. Having decided what it is that he designs to work out, he will mould his story accordingly; but before he begin to execute, he will have clearly informed his mind of the conception that induces the work itself.

INTEREST

No fiction can be first-rate if it fail to create INTEREST. But the merit of the fiction is not, by any means, proportioned to the *degree* of excitement it produces, but to the *quality* of the excitement. It is certainly some merit to make us weep; but the great artist will consider from what sources our tears are to be drawn. We may weep as much at the sufferings of a beggar as at the agonies of Lear; but from what sublime sympathies arise our tears for the last! what commonplace pity will produce the first! We may have our interest much more acutely excited by the 'Castle of Udolpho'[8] than by 'Anastasius,'[9] but in the one, it is a melo-dramatic arrangement of hair-breadth escapes and a technical skill in the arrangement of vulgar mysteries – in the other; it is the consummate knowledge of actual life, that fascinates the eye to the page. It is necessary, then, that every novel should excite interest; but one novel may produce a much more gradual, gentle, and subdued interest than another, and yet have infinitely more merit in the *quality* of the interest it excites.

TERROR AND HORROR

True art never disgusts. If, in descriptions intended to harrow us, we feel sickened and revolted by the very power with which the description is drawn, the author has passed the boundary of his province; he does not appal – he shocks. Thus, nothing is more easy than to produce a feeling of intense pain by a portrait of great bodily suffering. The vulgarest mind can do this, and the mistaken populace of readers will cry, 'See the power of this author!' But all sympathy with bodily torture is drawn from our basest infirmities; all sympathy with mental torture from our deepest passions and our most spiritual nature. HORROR is generally produced by the one, TERROR by the other. If you describe a man hanging by a breaking bough over a precipice – if you paint his starting eyeballs, his erect hair, the death-sweat on his brow, the cracking of the bough, the depth of the abyss, the sharpness of the rock, the roar of the cataract below, you may make us dizzy and sick with sympathy; but you operate on the physical nerves, and our sensation is that of coarse and revolting pain. But take a *moral* abyss: Œdipus, for instance, on the brink of learning the awful secret which proclaims him an incestuous parricide. Show the splendour of his power, the depth of his wisdom, the loftiness of his pride, and then gradually, step by step, reveal the precipice on which he stands – and you work not on the body but the mind; you produce the true tragic emotion, *terror*. Even in this, you must stop short of all that could make terror revolt while it thrills us. This, Sophocles has done by one of those fine perceptions of nature which opens the sublimest mysteries of art; we are not allowed time to 'suffer our thoughts to dwell upon the incest and self-assault of Œdipus, or upon the suicide of Jocasta, before, by the introduction of the Children, terror melts into pity, and the parricide son assumes the new aspect of the broken-hearted father.[10] A modern French writer, if he had taken this subject, would have disgusted us by details of the incest itself, or forced us from the riven heart to gaze on the bloody and eyeless sockets of the blind king; and the more he disgusted us the more he would have thought that he excelled the tragedian of Colonos. Such of the Germans, on the contrary, as follow the School of Schiller,[11] will often stop as far short of the true boundaries of Terror as the French romanticists would go beyond it. Schiller held it a principle of art never to leave the complete and entire effects of a work of art one of pain. According to him, the pleasure of the art should exceed the sympathy with the suffering. He sought to vindicate this principle by a reference to the Greek drama, but in this he confounded the sentiments with which we, moderns, read the works of Æschylus and Sophocles, with the sentiments with which a *Greek* would have read them. No doubt, to a Greek religiously impressed with the truth and reality of the woes or the terror depicted, the 'Agamemnon' of Æeschylus, the 'Œdipus Tyrannus' of Sophocles, and the 'Medea' of Euripides, would have left a far more unqualified and over-powering sentiment of awe and painful sympathy than we now can entertain for victims, whom we believe to be shadows, to deities and destinies that we know to be chimeras. Were Schiller's rule universally adopted, we should condemn Othello and Lear.

Terror may then be carried up to its full extent, provided that it work upon us through the mind, not the body, and stop short of the reaction of recoil and disgust.

DESCRIPTION

One of the greatest and most peculiar arts of the Novelist is DESCRIPTION. It is in this that he has a manifest advantage over the dramatic poet. The latter will rarely describe scenery, costume, *personals*, for they ought to be placed before the eyes of the audience by the theatre and the actors. When he does do so, it is generally understood by an intelligent critic, to be an episode introduced for the sake of some poetical beauty, which, without absolutely carrying on the plot, increases the agreeable and artistical effect of the whole performance. This is the case with the description of Dover cliff, in 'Lear', or with that of the chasm which adorns, by so splendid a passage, the monstrous tragedy of 'The Cenci'.[12] In the classical French theatre, as in the Greek, Description, it is true, becomes an essential part of the play itself, since the catastrophe is thrown into description. Hence the celebrated picture of the death of Hippolyte, in the 'Phedre' of Racine – of the suicide of Hæmon in the 'Antigone' of Sophocles. But it may be doubted whether both Sophocles and his French imitator did not, in this transfer of actions to words, strike at the very core of dramatic art, whether ancient or modern; for it may be remarked – and we are surprised that it has not been remarked before, that Æschylus preferred placing the catastrophe before the eyes of the reader; and he who remembers the sublime close of the Prometheus,[13] the storm, the lightning, the bolt, the shivered rock, and the mingled groans and threats of the Titan himself, must acknowledge that the effect is infinitely more purely tragical than it would have been if we had been told how it all happened by the Aggelos or Messenger. So in the 'Agamemnon' of the same sublime poet, though we do not see the blow given, the scene itself, opening, places before us the murderess and the corpse. No messenger intervenes – no description is required for the action. 'I stand where I struck him', says Clytæmnestra. 'The deed is done!'

But without recurring farther to the Drama of other nations, we may admit at once that in our own it is the received and approved rule that Action, as much as possible, should dispense with Description. With Narrative Fiction it is otherwise: the novel writer is his own scene painter; description is as essential to him as canvass is to the actor – description of the most various character.

In this art, none ever equalled Scott. In the comparison we made between him and Shakspeare, we meant not to censure the former for indulging in what the latter shunned; each did that which his art required. We only lament that Scott did not combine with external description an equal, or, at least, not very inferior, skill in metaphysical analysis. Had he done so, he would have achieved all of which the novelist is capable.

In the description of natural scenery, the author will devote the greatest care to such landscapes as are meant for the localities of his principal events. There is nothing, for instance, very attractive in the general features of a common; but if the author lead us through a common, on which, in a later portion of his work, a deed of murder is to be done, he will strive to fix deeply in our remembrance the character of the landscape, the stunted tree, or the mantling pool, which he means to associate in our minds with an act of terror.

If the duration of time in a fiction be limited to a year, the author may be enabled artfully to show us the progress of time by minute descriptions of the gradual change in the seasons. This is attempted to be done in the tale of 'Eugene Aram';[14] instead of telling us when it is July, and when it is

October, the author of that fiction describes the signs and characteristics of the month, and seeks to identify our interest in the natural phenomena, with the approaching fate of the hero, himself an observer and an artist of the 'clouds that pass to and fro', and the 'herbs that wither and are renewed'. Again, in description, if there be any natural objects that will bear upon the catastrophe, if, for instance, the earthquake or the inundation be intended as an agent in the fate of those whose history the narrative relates, incidental descriptions of the state of the soil, frequent references to the river or the sea, will serve to make the elements themselves minister to the interest of the plot; and the final catastrophe will be made at once more familiar, yet more sublime, if we have been prepared and led to believe that you have from the first designed to invoke to your aid the awful agencies of Nature herself. Thus, in the Œdipus at Colonos, the Poet, at the very opening of the tragedy, indulges in the celebrated description of the seats of the Dread Goddesses, because the place, and the deities themselves, though invisible, belong yet more essentially to the crowning doom of the wanderer than any of the characters introduced.

The description of *feelings* is also the property of the novelist. The dramatist throws the feelings into dialogue, – the novelist goes at once to the human heart, and calmly scrutinises, assorts, and dissects them. Few, indeed, are the writers who have hitherto attempted this – the master mystery of the hierophant! Godwin[15] has done so the most elaborately; Goethe[16] the most skilfully. The first writer is, indeed, so minute, that he is often frivolous – so lengthened, that he is generally tedious; but the cultivator of the art, and not the art itself, is to be blamed for such defects. A few words will often paint the precise state of emotion as faithfully as the most voluminous essay; and in this department condensation and brevity are to be carefully studied. Conduct us to the cavern, light the torch, and startle and awe us by what you reveal; but if you keep us all day in the cavern, the effect is lost, and our only feeling is that of impatience and desire to get away.

ARRANGEMENT OF INCIDENTS

Distinctions between the Novel and the Drama

In the arrangements of incidents, the reader will carefully study the distinctions between the novel and the drama – distinctions the more important, because they are not, at the first glance, very perceptible.

In the first place, the incidents of a play must grow, progressively, out of each other. Each scene should appear the necessary consequence of the one that precedes it. This is far from being the case with the novel; in the last, it is often desirable to go back instead of forward – to wind, to vary, to shift the interest from person to person – to keep even your principal hero, your principal actor, in the background. In the novel, you see more of Frank Osbaldistone than you do of Rob Roy,[17] but bring Rob Roy on the stage, and Frank Osbaldistone must recede at once into a fifth-rate personage.

In our closets we should be fatigued with the incessant rush of events that we desire when we make one of a multitude. Oratory and the drama in this resemble each other – that the things best to hear are not always the best to read. In the novel, we address ourselves to the one person – on the stage we address ourselves to a crowd: more rapid effects, broader and more popular sentiments, more condensed grasp of the universal passions are required for the last. The calm advice which persuades our friend would only tire out the patience of the crowd. The man who writes a play for Covent Garden ought to remember that the Theatre is but a few paces distant from the Hustings: success at either place, the Hustings or the Theatre, will depend upon a mastery over feelings, not perhaps the most commonplace, but the most commonly felt. If with his strong effects on the stage, the dramatic poet can, like Shakspeare, unite the most delicate and subtle refinement, like Shakspeare he will be a consummate artist. But the refinement will not do without the effects. In the novel it is different: the most enchanting and permanent kind of interest, in the latter, is often gentle, tranquillising, and subdued. The novelist can appeal to those delicate and subtle emotions, which are easily awakened when we are alone, but which are torpid and unfelt in the electric contagion of popular sympathies. The most refining amongst us will cease to refine when placed in the midst of a multitude.

There is a great distinction between the plot of a novel and that of a play; a distinction which has been indicated by Goethe in the 'Wilhelm Meister'. The novel allows *accident*, the drama never. In the former, your principal character may be thrown from his horse, and break his neck; in the latter, this would be a gross burlesque on the first laws of the drama; for in the drama the incidents must bring about the catastrophe; in the novel there is no such necessity. Don Quixote at the last falls ill and dies in his bed; but in order that he should fall ill and die in his bed, there was no necessity that he should fight windmills, or mistake an inn for a castle. If a novelist had taken for his theme the conspiracy of Fiesco,[18] he might have adhered to history with the most perfect consistency to his art. In the history, as Fiesco, after realising his ambitious projects, is about to step into the ship, he slips from the plank, and the weight of his armour drowns him. This is accident, and this catastrophe would not only have been admissible in the novel, but would have conveyed, perhaps, a sublimer moral than any that fiction could invent. But when Schiller adapted Fiesco for the stage, he felt that accident was not admissible, and his Fiesco falls by the hand of the patriot Verrina. The whole dialogue preceding the fatal blow is one of the most masterly adaptations of moral truth to the necessity of historical infidelity, in European literature.

In the 'Bride of Lammermoor',[19] Ravenswood is swallowed up by a quicksand. This catastrophe is singularly grand in romance; it could not be allowable on the stage; for this again is *accident*, and not *result*.

The distinctions, then, between the novel and the drama, so far as the management of incidents is concerned, are principally these: that in the one the interest must always progress – that in the other, it must often go back and often halt; that dealing with human nature in a much larger scale in the novel, you will often introduce events and incidents, not necessarily growing one out of the other, though all conducing to the completeness of the whole; that in the drama you have more impatience to guard against – you are addressing men in numbers, not the individual man; your effects must be more rapid and more startling; that in the novel you may artistically have recourse to accident for the working out of your design – in the drama, never.

The ordinary faults of a play by the novelist, and of a novel by the play-writer, will serve as an illustration of the principles which have insensibly regulated each. The novelist will be too diffuse, too narrative, and too refined in his effects for the stage; the play-writer will be too condensed, abrupt, and, above all, too exaggerated, for our notions of the Natural when we are in the closet. Stage effect is a vice in the novel; but, how can we expect a man trained to write for the stage to avoid what on the stage is a merit? A certain exaggeration of sentiment is natural, and necessary, for sublime and truthful effects when we address numbers; it would be ludicrous uttered to our friend in his easy chair. If Demosthenes, urging a young Athenian to conduct himself properly, had thundered out that sublime appeal to the shades of Marathon, Platea, and Salamis, which thrilled the popular assembly,[20] the young Athenian would have laughed in his face. If the dialogue of 'Macbeth' were the dialogue of a romance on the same subject, it would be equally good in itself, but it would seem detestable bombast. If the dialogue in 'Ivanhoe', which is matchless of its kind for spirit and fire, were shaped into blank verse, and cut up into a five-act play, it would be bald and pointless. As the difference between the effective oration and the eloquent essay – between Pitt so great to hear, and Burke so great to read, so is the difference between the writing for the eye of one man, and the writing for the ears of three thousand.

MECHANISM AND CONDUCT

The mechanism and conduct of the story ought to depend upon the nature of the preconceived design. Do you desire to work out some definite end, through the passions or through the characters you employ? Do you desire to carry on the interest less through character and passion than through incident? Or, do you rather desire to entertain and instruct by a general and wide knowledge of living manners or human nature? or, lastly, would you seek to incorporate all these objects? As you are faithful to your conception, will you be attentive to, and precise in, the machinery you use? In other words, your *progress* must depend upon the order of interest you mean to be predominant. It is by not considering this rule that critics have often called that episodical or extraneous, which is in fact a part of the design. Thus, in 'Gil Blas',[21] the object is to convey to the reader a complete picture of the surface of society; the manners, foibles, and peculiarities of the time: elevated by a general, though not very profound, knowledge of the more durable and universal elements of human nature in the abstract. Hence, the numerous takes and nouvelletes scattered throughout the work, though episodical to the adventures of Gil Blas, are not episodical to the design of Le Sage. They all serve to complete and furnish out the conception, and the whole would be less rich and consummate in its effect without them. They are not passages which lead to nothing, but conduce to many purposes we can never comprehend, unless we consider well for what end the building was planned. So if you wish to bring out all the peculiarities of a certain character, you will often seem to digress into adventures which have no palpable bearing on the external plot of incident and catastrophe. This is constantly the case with Cervantes and Fielding; and the critic who blames you for it, is committing the gross blunder of judging the novel by the laws of the drama.

But as an ordinary rule, it may be observed that, since, both in the novel and the play, human life is represented by an epitome, so in both it is desirable that all your characters should more or less be brought to bear on the conclusions you have in view. It is not necessary in the novel that they should bear on the physical events; they may sometimes bear on the mental and interior changes in the minds and characters of the persons you introduce. For instance, if you design in the life of your hero to illustrate the Passion of Jealousy upon a peculiar conformation of mind, you may introduce several characters and several incidents, which will serve to ripen his tendencies, but not have the least bearing on the actual catastrophe in which those tendencies are confirmed into deeds. This is but fidelity to real life, in which it seldom happens that they who foster the passion are the witnesses or sufferers of the effects. This distinction between interior and external agencies will be made apparent by a close study of the admirable novel of Zeluco.[22]

In the mechanism of external incidents, Scott is the greatest model that fiction possesses; and if we select from his works that in which this mechanism is most artistical, we instance not one of his most brilliant and popular, but one in which he combined all the advantages of his multiform and matured experience in the craft: we mean the 'Fair Maid of Perth'. By noting well the manner in which, in this tale, the scene is ever varied at the right moment, and the exact medium preserved between abruptness and *longueur*, how all the incidents are complicated, so as to appear inextricable, yet the solution obtained by the simplest and shortest process, the reader will learn more of the art of *mechanical* construction, than by all the rules that Aristotle himself, were he living, could lay down.

DIVISIONS OF THE WORK

In the Drama, the DIVISIONS of the plot into *Acts* are of infinite service in condensing and simplifying the design of the author. The novelist will find it convenient to himself to establish analogous divisions in the conduct of his story. The division into volumes is but the affair of the printer, and affords little help to the intellectual purposes of the author.

Hence, most of our greatest novelists have had recourse to the more definite sub-partition of the work into *Books*; and if the student use this mode of division, not from capricious or arbitrary pleasure, but with the same purposes of art, for which, in the drama, recourse is had to the division into Acts, he will find it of the greatest service. Properly speaking, each Book should be complete in itself, working out the exact and whole purpose that the author meditates in that portion of his work. It is clear, therefore, that the number of his Books will vary according to the nature of his design. Where you have shaped your story after a dramatic fashion, you will often be surprised to find how greatly you serve to keep your construction faithful to your design by the mere arrangement of the work into the same number of sub-divisions as are adopted in the drama, viz., five books instead of five acts. Where, on the other hand, you avoid the dramatic construction, and lead the reader through great varieties of life and action, meaning in each portion of the history of your hero, to illustrate separate views of society or human nature, you will probably find a much greater number of sub-divisions requisite. This must depend upon your design. Another advantage in these divisions consists in the rules that your own common sense will suggest to you with respect to the introduction of Characters. It is seldom advisable to admit any new character of importance, after the interest has arrived at a certain point of maturity. As you would not introduce a new character of consequence to the catastrophe, in the fifth act of a play, so, though with more qualification and reserve, it will be inartistical to make a similar introduction in the corresponding portion of a novel. The most illustrious exception to this general rule is in 'Clarissa',[23] in which the Avenger, the brother of the heroine, and the executioner of Lovelace, only appears at the close of the story, and for the single purpose of revenge; and here the effect is heightened by the lateness and suddenness of the introduction of the very person to whom the catastrophe is confided.

THE CATASTROPHE

The distinction between the novel and the drama is usually very visible in the Catastrophe. The stage effect of bringing all the characters together in the closing chapter, to be married or stabbed as the thing may require, is, to a fine taste, eminently displeasing in a novel. It introduces into the very place where we most desire verisimilitude, a clap-trap and theatrical effect. For it must be always remembered, that in prose fiction we require more of the Real than we do in the drama (which belongs, of right, to the regions of pure poetry), and if the very last effect bequeathed to us be that of palpable delusion and trick, the charm of the whole work is greatly impaired. Some of Scott's romances may be justly charged with this defect.

Usually, the author is so far aware of the inartist-like effect of a final grouping of all the characters before the fall of the curtain, that he brings but few of the agents he has employed to be *present* at the catastrophe, and follows what may be called the wind-up of the main interest, by one or more epilogical chapters, in which we are told how Sir Thomas married and settled at his country seat, how Miss Lucy died an old maid, and how the miser Grub was found dead on his money chest; disposing in a few sentences of the lives and deaths of all to whom we have been presented – a custom that we think might now give place to less hacknied inventions.

The drama will bear but one catastrophe; the novel will admit of more. Thus, in 'Ivanhoe', the more vehement and apparent catastrophe is the death of Bois Guilbert; but the marriage of Ivanhoe, the visit of Rebecca to Rowena, and the solemn and touching farewell of the Jewess, constitute, properly speaking, a catastrophe no less capital in itself, and no less essential to the completion of the incidents. So also there is often a moral catastrophe, as well as a physical one, sometimes identified each with the other, sometimes distinct. If you have been desirous to work out some conception of a principle or a truth, the design may not be completed till after the more violent effects which form the physical catastrophe. In the recent novel of 'Alice, or the Mysteries',[24] the external catastrophe is in the vengeance of Cæsarini and the death of Vargrave, but the complete *denouement* and completion of the more typical meanings and ethical results of the fiction are reserved to the moment when Maltravers recognises the Natural to be the true Ideal, and is brought, by the faith and beauty of simple goodness, to affection and respect for mankind, itself. In the drama, it would be necessary to incorporate in one scene all the crowning results of the preceding events. We could not bear a new interest after the death of Bois Guilbert; and a new act of mere dialogue between Alice and Maltravers, after the death of Vargrave, would be unsufferably tame and frigid. The perfection of a catastrophe is not so much in the power with which it is told, as in the feeling of completeness which it should leave on the mind. On closing the work, we ought to feel that we have read a *whole* – that there is an harmonious unity in all its parts – that its close, whether it be pleasing or painful, is that which is essentially appropriate to all that has gone before; and not only the mere isolated thoughts in the work, but the unity of the work itself, ought to leave its single and deep impression on the mind. The book itself should be a thought.

There is another distinction between the catastrophe of a novel and that of a play. In the last, it ought to be the most permanent and striking events that lead to the catastrophe; in the former, it will often be highly artistical to revive for the consummating effect, many slight details – incidents the author had but dimly shadowed out – mysteries, that you had judged, till then, he had forgotten to clear up; and to bring a thousand rivulets, that had seemed merely introduced to relieve or adorn the way, into the rapid gulf which closes over all. The effect of this has a charm not derived from mere trick, but from its fidelity to the natural and lifelike order of events. What more common in the actual world than that the great crises of our fate are influenced and coloured, not so much by the incidents and persons we have deemed most important, but by many things of remote date, or of seeming insignificance. The feather the eagle carelessly sheds by the way-side plumes the shaft that transfixes him. In this management and combination of incidents towards the grand end, knowledge of Human Nature can alone lead the student to the knowledge of Ideal Art.

These remarks from the summary of the hints and suggestions that, after a careful study of books, we submit to the consideration of the student in a class of literature now so widely cultivated, and hitherto almost wholly unexamined by the critic. We presume not to say that they form an entire code of laws for the art. Even Aristotle's immortal treatise on Poetry, were it bequeathed to us complete, would still be but a skeleton; and though no poet could read that treatise without advantage, the most glorious poetry might be, and has been, written in defiance of nearly all its laws. Genius will arrive at fame by the light of its own star; but Criticism can often serve as a sign-post to save many an unnecessary winding, and indicate many a short way. He who aspires to excel in that fiction which is the glass of truth, may learn much from books and rules, from the lecturer and the critic; but he must be also the Imaginer, the Observer. He will be ever examining human life in its most catholic and comprehensive aspects. Nor is it enough to observe, – it is necessary to feel. We must let the heart be a student as well as the head. No man who is a passionless and cold spectator, will ever be an accurate analyst, of all the motives and springs of action. Perhaps, if we were to search for the true secret of CREATIVE GENIUS, we should find that secret in the intenseness of its SYMPATHIES.

1   Vittorio Alfieri was an Italian dramatist; in his *Viluppo* (1783) Don Carlos is a central character.
2   Thucydides, *History of the Peloponnesian War*, I, xxii, 4 (mis-spelt); the phrase is translated in the following words of the text.
3   Henry Fielding (1707–54), *Jonathan Wild the Great* (1743).
4   In Fielding's *Tom Jones* (1749).
5   Scott, *Kenilworth* (1821), Ch. 34.
6   *Othello*, III, iii, 334.
7   Ibid., 473.

8   Ann Radcliffe's Gothic novel, *The Mysteries of Udolpho* (1794).
9   Thomas Hope's *Anastasius: or Memoirs of a Modern Greek* (1819).
10   In Sophocles' *Oedipus the King*.
11   Johann Christoph Friedrich von Schiller (1759–1805), the German
     poet and dramatist of the 'Sturm und Drang' (storm and stress)
     period.
12   The play by Shelley (1819).
13   Aeschylus, *Prometheus Bound*.
14   Bulwer Lytton's own novel of 1832.
15   William Godwin (1756–1836), the philosophical anarchist, wrote
     novels of psychological analysis, especially *Caleb Williams* (1794) and
     Fleetwood (1805).
16   Johann Wolfgang von Goethe (1749–1832), the great German writer,
     especially in his novel *Wilhelm Meister* (1829).
17   In Scott's *Rob Roy* (1817).
18   The theme of a play by Schiller; Bulwer Lytton has a footnote
     referring to *Die Verschwörung des Fiesco zu Genua* (1784): ' "The
     nature of this Drama", observes Schiller in his preface to *Fiesco* and
     in excuse for his corruption of history, "does not admit the hand of
     Chance".'
19   The novel by Scott (1819).
20   Demosthenes, the Greek orator, in his speech 'De Corona'.
21   The picaresque novel *Gil Blas* (1715–35) by Alain René Le Sage
     (1668–1747) was greatly admired in the eighteenth and early nine-
     teenth centuries.
22   A novel by Dr John Moore (1786).
23   Samuel Richardson (1689–1761) wrote *Clarissa Harlowe* (1747–8).
24   By Bulwer Lytton himself (1838).

THOMAS CARLYLE

Carlyle (1795–1881) was one of the most influential moralists of the age, expressing his anti-Utilitarian view of life in *Sartor Resartus* (1833–4), *The French Revolution* (1837), *Past and Present* (1843), *Latter-Day Pamphlets* (1850) and many other works. In 1840 he gave a series of lectures, of which two were devoted to literature: III was on 'The Hero as Poet', concentrating on Dante and Shakespeare and arguint that 'All deep things are Song', while V discussed, in terms of the unusual trio of Dr Johnson, Rousseau and Burns, the new idea of the category to which Carlyle himself belonged, that of the man of letters; Carlyle makes very high claims for the writer who takes his vocation seriously.

The lectures were published as *On Heroes, Hero-Worship and the Heroic in History* (1841).

6 From 'The Hero as Man of Letters', 19 May 1840

Hero-gods, Prophets, Poets, Priests are forms of Heroism that belong to the old ages, make their appearance in the remotest times; some of them have ceased to be possible long since, and cannot any more show themselves in the world. The Hero as *Man of Letters*, again, of which class we are to speak today, is altogether a product of these new ages; and so long as the wondrous art of *Writing*, or of Ready-writing which we call *Printing*, subsists, he may be expected to continue, as one of the main forms of Heroism for all future ages. He is, in various respects, a very singular phenomenon.

He is new, I say; he has hardly lasted above a century in the world yet. Never, till about a hundred years ago, was there seen any figure of a Great Soul living apart in that anomalous manner; endeavouring to speak-forth the inspiration that was in him by Printed Books, and find place and subsistence by what the world would please to give him for doing that. Much had been sold and bought, and left to make its own bargain in the marketplace; but the inspired wisdom of a Heroic Soul never till then, in that naked manner. He, with his copy-rights and copy-wrongs, in his squalid garret, in his rusty coat; ruling (for this is what he does), from his grave, after death, whole nations and generations who would, or would not, give him bread while living, – is a rather curious spectacle! Few shapes of Heroism can be more unexpected.

Alas, the Hero from of old has had to cramp himself into strange shapes: the world knows not well at any time what to do with him, so foreign is his aspect in the world! It seemed absurd to us, that men, in their rude admiration, should take some wise great Odin for a god, and worship him as such; some wise great Mahomet for one god-inspired, and religiously follow his Law for twelve centuries; but that a wise great Johnson,[1] a Burns,[2] a Rousseau,[3] should be taken for some idle nondescript, extant in the world to amuse idleness, and have a few coins and applauses thrown in, that he might live thereby; *this* perhaps, as before hinted, will one day seem a still absurder phasis of things! – Meanwhile, since it is the spiritual always that determines the material, this same Man-of-Letters Hero must be regarded as our most important modern person. He, such as he may be, is the soul of all. What he teaches, the whole world will do and make. The world's manner of dealing with him is the most significant feature of the world's general position. Looking well at his life, we may get a glance, as deep as is readily possible for us, into the life of those singular centuries which have produced him, in which we ourselves live and work.

There are genuine Men of Letters, and not genuine; as in every kind there is a genuine and a spurious. If *Hero* be taken to mean genuine, then I say the Hero as Man of Letters will be found discharging a function for us which is ever honourable, ever the highest; and was once well known to be the highest. He is uttering forth, in such a way as he has, the inspired soul of him; all that a man, in any case, can do. I say *inspired*; for what we call 'originality', 'sincerity', 'genius', the heroic quality we have no good name for, signifies that. The Hero is he who lives in the inward sphere of things, in the True, Divine and Eternal, which exists always, unseen to most, under the Temporary, Trivial: his being is in that; he declares that abroad, by act or speech as it may be, in declaring himself abroad. His life, as we said before, is a piece of the everlasting heart of Nature herself: all men's life is, – but the weak many know not the fact, and are untrue to it, in most times; the strong few are strong, heroic, perennial, because it cannot be hidden from them. The Man of Letters, like every Hero, is there to proclaim this in such sort as he can. Intrinsically it is the same function which the old generations named a man Prophet, Priest, Divinity for doing; which all manner of Heroes, by speech or by act, are sent into the world to do.

Fichte the German Philosopher[4] delivered, some forty years ago at Erlangen, a highly remarkable Course of Lectures on this subject: '*Ueber das Wesen des Gelehrten,* On the Nature of the Literary Man.' Fichte, in conformity with the Transcendental Philosophy, of which he was a distinguished teacher, declares first: That all things which we see or work with in this Earth, especially we ourselves and all persons, are as a kind of vesture or sensuous Appearance: that under all there lies, as the essence of them, what he calls the 'Divine Idea of the World'; this is the Reality which 'lies at the bottom of all Appearance'. To the mass of men no such Divine Idea is recognisable in the world; they live merely, says Fichte, among the superficialities, practicalities and shows of the world, not dreaming that there is anything divine under them. But the Man of Letters is sent hither specially that he may discern for himself, and make manifest to us, this same Divine Idea: in every new generation it will manifest itself in a new dialect; and he is there for the purpose of doing that. Such is Fichte's phraseology; with which we need not quarrel. It is his way of naming what I here, by other words, am striving imperfectly to name; what there is at present no name for: The unspeakable Divine Significance, full of splendour, of wonder and terror, that lies in the being of every man, of every thing, – the Presence of the God who made every man and thing. Mahomet taught this in his dialect; Odin in his: it is the thing which all thinking hearts, in one dialect or another, are here to teach.

Fichte calls the Man of Letters, therefore, a Prophet, or as he prefers to phrase it, a Priest, continually unfolding the Godlike to men: Men of Letters are a perpetual Priesthood, from age to age, teaching all men that a God is still present in their life; that all 'Appearance,' whatsoever we see in the world, is but as a vesture for the 'Divine Idea of the World'. for 'that which lies at the bottom of Appearance'. In the true Literary Man there is thus ever, acknowledged or not by the world, a sacredness: he is the light of the world; the world's Priest: – guiding it, like a sacred Pillar of Fire, in is dark pilgrimage through the waste of Time. Fichte discriminates with sharp zeal the *true* Literary Man, what we here call the *Hero* as Man of Letters, from multitudes of false unheroic. Whoever lives not wholly in this Divine Idea, or living partially in it, struggles not, as for the one good, to live wholly in it, – he is, let him live where else he like, in what pomps and prosperities he like, no Literary Man; he is, says Fichte, a 'Bungler, *Stümper*'. Or at best, if he belong to the prosaic provinces, he may be a 'Hodman'; Fichte even calls him elsewhere a 'Nonentity', and has in short no mercy for him, no wish that *he* should continue happy among us! This is Fichte's notion of the Man of Letters. It means, in its own form, precisely what we here mean.

1   Samuel Johnson (1709–84) the great eighteenth-century moralist.
2   Robert Burns (1759–96), the Scots poet.
3   Jean-Jaques Rousseau (1712–78), the French social thinker and auto-biographical writer.
4   Johann Gottlieb Fichte (1762–1814), the German Idealist philosopher.

CHARLES DICKENS

Dickens was of course the most popular novelist of the age. This retrospective introduction to one of his earliest novels shows him taking up a position in the line of the English satirists and social critics, and asserting the accuracy of his observation of the world described.

7 The Author's Introduction to the Third Edition of *Oliver Twist*, 1841

'Some of the author's friends cried, "Lookee, gentlemen, the man is a villain; but it is Nature for all that;" and the young critics of the age, the clerks, apprentices, &c., called it low, and fell a groaning.' – FIELDING

The greater part of this Tale was originally published in a magazine. When I completed it, and put it forth in its present form three years ago, I fully expected it would be objected to on some very high moral grounds in some very high moral quarters. The result did not fail to prove the justice of my anticipations.

I embrace the present opportunity of saying a few words in explanation of my aim and object in its production. It is in some sort a duty with me to do so, in gratitude to those who sympathised with me and divined my purpose at the time, and who, perhaps, will not be sorry to have their impression confirmed under my own hand.

It is, it seems, a very coarse and shocking circumstance, that some of the characters in these pages are chosen from the most criminal and degraded of London's population;

that Sikes is a thief, and Fagin a receiver of stolen goods; that the boys are pickpockets, and the girl is a prostitute.

I confess I have yet to learn that a lesson of the purest good may not be drawn from the vilest evil. I have always believed this to be a recognised and established truth, laid down by the greatest men the world has ever seen, constantly acted upon by the best and wisest natures, and confirmed by the reason and experience of every thinking mind. I saw no reason, when I wrote this book, why the very dregs of life, so long as their speech did not offend the ear, should not serve the purpose of a moral, at least as well as its froth and cream. Nor did I doubt that there lay festering in Saint Giles's as good materials towards the truth as any flaunting in Saint James's.[1]

In this spirit, when I wished to shew, in little Oliver, the principle of Good surviving through every adverse circumstance, and triumphing at last; and when I considered among what companions I could try him best, having regard to that kind of men into whose hands he would most naturally fall; I bethought myself of those who figure in these volumes. When I came to discuss the subject more maturely with myself, I saw many strong reasons for pursuing the course to which I was inclined. I had read of thieves by scores – seductive fellows (amiable for the most part), faultless in dress, plump in pocket, choice in horseflesh, bold in bearing, fortunate in gallantry, great at a song, a bottle, pack of cards or dice-box, and fit companions for the bravest. But I had never met (except in HOGARTH)[2] with the miserable reality. It appeared to me that to draw a knot of such associates in crime as really do exist; to paint them in all their deformity, in all their wretchedness, in all the squalid poverty of their lives; to shew them as they really are, for ever skulking uneasily through the dirtiest paths of life, with the great, black, ghastly gallows closing up their prospect, turn them where they may; it appeared to me that to do this, would be to attempt a something which was greatly needed, and which would be a service to society. And therefore I did it as I best could.

In every book I know, where such characters are treated of at all, certain allurements and fascinations are thrown around them. Even in the Beggar's Opera,[3] the thieves are represented as leading a life which is rather to be envied than otherwise; while MACHEATH, with all the captivations of command, and the devotion of the most beautiful girl and only pure character in the piece, is as much to be admired and emulated by weak beholders, as any fine gentleman in a red coat who has purchased, as VOLTAIRE says, the right to command a couple of thousand men, or so, and to affront death at their head. Johnson's question, whether any man will turn thief because Macheath is reprieved, seems to me beside the matter. I ask myself, whether any man will be deterred from turning thief because of his being sentenced to death, and because of the existence of Peachum and Lockit; and remembering the captain's roaring life, and great appearance, vast success, and strong advantages, I feel assured that nobody having a bent that way will take any warning from him, or will see anything in the play but a very flowery and pleasant road, conducting an honourable ambition in course of time, to Tyburn Tree.

In fact, Gay's witty satire on society had a general object, which made him careless of example in this respect, and gave him other, wider, and higher aims. The same may be said of Sir Edward Bulwer's admirable and most powerful novel of Paul Clifford,[4] which cannot be fairly considered as having, or being intended to have, any bearing on this part of the subject, one way or other.

What manner of life is that which is described in these pages, as the every-day existence of a Thief? What charms has it for the young and ill-disposed, what allurements for the most jolter-headed of juveniles? Here are no canterings upon moonlit heaths, no merry-makings in the snuggest of all possible caverns, none of the attractions of dress, no embroidery, no lace, no jack-boots, no crimson coats and ruffles, none of the dash and freedom with which 'the road' has been, time out of mind, invested. The cold, wet, shelterless midnight streets of London; the foul and frowsy dens, where vice is closely packed and lacks the room to turn; the haunts of hunger and disease, the shabby rags that scarcely hold together: where are the attractions of these things? Have they no lesson, and do they not whisper something beyond the little-regarded warning of a moral precept?

But there are people of so refined and delicate a nature, that they cannot bear the contemplation of these horrors. Not that they turn instinctively from crime; but that criminal characters, to suit them, must be, like their meat, in delicate disguise. A Massaroni[5] in green velvet is quite an enchanting creature; but a Sikes in fustian is insupportable. A Mrs. Massaroni, being a lady in shot petticoats and a fancy dress, is a thing to imitate in tableaux and have in lithograph on pretty songs; but a Nancy, being a creature in a cotton gown and cheap shawl, is not to be thought of. It is wonderful how Virtue turns from dirty stockings; and how Vice, married to ribbons and a little gay attire, changes her name, as wedded ladies do, and becomes Romance.

Now, as the stern and plain truth, even in the dress of this (in novels) much exalted race, was a part of the purpose of this book, I will not, for these readers, abate one hole in the Dodger's coat, or one scrap of curlpaper in the girl's dishevelled hair. I have no faith in the delicacy which cannot bear to look upon them. I have no desire to make proselytes among such people. I have no respect for their opinion, good or bad; do not covet their approval; and do not write for their amusement. I venture to say this without reserve; for I am not aware of any writer in our language having a respect for himself, or held in any respect by his posterity, who ever has descended to the taste of this fastidious class.

On the other hand, if I look for examples, and for precedents, I find them in the noblest range of English literature. Fielding, De Foe, Goldsmith, Smollett, Richardson, Mackenzie[6] – all these for wise purposes, and especially the two first, brought upon the scene the very scum and refuse of the land. Hogarth, the moralist, and censor of his age – in whose great works the times in which he lived, and the characters of every time, will never cease to be reflected – did the like, without the compromise of a hair's breadth; with a power and depth of thought which belonged to few men before him, and will probably appertain to fewer still in time to come. Where does this giant stand now in the estimation of his countrymen? And yet, if I turn back to the days in which he or any of these men flourished, I find the same reproach levelled against them every one, each in his turn, by the insects of the hour, who raised their little hum, and died, and were forgotten.

Cervantes laughed Spain's chivalry away, by showing Spain its impossible and wild absurdity. It was my attempt, in my humble and far-distant sphere, to dim the false glitter surrounding something which really did exist, by shewing it in its unattractive and repulsive truth. No less consulting my own taste, than the manners of the age, I endeavoured, while I painted it in all its fallen and degraded aspect, to banish from the lips of the lowest character I introduced, any expression that could by possibility offend; and rather to lead to the unavoidable inference that its existence was the most debased and vicious kind, than to prove it elaborately by words and deeds. In the case of the girl, in particular, I kept this intention constantly in view. Whether it is apparent in the narrative, and how it is executed, I leave my readers to determine.

It has been observed of this girl, that her devotion to the brutal housebreaker does not seem natural, and it has been objected to Sikes in the same breath – with some inconsistency, as I venture to think – that he is surely overdrawn, because in him there would appear to be none of those redeeming traits which are objected to as unnatural in his mistress. Of the latter objection I will merely say, that I fear there are in the world some insensible and callous natures that do become, at last, utterly and irredeemably bad. But whether this be so or not, of one thing I am certain: that there are such men as Sikes, who, being closely followed through the same space of time, and through the same current of circumstances, would not give, by one look or action of a moment, the faintest indication of a better nature. Whether every gentler human feeling is dead within such bosoms, or the proper chord to strike has rusted and is hard to find, I do not know, but that the fact is so, I am sure.

It is useless to discuss whether the conduct and character of the girl seems natural or unnatural, probably or improbable, right or wrong. IT IS TRUE. Every man who has watched these melancholy shades of life knows it to be so. Suggested to my mind long ago – long before I dealt in fiction – by what I often saw and read of, in actual life around me, I have, for years, tracked it through many profligate and noisome ways, and found it still the same. From the first introduction of that poor wretch, to her laying her bloody head upon the robber's breast, there is not one word exaggerated or over-wrought. It is emphatically God's truth, for it is the truth He leaves in such depraved and miserable breasts; the hope yet lingering behind; the last fair drop of water at the bottom of the dried-up weed-choked well. It involves the best and worst shades of our common nature; much of its ugliest hues, and something of its most beautiful; it is a contradiction, an anomaly, an apparent impossibility, but it is a truth. I am glad to have had it doubted, for in that circumstance I find a sufficient assurance that it needed to be told.

1 Poorer and richer parts of London respectively.
2 William Hogarth (1697–1764), the painter and engraver whose series of moral commentaries like the 'Harlot's Progress' and the 'Rake's Progress' Dickens greatly admired.
3 John Gay (1685–1732) produced *The Beggar's Opera* in 1728; it involves the story of the highwayman Macheath, who is reprieved at the last moment; Peachum and Lockit are other characters in the opera.
4 Bulwer Lytton's *Paul Clifford* (1830) tells an exciting story about a young man who becomes unwillingly involved in crime.
5 The Massaronis are glamorous criminal figures from the upper class, unlike Sikes and Nancy, the working-class characters in Dickens's novel.
6 Dickens shows his awareness of the leading novelists of the eighteenth century; least known today is Henry Mackenzie (1745–1831), whose *The Man of Feeling* (1771) was a great success at the time.

CHARLOTTE BRONTË

Charlotte Brontë (1816–55) published *Jane Eyre* (1847), *Shirley* (1849) and *Villette* (1853) under the pseudonym Currer Bell. She was a deliberately Romantic novelist, as can be seen from these three passages.

8 Preface to the Second Edition of *Jane Eyre*, 1847

A Preface to the first edition of 'Jane Eyre' being unnecessary, I gave none: this second edition demands a few words both of acknowledgment and miscellaneous remark.

My thanks are due in three quarters.

To the Public, for the indulgent ear it has inclined to a plain tale with few pretensions.

To the Press, for the fair field its honest suffrage has opened to an obscure aspirant.

To my Publishers, for the aid their tact, their energy, their practical sense, and frank liberality have afforded an unknown and unrecommended Author.

The Press and the Public are but vague personifications for me, and I must thank them in vague terms; but my Publishers are definite: so are certain generous critics who have encouraged me as only large-hearted and high-minded men know how to encourage a struggling stranger; to them, *i.e.* to my Publishers and the select Reviewers, I say cordially, Gentlemen, I thank you from my heart.

Having thus acknowledged what I owe those who have aided and approved me, I turn to another class; a small one, so far as I know, but not, therefore, to be overlooked. I mean the timorous or carping few who doubt the tendency of such books as 'Jane Eyre:' in whose eyes whatever is unusual is wrong; whose ears detect in each protest against bigotry – that parent of crime – an insult to piety, that regent of God on earth. I would suggest to such doubters certain obvious distinctions; I would remind them of certain simple truths.

Conventionality is not morality. Self-righteousness is not religion. To attack the first is not to assail the last. To pluck the mask from the face of the Pharisee, is not to lift an impious hand to the Crown of Thorns.

These things and deeds are diametrically opposed: they are as distinct as is vice from virtue. Men too often confound them; they should not be confounded: appearance should not be mistaken for truth; narrow human doctrines, that only tend to elate and magnify a few, should not be substituted for the world-redeeming creed of Christ. There is – I repeat it – a difference; and it is a good, and not a bad action to mark broadly and clearly the line of separation between them.

The world may not like to see these ideas dissevered, for it has been accustomed to blend them; finding it convenient to make external show pass for sterling worth – to let white-washed walls vouch for clean shrines. It may hate him who dares to scrutinize and expose – to raise the gilding, and show base metal under it – to penetrate the sepulchre, and reveal charnel relics: but hate as it will, it is indebted to him.

Ahab did not like Micaiah,[1] because he never prophesied good concerning him, but evil: probably he liked the sycophant son of Chenaannah better; yet might Ahab have escaped a bloody death, had he but stopped his ears to flattery, and opened them to faithful counsel.

There is a man in our own days whose words are not framed to tickle delicate ears: who, to my thinking, comes before the great ones of society, much as the son of Imlah[2] came before the throned Kings of Judah and Israel; and who speaks truth as deep, with a power as prophet-like and as

vital – a mien as dauntless and as daring. Is the satirist of
'Vanity Fair' admired in high places? I cannot tell; but I
think if some of those amongst whom he hurls the Greek fire
of his sarcasm, and over whom he flashes the levin-brand[3] of
his denunciation, were to take his warnings in time – they or
their seed might yet escape a fatal Ramoth-Gilead.[4]

Why have I alluded to this man? I have alluded to him,
Reader, because I think I see in him an intellect profounder
and more unique than his contemporaries have yet recognised; because I regard him as the first social regenerator of
the day – as the very master of that working corps who
would restore to rectitude the warped system of things;
because I think no commentator on his writings has yet
found the comparison that suits him, the terms which rightly
characterize his talent. They say he is like Fielding: they talk
of his wit, humour, comic powers. He resembles Fielding as
an eagle does a vulture: Fielding could stoop on carrion, but
Thackeray never does. His wit is bright, his humour attractive, but both bear the same relation to his serious genius,
that the mere lambent sheet-lightning playing under the
edge of the summer-cloud, does to the electric death-spark
hid in its womb. Finally; I have alluded to Mr Thackeray,
because to him – if he will accept the tribute of a total
stranger – I have dedicated this second edition of 'Jane Eyre.'

1 I Kings 22 tells the story of how Ahab, King of Israel, ignored the
   prophecy of Micaiah that he would be defeated in battle by the
   Syrians; Zedekiah, the son of Chenaannah, gave an opposing prophecy of success.
2 i.e. Micaiah.
3 Lightning-flash.
4 Where the disastrous battle took place.

9 From a letter to W. S. Williams, 1850

[W. S. Williams was the publisher's reader who had brought
about the acceptance of *Jane Eyre* by Smith and Elder; she
had already found herself in disagreement with G. H. Lewes

(see No. 28) for his high evaluation of Jane Austen's novels, which she found to be limited by their avoidance of passion.]

I have likewise read one of Miss Austen's works *Emma* – read it with interest and with just the degree of admiration which Miss Austen herself would have thought sensible and suitable – anything like warmth or enthusiasm; anything energetic, poignant, heartfelt, is utterly out of place in commending these works: all such demonstration the authoress would have met with a well-bred sneer, would have calmly scorned as outré and extravagant. She does her business of delineating the surface of the lives of genteel English people curiously well; there is a Chinese fidelity, a miniature delicacy in the painting: she ruffles her reader by nothing vehement, disturbs him by nothing profound: the Passions are perfectly unknown to her; she rejects even a speaking acquaintance with that stormy Sisterhood; even to the Feelings she vouchsafes no more than an occasional graceful but distant recognition; too frequent converse with them would ruffle the smooth elegance of her progress. Her business is not half so much with the human heart as with the human eyes, mouth, hands and feet; what sees keenly, speaks aptly, moves flexibly, it suits her to study, but what throbs fast and full, though hidden, what the blood rushes through, what is the unseen seat of Life and the sentient target of death – *this* Miss Austen ignores; she no more, with her mind's eye, beholds the heart of her race than each man, with bodily vision sees the heart in his heaving breast. Jane Austen was a complete and most sensible lady, but a very incomplete, and rather insensible (*not senseless*) woman, if this is heresy – I cannot help it. If I said it to some people (Lewes for instance) they would directly accuse me of advocating exaggerated heroics, but I am not afraid of your falling into any such vulgar error.

10 Editor's Preface to the New Edition of *Wuthering Heights*, 1850

I have just read over 'Wuthering Heights' and, for the first time, have obtained a clear glimpse of what are termed (and,

perhaps, really are) its faults; have gained a definite notion
of how it appears to other people – to strangers who knew
nothing of the author; who are unacquainted with the
locality where the scenes of the story are laid; to whom the
inhabitants, the customs, the natural characteristics of the
outlying hills and hamlets in the West-Riding of Yorkshire
are things alien and unfamiliar.

To all such 'Wuthering Heights' must appear a rude and
strange production. The wild moors of the north of England
can for them have no interest; the language, the manners,
the very dwellings and household customs of the scattered
inhabitants of those districts, must be to such readers in a
great measure unintelligible, and – where intelligible –
repulsive. Men and women who, perhaps, naturally very
calm, and with feelings moderate in degree, and little
marked in kind, have been trained from their cradle to
observe the utmost evenness of manner and guardedness of
language, will hardly know what to make of the rough,
strong utterance, the harshly manifested passions, the un-
bridled aversions, and headlong partialities of unlettered
moorland hinds and rugged moorland squires, who have
grown up untaught and unchecked, except by mentors as
harsh as themselves. A large class of readers, likewise, will
suffer greatly from the introduction into the pages of this
work of words printed with all their letters, which it has
become the custom to represent by the initial and final letter
only – a blank line filling the interval. I may as well say at
once that, for this circumstance, it is out of my power to
apologize; deeming it, myself, a rational plan to write words
at full length. The practice of hinting by single letters those
expletives with which profane and violent persons are wont
to garnish their discourse, strikes me as a proceeding which,
however well meant, is weak and futile. I cannot tell what
good it does – what feeling it spares – what horror it
conceals.

With regard to the rusticity of 'Wuthering Heights' I admit
the charge, for I feel the quality. It is rustic all through. It is
moorish, and wild, and knotty as a root of heath. Nor was it

natural that it should be otherwise; the author being herself a native and nursling of the moors. Doubtless, had her lot been cast in a town, her writings, if she had written at all, would have possessed another character. Even had chance or taste led her to choose a similar subject, she would have treated it otherwise. Had Ellis Bell[1] been a lady or a gentleman accustomed to what is called 'the world', her view of a remote and unreclaimed region, as well as of the dwellers therein, would have differed greatly from that actually taken by the homebred country girl. Doubtless it would have been wider – more comprehensive: whether it would have been more original or more truthful is not so certain. As far as the scenery and locality are concerned, it could scarcely have been so sympathetic: Ellis Bell did not describe as one whose eye and taste alone found pleasure in the prospect; her native hills were far more to her than a spectacle; they were what she lived in, and by, as much as the wild birds, their tenants, or as the heather, their produce. Her descriptions, then, of natural scenery, are what they should be, and all they should be.

Where delineation of human character is concerned, the case is different. I am bound to avow that she had scarcely more practical knowledge of the peasantry amongst whom she lived, than a nun has of the country people who sometimes pass her convent gates. My sister's disposition was not naturally gregarious; circumstances favoured and fostered her tendency to seclusion; except to go to church or take a walk on the hills, she rarely crossed the threshold of home. Though her feeling for the people round was benevolent, intercourse with them she never sought; nor, with very few exceptions, ever experienced. And yet she knew them: knew their ways, their language, their family histories; she could hear of them with interest, and talk of them with detail, minute, graphic, and accurate; but *with* them, she rarely exchanged a word. Hence it ensued that what her mind had gathered of the real concerning them, was too exclusively confined to those tragic and terrible traits of which, in listening to the secret annals of every rude vicinage, the memory is sometimes compelled to receive the impress. Her imagination, which was a spirit more sombre than sunny, more powerful than sportive, found in such traits material whence it wrought creations like Heathcliff, like Earnshaw, like Catherine. Having formed these beings, she did not know what she had done. If the auditor of her work when read in manuscript, shuddered under the grinding influence of natures so relentless and implacable, of spirits so lost and fallen; if it was complained that the mere hearing of certain vivid and fearful scenes banished sleep by night, and disturbed mental peace by day, Ellis Bell would wonder what was meant, and suspect the complainant of affectation. Had she but lived, her mind would of itself have grown like a strong tree, loftier, straighter, wider-spreading, and its matured fruits would have attained a mellower ripeness and sunnier bloom; but on that mind time and experience alone could work: to the influence of other intellects, it was not amenable.

Having avowed that over much of 'Wuthering Heights' there broods 'a horror of great darkness'; that, in its storm-heated and electrical atmosphere, we seem at times to breathe lightning, let me point to those spots where clouded daylight and the eclipsed sun still attest their existence. For a specimen of true benevolence and homely fidelity, look at the character of Nelly Dean; for an example of constancy and tenderness, remark that of Edgar Linton. (Some people will think these qualities do not shine so well incarnate in a man as they would do in a woman, but Ellis Bell could never be brought to comprehend this notion: nothing moved her more than any insinuation that the faithfulness and clemency, the long-suffering and loving-kindness which are esteemed virtues in the daughters of Eve, become foibles in the sons of Adam. She held that mercy and forgiveness are the divinest attributes of the Great Being who made both man and woman, and that what clothes the Godhead in glory, can disgrace no form of feeble humanity.) There is a dry saturnine humour in the delineation of old Joseph, and some glimpses of grace and gaiety animate the younger Catherine.

Nor is even the first heroine of the name destitute of a certain strange beauty in her fierceness, or of honesty in the midst of perverted passion and passionate perversity.

Heathcliff, indeed, stands unredeemed; never once swerving in his arrow-straight course to perdition, from the time when 'the little black-haired, swarthy thing, as dark as if it came from the Devil', was first unrolled out of the bundle and set on its feet in the farm-house kitchen, to the hour when Nelly Dean found the grim, stalwart corpse laid on its back in the panel-enclosed bed, with wide-gazing eyes that seemed 'to sneer at her attempt to close them, and parted lips and sharp white teeth that sneered too'.

Heathcliff betrays one solitary human feeling, and that is *not* his love for Catherine; which is a sentiment fierce and inhuman: a passion such as might boil and glow in the bad essence of some evil genius; a fire that might form the tormented centre – the ever-suffering soul of a magnate of the infernal world: and by its quenchless and easeless ravage effect the execution of the decree which dooms him to carry Hell with him wherever he wanders. No; the single link that connects Heathcliff with humanity is his rudely confessed regard for Hareton Earnshaw – the young man whom he has ruined; and then his half-implied esteem for Nelly Dean. These solitary traits omitted, we should say he was child neither of Lascar[2] nor gipsy, but a man's shape animated by demon life – a Ghoul – an Afreet.[3]

Whether it is right or advisable to create beings like Heathcliff, I do not know: I scarcely think it is. But this I know; the writer who possesses the creative gift owns something of which he is not always master – something that at times strangely wills and works for itself. He may lay down rules and devise principles, and to rules and principles it will perhaps for years lie in subjection; and then, haply without any warning of revolt, there comes a time when it will no longer consent to 'harrow the vallies, or be bound with a band in the furrow' – when it 'laughs at the multitude of the city, and regards not the crying of the river' – when, refusing absolutely to make ropes out of sea-sand any longer, it sets to work on statue-hewing, and you have a Pluto or a Jove, a Tisiphone or a Psyche, a Mermaid or a Madonna, as Fate or Inspiration direct. Be the work grim or glorious, dread or divine, you have little choice left but quiescent adoption. As for you – the nominal artist – your share in it has been to work passively under dictates you neither delivered nor could question – that would not be uttered at your prayer, nor suppressed nor changed at your caprice. If the result be attractive, the World will praise you, who little deserve praise; if it be repulsive, the same World will blame you, who almost as little deserve blame.

'Wuthering Heights' was hewn in a wild workshop, with simple tools, out of homely materials. The statuary found a granite block on a solitary moor: gazing thereon, he saw how from the crag might be elicited a head, savage, swart, sinister; a form moulded with at least one element of grandeur – power. He wrought with a rude chisel, and from no model but the vision of his meditations. With time and labour, the crag took human shape; and there it stands colossal, dark, and frowning, half statue, half rock: in the former sense, terrible and goblin-like; in the latter, almost beautiful, for its colouring is of mellow grey, and moorland moss clothes it; and heath, with its blooming bells and balmy fragrance, grows faithfully close to the giant's foot.

1 The name under which Emily Brontë published *Wuthering Heights*.
2 An East Indian sailor.
3 A demon (in Islamic mythology).

WILLIAM MAKEPEACE THACKERAY

Thackeray (1811–63), best known for *Vanity Fair* (1847), was Dickens' major rival for the allegiance of the early Victorian reading public. Numerous comments on the writing of fiction can be found in the novels themselves, in lectures like *The English Humourists of the Eighteenth Century* (published 1853), and essays like *The Roundabout Papers* (1862). He often stresses the gap between fiction and reality, and the novelist's responsibility to the truth.

11 From *Catherine*, 1839–40

This being a good opportunity for closing Chapter I, we ought, perhaps, to make some apologies to the public for introducing them to characters that are so utterly worthless; as we confess all our heroes, with the exception of Mr. Bullock, to be. In this we have consulted nature and history, rather than the prevailing taste and the general manner of authors. The amusing novel of 'Ernest Maltravers',[1] for instance, opens with a seduction; but then it is performed by people of the strictest virtue on both sides: and there is so much religion and philosophy in the heart of the seducer, so much tender innocence in the soul of the seduced, that – bless the little dears! – their very peccadilloes make one interested in them; and their naughtiness becomes quite sacred, so deliciously is it described. Now, if we *are* to be interested by rascally actions, let us have them with plain faces, and let them be performed, not by virtuous philosophers, but by rascals. Another clever class of novelists adopt the contrary system, and create interest by making their rascals perform virtuous actions. Against these popular plans we here solemnly appeal. We say, let your rogues in novels act like rogues, and your honest men like honest men; don't let us have any juggling and thimblerigging with virtue and vice, so that, at the end of three volumes, the bewildered reader shall not know which is which; don't let us find ourselves kindling at the generous qualities of thieves, and sympathising with the rascalities of noble hearts. For our own part, we know what the public likes, and have chosen rogues for our characters, and have taken a story from the 'Newgate Calendar',[2] which we hope to follow out to edification. Among the rogues, at least, we will have nothing that shall be mistaken for virtues. And if the British public (after calling for three or four editions) shall give up, not only our rascals, but the rascals of all other authors, we shall be content:– we shall apply to Government for a pension, and think that our duty is done.

1 By Bulwer Lytton (1837).
2 A publication giving information about criminals in Newgate Prison.

12 From a letter to Mark Lemmon, 24 February 1847

What I mean applies to my own case & that of all of us – who set up as Satirical-Moralists – and having such a vast multitude of readers whom we not only amuse but teach. And indeed, a solemn prayer to God Almighty was in my thoughts that we may never forget truth & Justice and kindness as the great ends of our profession. There's something of the same strain in Vanity Fair. A few years ago I should have sneered at the idea of setting up as a teacher at all, and perhaps at this pompous and pious way of talking about a few papers of jokes in Punch[1] – but I have got to believe in the business, and in many other things since then. And our profession seems to me to be as serious as the

Parson's own. Please God we'll be honest & kind was what I meant and all I meant. I swear nothing more.

1   The comic magazine, to which Thackeray was a regular contributor.

13 The Preface to *Pendennis* 1850

If this kind of composition, of which the two years' product is now laid before the public, fail in art, as it constantly does and must, it at least has the advantage of a certain truth and honesty, which a work more elaborate might lose. In his constant communication with the reader, the writer is forced into frankness of expression, and to speak out his own mind and feelings as they urge him. Many a slip of the pen and the printer, many a word spoken in haste, he sees and would recall as he looks over his volume. It is a sort of confidential talk between writer and reader, which must often be dull, must often flag. In the course of his volubility, the perpetual speaker must of necessity lay bare his own weaknesses, vanities, peculiarities. And as we judge a man's character, after long frequenting his society, not by one speech, or by one mood or opinion, or by one day's talk, but by the tenor of his general bearing and conversation; so of a writer, who delivers himself up to you perforce unreservedly, you say, Is he honest? Does he tell the truth in the main? Does he seem actuated by a desire to find out and speak it? Is he a quack, who shams sentiment, or mouths for effect? Does he seek popularity by claptraps or other arts? I can no more ignore good fortune than any other chance which has befallen me. I have found many thousands more readers than I ever looked for. I have no right to say to these, You shall not find fault with my art, or fall asleep over my pages; but I ask you to believe that this person writing strives to tell the truth. If there is not that, there is nothing.

Perhaps the lovers of 'excitement' may care to know that this book began with a very precise plan, which was entirely put aside. Ladies and gentlemen, you were to have been

treated, and the writer's and the publishers' pocket bene-
fited, by the recital of the most active horrors. What more
exciting than a ruffian (with many admirable virtues) in
St Giles's visited constantly by a young lady from Belgravia?
What more stirring than the contrasts of society? the mixture
of slang and fashionable language? the escapes, the battles,
the murders? Nay, up to nine o'clock this very morning, my
poor friend, Colonel Altamont,[1] was doomed to execution,
and the author only relented when his victim was actually at
the window.

The 'exciting' plan was laid aside (with a very honourable
forbearance on the part of the publishers) because, on
attempting it, I found that I failed from want of experience
of my subject; and never having been intimate with any
convict in my life, and the manners of ruffians and gaol-birds
being quite unfamiliar to me, the idea of entering into
competition with M. Eugène Sue[2] was abandoned. To
describe a real rascal, you must make him so horrible that he
would be too hideous to show; and unless the painter paints
him fairly, I hold he has no right to show him at all.

Even the gentlemen of our age – this is an attempt to
describe one of them, no better nor worse than most
educated men – even these we cannot show as they are, with
the notorious foibles and selfishness of their lives and their
education. Since the author of 'Tom Jones' was buried, no
writer of fiction among us has been permitted to depict to his
utmost power a MAN.[3] We must drape him, and give him a
certain conventional simper. Society will not tolerate the
Natural in our Art. Many ladies have remonstrated and
subscribers left me, because, in the course of the story, I
described a young man resisting and affected by temptation.
My object was to say, that he had the passions to feel, and
the manliness and generosity to overcome them. You will
not hear – it is best to know it – what moves in the real
world, what passes in society, in the clubs, colleges, mess-
rooms, – what is the life and talk of your sons. A little more
frankness than is customary has been attempted in this story;
with no bad desire on the writer's part, it is hoped, and with

no ill consequence to any reader. If the truth is not always pleasant; at any rate truth is best, from whatever chair – from those whence graver writers or thinkers argue, as from that at which the storyteller sits as he concludes his labour, and bids his kind reader farewell.

1   A character in *Pendennis*.
2   Eugène Sue (1804–57) was a prolific and popular novelist of Paris underworld life.
3   Fielding published *Tom Jones* in 1749, and died in 1754.

14 From *The Newcomes* 1855

What about Sir Barnes Newcome ultimately?[1] My impression is that he is married again, and it is my fervent hope that his present wife bullies him. Mrs. Mackenzie cannot have the face to keep that money which Clive paid over to her, beyond her lifetime; and will certainly leave it and her savings to little Tommy. I should not be surprised if Madame de Montcontour left a smart legacy to the Pendennis children; and Lord Kew stood godfather in case – in case Mr. and Mrs. Clive wanted such an article. But have they any children? I, for my part, should like her best without, and entirely devoted to little Tommy. But for you, dear friend, it is as you like. You may settle your fable-land in your own fashion. Anything you like happens in fable-land. Wicked folks die à propos (for instance, that death of Lady Kew was most artful, for if she had not died, don't you see that Ethel would have married Lord Farintosh the next week?) – annoying folks are got out of the way; the poor are rewarded – the upstarts are set down in fable-land, – the frog bursts with wicked rage, the fox is caught in his trap, the lamb is rescued from the wolf, and so forth, just in the nick of time. And the poet of fable-land rewards and punishes absolutely. He splendidly deals out bags of sovereigns, which won't buy anything; belabours wicked backs with awful blows, which do not hurt: endows heroines with

preternatural beauty, and creates heroes, who, if ugly sometimes, yet possess a thousand good qualities, and usually end
by being immensely rich; makes the hero and heroine happy
at last, and happy ever after. Ah, happy, harmless fable-
land, where these things are! Friendly reader! may you and
the author meet there on some future day! He hopes so; as
he yet keeps a lingering hold on your hand, and bids you
farewell with a kind heart.

1 This and the following references are to characters in the novel itself;
   Thackeray is challenging the Victorian reader's assumed desire for
   poetic justice at the end of a story.

ELIZABETH CLEGHORN GASKELL

Mrs Gaskell (1810–65) lived most of her adult life in Manchester, and her early novels – especially *Mary Barton* (1848) and *North and South* (1855) – attempt to depict sympathetically the lives of the working people of this city.

15 The Preface to *Mary Barton*, 1848

Three years ago I became anxious (from circumstances that need not be more fully alluded to) to employ myself in writing a work of fiction. Living in Manchester, but with a deep relish and fond admiration for the country, my first thought was to find a frame-work for my story in some rural scene; and I had already made a little progress in a tale, the period of which was more than a century ago, and the place on the borders of Yorkshire, when I bethought me how deep might be the romance in the lives of some of those who elbowed me daily in the busy streets of the town in which I resided. I had always felt a deep sympathy with the care-worn men, who looked as if doomed to struggle through their lives in strange alternations between work and want; tossed to and fro by circumstances, apparently in even a greater degree than other men. A little manifestation of this sympathy and a little attention to the expression of feelings on the part of some of the work-people with whom I was acquainted, had laid open to me the hearts of one or two of the more thoughtful among them; I saw that they were sore and irritable against the rich, the even tenor of whose seemingly happy lives appeared to increase the anguish caused by the lottery-like nature of their own. Whether the bitter complaints made by them, of the neglect which they experienced from the prosperous – especially from the masters whose fortunes they had helped to build up – were well-founded or no, it is not for me to judge. It is enough to say, that this belief of the injustice and unkindness which they endure from their fellow-creatures, taints what might be resignation to God's will, and turns it to revenge in too many of the poor uneducated factory-workers of Manchester.

The more I reflected on this unhappy state of things between those so bound to each other by common interests, as the employers and the employed must ever be, the more anxious I became to give some utterance to the agony which, from time to time, convulses this dumb people; the agony of suffering without the sympathy of the happy, or of erroneously believing that such is the case. If it be an error, that the woes, which come with ever-returning tide-like flood to overwhelm the workmen in our manufacturing towns, pass unregarded by all but the sufferers, it is at any rate an error so bitter in its consequences to all parties, that whatever public effort can do in the way of legislation, or private effort in the way of merciful deeds, or helpless love in the way of widow's mites, should be done, and that speedily, to disabuse the work-people of so miserable a misapprehension. At present they seem to me to be left in a state, wherein lamentations and tears are thrown aside as useless, but in which the lips are compressed for curses, and the hands clenched and ready to smite.

I know nothing of Political Economy, or the thories of trade. I have tried to write truthfully; and if my accounts agree or clash with any system, the agreement or disagreement is unintentional.

To myself the idea which I have formed of the state of feeling among too many of the factory-people in Manchester, and which I endeavoured to represent in this tale (completed above a year ago), has received some confirmation from the events which have so recently occurred among a similar class on the Continent.[1]

1   A reference to the uprisings which took place in many parts of Europe
     in 1848, known as the Year of Revolutions.

16 A letter to a young novelist, 1859

As you ask me for my opinion I shall try and give it as truly
as I can; otherwise it will be of no use; as it is I think that it
may be of use, as the experience of any one who has gone
before the path you are following must always have some
value in it. In the first place you say you do not call The
3 paths[1] a novel; but the work is in the form which always
assumes that name, nor do I think it is one to be quarrelled
with. I suppose you mean that you used the narrative form
merely to introduce certain opinions & thoughts. If so you
had better have condensed them into the shape of an Essay.
Those in Friends in Council[2] &c. are admirable examples of
how much may be said on both sides of any question,
without any decision being finally arrived at, & certainly
without any dogmatism. Besides if you have thought (the
result of either introspection or experience, – & the latter is
the best & likely to be the most healthy –) to communicate,
the neatness pithiness, & conciseness of expression required
by the Essay form is a capital training of style. In all
conversation there is a great deal of nothing talked – and in a
written conversation on thoughtful subjects these nothings
come in with a jar, & cause impatience.

But I believe in spite of yr objection to the term 'novel'
you do wish to 'narrate,' – and I believe you can do it if you
try, – but I think you must observe what is *out* of you,
instead of examining what is *in* you. It is always an unhealthy
sign where we are too conscious of any of the physical
processes that go on within us; & I believe in like manner
that we ought not to be too cognizant of our mental
proceedings, only taking note of the results. But certainly –
whether introspection be morbid or not, – it is not a safe
training for a novelist. It is a weakening of the art which has
crept in of late years. Just read a few pages of De Foe &c

– and you will see the healthy way in which he sets *objects* not *feelings* before you. I am sure the right way is this. You are an Electric telegraph something or other, –

Well! every day your life brings you into contact with live men & women, – of whom I yr reader, know nothing about: (and I, Mrs Gaskell for instance, do know nothing about the regular work & daily experience of people working for their bread with head-labour, – & that not professional, – in London.) Think if you can not imagine a complication of events in their life which would form a good plot. (Your plot in The Three paths is very poor; you have not thought enough about it, – simply used it as a medium. The plot must grow, and culminate in a crisis; not a character must be introduced who does not conduce to this growth & progress of events. The plot is like the anatomical drawing of an artist; he must have an idea of his skeleton, before he can clothe it with muscle & flesh, much more before he can drape it. Study hard at your plot. I have been told that those early Italian Tales from which Shakspeare took so many of his stories are models of plots, – a regular storehouse. See how they – how the great tragedies of all time, – how the grandest narrations of all languages are worked together, – & really make this sketch of your story a subject of labour & thought. Then set to & imagine yourself a spectator & auditor of every scene & event! Work hard at this till it become a reality to you, – a thing you have to recollect & describe & report fully & accurately as it struck you, in order that your reader may have it equally before him. Don't intrude yourself into your description. If you but think eagerly of your story till *you see it in action*, words, good simple strong words, will come, – just as if you saw an accident in the street that impressed you strongly you would describe it forcibly.

Cut your epithets short. Find one, whenever you can, that will do in the place of two. Of two words choose the simplest. But yr style seemed to me good. It was the want of a plot, – & the too great dwelling on feelings &c, – & the length of the conversations, which *did not advance the action* of the story, – & the too great reference to books &c – which only impede the narration – that appeared to me the prevalent faults in your book.

You see I am very frank-spoken. But I believe you are worth it. I judge from yr letter which I like –

Please don't thank me. But try & follow my advice for I am pretty sure it is good. You know everybody can preach better than they can practise.

1 *The Three Paths* by H. Grey was published in 1859; the tone of the letter suggests that Mrs Gaskell did not know the author.
2 Sir Arthur Phelps (1817–75) published *Friends in Council*, the first series in 1847, the second in 1859.

ROBERT BROWNING

Browning (1812–89) published his first poem, *Pauline*, in 1833, followed by *Paracelsus* (1835), *Sordello* (1840), *Men and Women* (1855), *Dramatis Personae* (1864) and *The Ring and the Book* (1868–9). The *Essay on Shelley*, his most extended piece of criticism, was written as an introduction to some recently discovered letters, believed to be by Shelley though soon found to be spurious. In it he discusses the two main types of poet, perhaps at this early stage in his career pondering his own vocation.

From *Essay on Shelley*, 1852

An opportunity having presented itself for the acquisition of a series of unedited letters by Shelley, all more or less directly supplementary to and illustrative of the collection already published by Mr. Moxon,[1] that gentleman has decided on securing them. They will prove an acceptable addition to a body of correspondence, the value of which towards a right understanding of its author's purpose and work, may be said to exceed that of any similar contribution exhibiting the worldly relations of a poet whose genius has operated by a different law.

Doubtless we accept gladly the biography of an objective poet, as the phrase now goes: one whose endeavour has been to reproduce things external (whether the phenomena of the scenic universe, or the manifested action of the human heart and brain) with an immediate reference, in every case, to the common eye and apprehension of his fellow men, assumed capable of receiving and profiting by this reproduction. It has been obtained through the poet's double faculty of seeing external objects more clearly, widely, and deeply, than is possible to the average mind, at the same time that he is so acquainted and in sympathy with its narrower comprehension as to be careful to supply it with no other materials than it can combine into an intelligible whole. The auditory of such a poet will include, not only the intelligences which, save for such assistance, would have missed the deeper meaning and enjoyment of the original objects, but also the spirits of a like endowment with his own, who, by means of his abstract, can forthwith pass to the reality it was made from, and either corroborate their impressions of things known already, or supply themselves with new from whatever shows in the inexhaustible variety of existence may have hitherto escaped their knowledge. Such a poet is properly the ποιητης[1] the fashioner; and the thing fashioned, his poetry, will of necessity be substantive, projected from himself and distinct. We are ignorant what the inventor of 'Othello' conceived of that fact as he beheld it in completeness, how he accounted for it, under what known law he registered its nature, or to what unknown law he traced its coincidence. We learn only what he intended we should learn by that particular exercise of his power, – the fact itself, – which, with its infinite significances, each of us receives for the first time as a creation, and is hereafter left to deal with, as, in proportion to his own intelligence, he best may. We are ignorant, and would fain be otherwise.

Doubtless, with respect to such a poet, we covet his biography. We desire to look back upon the process of gathering together in a lifetime, the materials of the work we behold entire; of elaborating, perhaps under difficulty and with hindrance, all that is familiar to our admiration in the apparent facility of success. And the inner impulse of this effort and operation, what induced it? Did a soul's delight in its own extended sphere of vision set it, for the gratification of an insuppressible power, on labour, as other men are set on rest? Or did a sense of duty or of love lead it to communicate its own sensations of mankind? Did an irresistible sympathy with men compel it to bring down and suit its own provision of knowledge and beauty to their narrow scope? Did the personality of such an one stand like an open watch-tower in the midst of the territory it is erected to gaze on, and were the storms and calms, the stars and meteors, its watchman was wont to report of, the habitual variegation of his every-day life, as they glanced across its open roof or lay reflected on its four-square parapet? Or did some sunken and darkened chamber of imagery witness, in the artificial illumination of every storied compartment we are permitted to contemplate, how rare and precious were the outlooks through here and there an embrasure upon a world beyond, and how blankly would have pressed on the artificer the boundary of his daily life, except for the amorous diligence with which he had rendered permanent by art whatever came to diversify the gloom? Still, fraught with instruction and interest as such details undoubtedly are, we can, if needs be, dispense with them. The man passes, the work remains. The work speaks for itself, as we say: and the biography of the worker is no more necessary to an understanding or enjoyment of it, than is a model or anatomy of some tropical tree, to the right tasting of the fruit we are familiar with on the market-stall, – or a geologist's map and stratification, to the prompt recognition of the hill-top, our land-mark of every day.

We turn with stronger needs to the genius of an opposite tendency – the subjective poet of modern classification. He, gifted like the objective poet with the fuller perception of nature and man, is impelled to embody the thing he perceives, not so much with reference to the many below as to the one above him, the supreme Intelligence which apprehends all things in their absolute truth, – an ultimate view ever aspired to, if but partially attained, by the poet's own soul. Not what man sees, but what God sees – the *Ideas* of Plato, seeds of creation lying burningly on the Divine hand – it is toward these that he struggles. Not with the combination of humanity in action, but with the primal elements of humanity he has to do; and he digs where he stands, – preferring to seek them in his own soul as the nearest reflex of that absolute Mind, according to the intuitions of which he desires to perceive and speak. Such a poet does not deal habitually with the picturesque groupings and tempestuous tossings of the forest-trees, but with their roots and fibres naked to the chalk and stone. He does not paint pictures and hang them on the walls, but rather carries them on the retina of his own eyes: we must look deep into his human eyes, to see those pictures on them. He is rather a seer, accordingly, than a fashioner, and what he produces will be less a work than an effluence. That effluence cannot be easily considered in abstraction from his personality, – being indeed the very radiance and aroma of his personality, projected from it but not separated. Therefore, in our approach to the poetry, we necessarily approach the personality of the poet; in apprehending it we apprehend him, and certainly we cannot love it without loving him. Both for love's and for understanding's sake we desire to know him, and as readers of his poetry must be readers of his biography also.

I shall observe, in passing, that it seems not so much from any essential distinction in the faculty of the two poets or in the nature of the objects contemplated by either, as in the more immediate adaptability of these objects to the distinct purpose of each, that the objective poet, in his appeal to the aggregate human mind, chooses to deal with the doings of men, (the result of which dealing, in its pure form, when even description, as suggesting a describer, is dispensed with, is what we call dramatic poetry), while the subjective poet, whose study has been himself, appealing through himself to the absolute Divine mind, prefers to dwell upon those external scenic appearances which strike out most abundantly and uninterruptedly his inner light and power, selects that silence of the earth and sea in which he can best hear the beating of his individual heart, and leaves the noisy, complex, yet imperfect exhibitions of nature in the manifold experience of man around him, which serve only to distract and suppress the working of his brain. These opposite tendencies of genius will be more readily descried in their artistic effect than in their moral spring and cause. Pushed to an extreme and manifested as a deformity, they wil be seen plainest of all in the fault of either artist, when subsidiarily to the human interest of his work his occasional illustrations from scenic nature are introduced as in the earlier works of the originative painters – men and women filling the fore-ground with consummate mastery, while mountain, grove and rivulet show an anticipatory revenge on that succeeding race of landscape-painters whose 'figures' disturb the perfec-tion of their earth and sky. It would be idle to inquire, of these two kinds of poetic faculty in operation, which is the higher or even rarer endowment. If the subjective might seem to be the ultimate requirement of every age, the objective, in the strictest state, must still retain its original value. For it is with this world, as starting point and basis alike, that we shall always have to concern ourselves: the world is not to be learned and thrown aside, but reverted to and relearned. The spiritual comprehension may be infinitely subtilised, but the raw material it operates upon, must remain. There may be no end of the poets who communicate to us what they see in an object with reference to their own individuality; what it was before they saw it, in reference to the aggregate human mind, will be as desirable to know as ever. Nor is there any reason why these two modes of poetic faculty may not issue hereafter from the same poet in successive perfect works, examples of which, according to what are now considered the exigences of art, we have hitherto possessed in distinct individuals only. A mere running-in of the one faculty upon the other, is, of course, the ordinary circumstance. Far more rarely it happens that either is found so decidedly prominent and superior, as to be pronounced comparatively pure: while of the perfect shield, with the gold and the silver side set up for all comers to challenge, there has yet been no instance. Either faculty in its eminent state is doubtless conceded by Providence as a best gift to men, according to their especial want. There is a time when the general eye has, so to speak, absorbed its fill of the phenomena around it, whether spiritual or material, and desires rather to learn the exacter significance of what it possesses, than to receive any augmentation of what is possessed. Then is the opportunity for the poet of loftier vision, to lift his fellows, with their half-apprehensions, up to his own sphere, by intensifying the import of details and rounding the universal meaning. The influence of such an achievement will not soon die out. A tribe of successors (Homerides)[3] working more or less in the same spirit, dwell on his discoveries and reinforce his doctrine; till, at unawares, the world is found to be subsisting wholly on the shadow of a reality, on sentiments diluted from passions, on the tradition of a fact, the convention of a moral, the straw of last year's harvest. Then is the imperative call for the appearance of another sort of poet, who shall at once replace this intellectual rumination of food swallowed long ago, by a supply of the fresh and living swathe; getting at new substance by breaking up the assumed wholes into parts of independent and unclassed value, careless of the unknown laws for recombining them (it will be the business of yet another poet to suggest those hereafter), prodigal of objects for men's outer and not inner sight, shaping for their uses a new and different creation from the last, which it displaces by the right of life over death, – to endure until, in the inevitable process, its very sufficiency to itself shall require, at length, an exposition of its affinity to something higher, – when the positive yet conflicting facts shall again precipitate themselves under a harmonising law, and one more degree will be apparent for a poet to climb in that mighty ladder, of which, however cloud-involved and undefined may glimmer the topmost step, the world dares no longer doubt that its gradations ascend.

1 Edward Moxon (1801–58) was a publisher and man of letters; he had brought out the first edition of Shelley's letters, edited by Mary Shelley, in 1840.
2 Usually translated 'maker': contrasted later in the essay with the subjective 'seer'.
3 'Little Homers'.

ARTHUR HUGH CLOUGH

Clough (1819–61) was an independent-minded poet and critic. He was a friend of Matthew Arnold at Rugby and Oxford, but differed from Arnold in his insistence on the need in poetry for direct reference to contemporary life. The opening part of the review, printed here, deals with *Poems* (1853) by Alexander Smith (1830–67), a young 'mechanic' from Glasgow.

The review, from the *North American Review* LXXVII, July 1853, 1–30, is reprinted in *The Prose Remains of Arthur Hugh Clough*, edited by his wife, 1888.

18 From a review of recent poetry, 1853

Studies of the literature of any distant age or country; all the imitations and *quasi*-translations which help to bring together into a single focus the scattered rays of human intelligence; poems after classical models, poems from Oriental sources, and the like, have undoubtedly a great literary value. Yet there is no question, it is plain and patent enough, that people much prefer 'Vanity Fair' and 'Bleak House'. Why so? Is it simply because we have grown prudent and prosaic, and should not welcome, as our fathers did, the Marmions and the Rokebys, the Childe Harolds and the Corsairs?[1] Or is it, that to be widely popular, to gain the ear of multitudes, to shake the hearts of men, poetry should deal, more than at present it usually does, with general wants, ordinary feelings, the obvious rather than the rare facts of human nature? Could it not attempt to convert into beauty and thankfulness, or at least into some form and shape, some feeling, at any rate, of content – the actual, palpable things with which our every-day life is concerned; introduce into business and weary task-work a character and a soul of purpose and reality; intimate to us relations which, in our unchosen, peremptorily appointed posts, in our grievously narrow and limited spheres of action, we still, in and through all, retain to some central, celestial fact? Could it not console us with a sense of significance, if not of dignity, in that often dirty, or at least dingy, work which it is the lot of so many of us to have to do, and which some one or other, after all, must do? Might it not divinely condescend to all infirmities; be in all points tempted as we are; exclude nothing, least of all guilt and distress, from its wide fraternisation; not content itself merely with talking of what may be better elsewhere, but seek also to deal with what *is* here? We could each one of us, alas, be so much that somehow we find we are not; we have all of us fallen away from so much that we still long to call ours. Cannot the Divine Song in some way indicate to us our unity, though from a great way off, with those happier things; inform us, and prove to us, that though we are what we are, we may yet, in some way, even in our abasement, even by and through our daily work, be related to the purer existence?

The modern novel is preferred to the modern poem, because we do here feel an attempt to include these indispensable latest addenda – these phenomena which, if we forget on Sunday, we must remember on Monday – these positive matters of fact, which people, who are not verse-writers, are obliged to have to do with.

> Et fortasse cupressum
> Scis simulare; quid hoc, si fractis enatat exspes
> Navibus, ære dato qui pingitur?[2]

The novelist does try to build us a real house to be lived in; and this common builder, with no notion of the orders, is more to our purpose than the student of ancient art who proposes to lodge us under an Ionic portico. We are, unhappily, not gods, nor even marble statues. While the poets, like the architects, are – a good thing enough in its way – studying ancient art, comparing, thinking, theorising, the common novelist tells a plain tale, often trivial enough, about this, that, and the other, and obtains one reading at any rate; is thrown away indeed to-morrow, but is devoured to-day.

We do not at all mean to prepare the reader for finding the great poetic desideratum in this present Life-Drama.[3] But it has at least the advantage, such as it is, of not showing much of the *littérateur* or connoisseur, or indeed the student; nor is it, as we have said, mere pastoral sweet piping from the country. These poems were not written among books and busts, nor yet

> By shallow rivers, to whose falls
> Melodious birds sing madrigals.[4]

They have something substantive and lifelike, immediate and first-hand, about them. There is a charm, for example, in finding, as we do, continual images drawn from the busy seats of industry; it seems to satisfy a want that we have long been conscious of, when we see the black streams that welter out of factories, the dreary lengths of urban and suburban dustiness,

> The squares and streets,
> And the faces that one meets,

irradiated with a gleam of divine purity.

There are moods when one is prone to believe that, in these last days, no longer by 'clear spring or shady grove,' no more upon any Pindus or Parnassus, or by the side of any Castaly,[5] are the true and lawful haunts of the poetic powers; but, we could believe it, if anywhere, in the blank and desolate streets, and upon the solitary bridges of the midnight city, where Guilt is, and wild Temptation, and the dire Compulsion of what has once been done – there, with these tragic sisters around him, and with pity also, and pure

Compassion, and pale Hope, that looks like despair, and Faith in the garb of doubt, there walks the discrowned Apollo, with unstrung lyre; nay, and could he sound it, those mournful Muses would scarcely be able, as of old, to respond and 'sing in turn with their beautiful voices'.

To such moods, and in such states of feeling, this 'Life Drama' will be an acceptable poem.

1　Scott's poem *Marmion* (1808) deals with the events leading to the battle of Flodden in 1513, and his *Rokeby* (1811) with events following the battle of Marston Moor in 1641. Byron's *Childe Harold's Pilgrimage* (1812–18) describes travels in exotic foreign countries, including Albania where Byron began to write it; his *The Corsair* (1814) deals with a pirate's adventures in the Aegean.
2　Horace, *De Arte Poetica*, lines 19–21: 'And perhaps you know how to paint a cypress; What of that, if your commission is to paint a sailor escaping from a shipwreck?'
3　The title of one of Smith's poems under review.
4　From Christopher Marlowe's 'The Passionate Shepherd to his Love.'
5　All classical allusions: Pindus is a range of mountains in Northern Greece; Parnassus the mountain sacred to Apollo and the Muses, and Castalia a spring on that mountain.

MATTHEW ARNOLD

Arnold (1822–88) was the leading Victorian literary critic, as well as a poet and, in his later prose writings, urbane critic of society. His letters to his friend Clough (see No. 18) – *The Letters of Matthew Arnold to Arthur Hugh Clough*, ed. H. F. Lowry, 1932 – often revert to the topic of the need for form, which Arnold found in the Classics, by contrast with the restless qualities of Romantic writers like Keats, whom Arnold believed to be dangerously influential. This continued to be the theme of much of his more formal criticism.

The *Complete Prose Works* are edited by R. H. Super in 11 volumes (1960–77).

19 From letters to A. H. Clough

FROM A LETTER OF LATE 1848, OR 1849

What a brute you were to tell me to read Keats' Letters.[1] However it is over now: and reflexion resumes her power over agitation.

What harm he has done in English Poetry. As Browning is a man with a moderate gift passionately desiring movement & fulness, and obtaining but a confused multitudinousness, so Keats with a very high gift, is yet also consumed by this desire: & cannot produce the truly living & moving, as his conscience keeps telling him. They will not be patient neither understand that they must begin with an Idea of the world in order not to be prevailed over by the world's multitudinousness: or if they cannot get that, at least with isolated ideas: & all other things shall (perhaps) be added unto them.

– I recommend you to follow up these letters with the Laocoon of Lessing.[2] It is not quite satisfactory, & a little mare's nesty – but very searching.

– I have had that desire of fulness without respect of the means, which may become almost maniacal: but nature had placed a bar thereto not only in the conscience (as with all men) but in a great numbness in that direction. But what perplexity Keats Tennyson et id genus omne[3] must occasion to young writers of the ὁπλίτης [4] sort: yes & those d-d Elizabethan poets generally. Those who cannot read G[ree]k sh[ou]ld read nothing but Milton & parts of Wordsworth: the state should see to it: for the failures of the στάσιμοι[5] may leave them good citizens enough, as Trench:[6] but the others go to the dogs failing or succeeding.

FROM A LETTER OF ABOUT 1 MARCH 1849

It is true about form: something of the same sort is in my letter which crossed yours on the road. On the other hand, there are two offices of Poetry – one to add to one's store of thoughts & feelings – another to compose & elevate the mind by a sustained tone, numerous allusions, and a grand style. What other process is Milton's than this last, in Comus for instance. There is no fruitful analysis of character: but a great effect is produced. What is Keats? A style & form seeker, & this with an impetuosity that heightens the effect of his style almost painfully. Nay in Sophocles what is valuable is not so much his contributions to psychology & the anatomy of sentiment, as the grand moral effects produced by *style*. For the style is the expression of the nobility of the poet's character, as the matter is the expression of the richness of his mind: but on men character produces as great an effect as mind.

FROM A LETTER OF 28 OCTOBER 1852

More and more I feel that the difference between a mature and a youthful age of the world compels the poetry of the former to use great plainness of speech as compared with that of the latter: and that Keats and Shelley were on a false track when they set themselves to reproduce the exuberance of expression, the charm, the richness of images, and the felicity, of the Elizabethan poets. Yet critics cannot get to learn this, because the Elizabethan poets are our greatest, and our canons of poetry are founded on their works. They still think that the object of poetry is to produce exquisite bits and images – such as Shelley's *clouds shepherded by the slow unwilling wind*,[7] and Keats passim: whereas modern poetry can only subsist by its *contents*: by becoming a complete magister vitae[8] as the poetry of the ancients did: by including, as theirs did, religion with poetry, instead of existing as poetry only, and leaving religious wants to be supplied by the Christian religion, as a power existing independent of the poetical power. But the language, style and general proceedings of a poetry which has such an immense task to perform, must be very plain direct and severe: and it must not lose itself in parts and episodes and ornamental work, but must press forwards to the whole.

1 R. Monkton Milnes had published *Life, Letters and Literary Remains of John Keats* in September 1848.
2 Gotthold Ephraim Lessing (1729–81), the German critic and dramatist, published *Laokoön* (1766) which considered the distinction between the plastic arts and literature.
3 and all that tribe.
4 Common (lit. infantryman).
5 Steady men.
6 Richard Chenevix Trench (1807–86), a friend of Arnold and Clough, and later Archbishop of Dublin.
7 *Prometheus Unbound*, II, i, 147.
8 ruler (director) of life.

20 Preface to the First Edition of *Poems*, 1853

In two small volumes of Poems, published anonymously, one in 1849, the other in 1852, many of the poems which compose the present volume have already appeared. The rest are now published for the first time.

I have, in the present collection, omitted the poem from which the volume published in 1852 took its title.[1] I have done so, not because the subject of it was a Sicilian Greek born between two and three thousand years go, although many persons would think this a sufficient reason. Neither have I done so because I had, in my own opinion, failed in the delineation which I intended to effect. I intended to delineate the feelings of one of the last of the Greek religious philosophers, one of the family of Orpheus and Musaeus,[2] having survived his fellows, living on into a time when the habits of Greek thought and feeling had begun fast to change, character to dwindle, the influence of the Sophists[3] to prevail. Into the feelings of a man so situated there entered much that we are accustomed to consider as exclusively modern; how much, the fragments of Empedocles himself which remain to us are sufficient at least to indicate. What those who are familiar only with the great monuments of early Greek genius suppose to be its exclusive characteristics, have disappeared: the calm, the cheerfulness, the disinterested objectivity have disappeared; the dialogue of the mind with itself has commenced; modern problems have presented themselves; we hear already the doubts, we witness the discouragement, of Hamlet and of Faust.

The representation of such a man's feelings must be interesting, if consistently drawn. We all naturally take pleasure, says Aristotle,[4] in any imitation or representation whatever: this is the basis of our love of poetry; and we take pleasure in them, he adds, because all knowledge is naturally agreeable to us; not to the philosopher only, but to mankind at large. Every representation, therefore, which is consistently drawn may be supposed to be interesting, inasmuch as it gratifies this natural interest in knowledge of all kinds. What is *not* interesting, is that which does not add to our knowledge of any kind; that which is vaguely conceived and loosely drawn; a representation which is general, indeterminate, and faint, instead of being particular, precise, and firm.

Any accurate representation may therefore be expected to be interesting; but, if the representation be a poetical one, more than this is demanded. It is demanded, not only that it shall interest, but also that it shall inspirit and rejoice the reader; that it shall convey a charm, and infuse delight. For the Muses, as Hesiod says,[5] were born that they might be 'a forgetfulness of evils, and a truce from cares': and it is not enough that the poet should add to the knowledge of men, it is required of him also that he should add to their happiness. 'All art', says Schiller, 'is dedicated to Joy, and there is no higher and no more serious problem, than how to make men happy. The right art is that alone, which creates the highest enjoyment.'[6]

A poetical work, therefore, is not yet justified when it has been shown to be an accurate, and therefore interesting representation; it has to be shown also that it is a representation from which men can derive enjoyment. In presence of the most tragic circumstances, represented in a work of art, the feeling of enjoyment, as is well known, may still subsist; the representation of the most utter calamity, of the liveliest anguish, is not sufficient to destroy it; the more tragic the situation, the deeper becomes the enjoyment; and the situation is more tragic in proportion as it becomes more terrible.

What then are the situations, from the representation of which, though accurate, no poetical enjoyment can be derived? They are those in which the suffering finds no vent in action; in which a continuous state of mental distress is prolonged, unrelieved by incident, hope, or resistance; in which there is everything to be endured, nothing to be done. In such situations there is inevitably something morbid, in the description of them something monotonous. When they occur in actual life, they are painful, not tragic; the representation of them in poetry is painful also.

To this class of situations, poetically faulty as it appears to me, that of Empedocles, as I have endeavoured to represent him, belongs; and I have therefore excluded the poem from the present collection.

And why, it may be asked, have I entered into this explanation respecting a matter so unimportant as the admission or exclusion of the poem in question? I have done so, because I was anxious to avow that the sole reason for its exclusion was that which has been stated above; and that it has not been excluded in deference to the opinion which many critics of the present day appear to entertain against subjects chosen from distant times and countries: against the choice, in short, of any subjects but modern ones.

'The poet', it is said,[7] and by an intelligent critic, 'the poet who would really fix the public attention must leave the exhausted past, and draw his subjects from matters of present import, and *therefore* both of interest and novelty.'

Now this view I believe to be completely false. It is worth examining, inasmuch as it is a fair sample of a class of critical dicta everywhere current at the present day, having a philosophical form and air, but no real basis in fact; and which are calculated to vitiate the judgment of readers of poetry, while they exert, so far as they are adopted, a misleading influence on the practice of those who make it.

What are the eternal objects of poetry, among all nations, and at all times? They are actions; human actions,[8] possessing an inherent interest in themselves, and which are to be communicated in an interesting manner by the art of the poet. Vainly will the latter imagine that he has everything in his own power; that he can make an intrinsically inferior action equally delightful with a more excellent one by his treatment of it. He may indeed compel us to admire his skill, but his work will possess, within itself, an incurable defect.

The poet, then, has in the first place to select an excellent action; and what actions are the most excellent? Those, certainly, which most powerfully appeal to the great primary human affections[9] to those elementary feelings which subsist permanently in the race, and which are independent of time. These feelings are permanent and the same; that which interests them is permanent and the same also. The modernness or antiquity of an action, therefore, has nothing to do with its fitness for poetical representation; this depends upon its inherent qualities. To the elementary part of our nature, to our passions, that which is great and passionate is eternally interesting; and interesting solely in proportion to its greatness and to its passion. A great human action of a thousand years ago is more interesting to it than a smaller human action of to-day, even though upon the representation of this last the most consummate skill may have been expended, and though it has the advantage of appealing by its modern language, familiar manners, and contemporary allusions, to all our transient feelings and interests. These, however, have no right to demand of a poetical work that it shall satisfy them; their claims are to be directed elsewhere. Poetical works belong to the domain of our permanent passions; let them interest these, and the voice of all subordinate claims upon them is at once silenced.

Achilles, Prometheus, Clytemnestra, Dido,[10] – what modern poem presents personages as interesting, even to us moderns, as these personages of an 'exhausted past'? We have the domestic epic dealing with the details of modern life which pass daily under our eyes; we have poems representing modern personages in contact with the problems of modern life, moral, intellectual, and social; these works have been produced by poets the most distinguished of their nation and time; yet I fearlessly assert that *Hermann and Dorothea, Childe Harold, Jocelyn, The Excursion*,[11] leave the reader cold in comparison with the effect produced upon him by the latter books of the *Iliad*, by the *Oresteia*, or by the episode of Dido. And why is this? Simply because in the three last-named cases the action is greater, the personages nobler, the situations more intense: and this is the true basis of the interest in a poetical work, and this alone.

It may be urged, however, that past actions may be

interesting in themselves, but that they are not to be adopted by the modern poet, because it is impossible for him to have them clearly present to his own mind, and he cannot therefore feel them deeply, nor represent them forcibly. But this is not necessarily the case. The externals of a past action, indeed, he cannot know with the precision of a contemporary; but his business is with its essentials. The outward man of Oedipus or of Macbeth, the houses in which they lived, the ceremonies of their courts, he cannot accurately figure to himself; but neither do they essentially concern him. His business is with their inward man; with their feelings and behaviour in certain tragic situations, which engage their passions as men; these have in them nothing local and casual; they are as accessible to the modern poet as to a contemporary.

The date of an action, then, signifies nothing: the action itself, its selection and construction, this is what is all-important. This the Greeks understood far more clearly than we do. The radical difference between their poetical theory and ours consists, as it appears to me, in this: that, with them, the poetical character of the action in itself, and the conduct of it, was the first consideration; with us, attention is fixed mainly on the value of the separate thoughts and images which occur in the treatment of an action. They regarded the whole; we regard the parts. With them, the action predominated over the expression of it; with us, the expression predominates over the action. Not that they failed in expression, or were inattentive to it; on the contrary, they are the highest models of expression, the unapproached masters of the *grand style*. But their expression is so excellent because it is so admirably kept in its right degree of prominence; because it is so simple and so well subordinated; because it draws its force directly for the pregnancy of the matter which it conveys. For what reason was the Greek tragic poet confined to so limited a range of subjects? Because there are so few actions which unite in themselves, in the highest degree, the conditions of excellence: and it was not thought that on any but an excellent subject could an excellent poem be constructed. A few actions, therefore, eminently adapted for tragedy, maintained almost exclusive possession of the Greek tragic stage. Their significance appeared inexhaustible; they were as permanent problems, perpetually offered to the genius of every fresh poet. This too is the reason of what appears to us moderns a certain baldness of expression in Greek tragedy; of the triviality with which we often reproach the remarks of the chorus, where it takes part in the dialogue that the action itself, the situation of Orestes, or Merope, or Alcmaeon,[12] was to stand the central point of interest, unforgotten, absorbing, principal; that no accessories were for a moment to distract the spectator's attention from this; that the tone of the parts was to be perpetually kept down, in order not to impair the grandiose effect of the whole. The terrible old mythic story on which the drama was founded stood, before he entered the theatre, traced in its bare outlines upon the spectator's mind; it stood in his memory, as a group of statuary, faintly seen, at the end of a long and dark vista: then came the poet, embodying outlines, developing situations, not a word wasted, not a sentiment capriciously thrown in: stroke upon stroke, the drama proceeded: the light deepened upon the group; more and more it revealed itself to the riveted gaze of the spectator: until at last, when the final words were spoken, it stood before him in broad sunlight, a model of immortal beauty.

This was what a Greek critic demanded; this was what a Greek poet endeavoured to effect. It signified nothing to what time an action belonged. We do not find that the *Persae*[13] occupied a particularly high rank among the dramas of Aeschylus, because it represented a matter of contemporary interest; this was not what a cultivated Athenian required. He required that the permanent elements of his nature should be moved; and dramas of which the action, though taken from a long-distant mythic time, yet was calculated to accomplish this in a higher degree than that of the *Persae*, stood higher in his estimation accordingly. The Greeks felt, no doubt, with their exquisite sagacity of taste,

that an action of present times was too near them, too much
mixed up with what was accidental and passing, to form a
sufficiently grand, detached, and self-subsistent object for a
tragic poem. Such objects belonged to the domain of the
comic poet, and of the lighter kinds of poetry. For the more
serious kinds, for *pragmatic* poetry, to use an excellent
expression of Polybius,[14] they were more difficult and severe
in the range of subjects which they permitted. Their theory
and practice alike, the admirable treatise of Aristotle, and
the unrivalled works of their poets, exclaim with a thousand
tongues – 'All depends upon the subject; choose a fitting
action, penetrate yourself with the feeling of its situations;
this done; everything else will follow.'

But for all kinds of poetry alike there was one point on
which they were rigidly exacting: the adaptability of the
subject to the kind of poetry selected, and the careful
construction of the poem.

How different a way of thinking from this is ours! We can
hardly at the present day understand what Menander meant,[15]
when he told a man who enquired as to the progress of his
comedy that he had finished it, not having yet written a
single line, because he had constructed the action of it in his
mind. A modern critic would have assured him that the
merit of his piece depended on the brilliant things which
arose under his pen as he went along. We have poems which
seem to exist merely for the sake of single lines and
passages; not for the sake of producing any total impression.
We have critics who seem to direct their attention merely to
detached expressions, to the language about the action, not
to the action itself. I verily think that the majority of them
do not in their hearts believe that there is such a thing as a
total impression to be derived from a poem at all, or to be
demanded from a poet; they think the term a commonplace
of metaphysical criticism. They will permit the poet to select
any action he pleases, and to suffer that action to go as it
will, provided he gratifies them with occasional bursts of fine
writing, and with a shower of isolated thoughts and images.
That is, they permit him to leave their poetical sense

ungratified, provided that he gratifies their rhetorical sense and their curiosity. Of his neglecting to gratify these, there is little danger. He needs rather to be warned against the danger of attempting to gratify these alone; he needs rather to be perpetually reminded to prefer his action to everything else; so to treat this, as to permit its inherent excellences to develop themselves, without interruption from the intrusion of his personal peculiarities; most fortunate, when he most entirely succeeds in effacing himself, and in enabling a noble action to subsist as it did in nature.

But the modern critic not only permits a false practice; he absolutely prescribes false aims. – 'A true allegory of the state of one's own mind in a representative history',[16] the poet is told, 'is perhaps the highest thing that one can attempt in the way of poetry.' And accordingly he attempts it. An allegory of the state of one's own mind, the highest problem of an art which imitates actions! No assuredly, it is not, it never can be so: no great poetical work has ever been produced with such an aim. *Faust* itself, in which something of the kind is attempted, wonderful passages as it contains, and in spite of the unsurpassed beauty of the scenes which relate to Margaret, *Faust* itself, judged as a whole, and judged strictly as a poetical work, is defective: its illustrious author, the greatest poet of modern times, the greatest critic of all times, would have been the first to acknowledge it; he only defended his work, indeed, by asserting it to be 'something incommensurable'.[17]

The confusion of the present times is great, the multitude of voices counselling different things bewildering, the number of existing works capable of attracting a young writer's attention and of becoming his models, immense. What he wants is a hand to guide him through the confusion, a voice to prescribe to him the aim which he should keep in view, and to explain to him that the value of the literary works which offer themselves to his attention is relative to their power of helping him forward on his road towards this aim. Such a guide the English writer at the present day will nowhere find. Failing this, all that can be looked for, all indeed that can be desired, is, that his attention should be fixed on excellent models; that he may reproduce, at any rate, something of their excellence, by penetrating himself with their works and by catching their spirit, if he cannot be taught to produce what is excellent independently.

Foremost among these models for the English writer stands Shakspeare: a name the greatest perhaps of all poetical names; a name never to be mentioned without reverence. I will venture, however, to express a doubt, whether the influence of his works, excellent and fruitful for the readers of poetry, for the great majority, has been of unmixed advantage to the writers of it. Shakspeare indeed chose excellent subjects; the world could afford no better than Macbeth, or Romeo and Juliet, or Othello; he had no theory respecting the necessity of choosing subjects of present import, or the paramount interest attaching to allegories of the state of one's own mind; like all great poets, he knew well what constituted a poetical action; like them, wherever he found such an action, he took it; like them, too, he found his best in past times. But to these general characteristics of all great poets he added a special one of his own; a gift, namely, of happy, abundant, and ingenious expression, eminent and unrivalled: so eminent as irresistably to strike the attention first in him, and even to throw into comparative shade his other excellences as a poet. Here has been the mischief. These other excellences were his fundamental excellences *as a poet*; what distinguishes the artist from the mere amateur, says Goethe,[18] is *Architectonicē* in the highest sense; that power of execution, which creates, forms, and constitutes: not the profoundness of single thoughts, not the richness of imagery, not the abundance of illustration. But these attractive accessories of a poetical work being more easily seized than the spirit of the whole, and these accessories being possessed by Shakspeare in an unequalled degree, a young writer having recourse to Shakspeare as his model runs great risk of being vanquished and absorbed by them, and, in consequence, of reproducing, according to the measure of his power, these, and these alone. Of this preponderating quality of Shakspeare's genius, accordingly, almost the whole of modern English poetry has, it appears to me, felt the influence. To the exclusive attention on the part of his imitators to this it is in a great degree owing, that of the majority of modern poetical works the details alone are valuable, the composition worthless. In reading them one is perpetually reminded of that terrible sentence on a modern French poet: – *Il dit tout ce qu'il veut, mais malheureusement il n'a rien à dire.*[19]

Let me give an instance of what I mean. I will take it from the works of the very chief among those who seem to have been formed in the school of Shakspeare: of one whose exquisite genius and pathetic death render him for ever interesting. I will take the poem of *Isabella, or the Pot of Basil*, by Keats. I choose this rather than the *Endymion*, because the latter work (which a modern critic has classed with the *Fairy Queen*!), although undoubtedly there blows through it the breath of genius, is yet as a whole so utterly incoherent, as not strictly to merit the name of a poem at all. The poem of *Isabella*, then, is a perfect treasure-house of graceful and felicitous words and images: almost in every stanza there occurs one of those vivid and picturesque turns of expression, by which the object is made to flash upon the eye of the mind, and which thrill the reader with a sudden delight. This one short poem contains, perhaps, a greater number of happy single expressions which one could quote than all the extant tragedies of Sophocles. But the action, the story? The action in itself is an excellent one; but so feebly is it conceived by the poet, so loosely constructed, that the effect produced by it, in and for itself, is absolutely null. Let the reader, after he has finished the poem of Keats, turn to the same story in the *Decameron*;[20] he will then feel how pregnant and interesting the same action has become in the hands of a great artist, who above all things delineates his object; who subordinates expression to that which it is designed to express.

I have said that the imitators of Shakspeare, fixing their attention on his wonderful gift of expression, have directed their imitation to this, neglecting his other excellences. These excellences, the fundamental excellences of poetical art, Shakspeare no doubt possessed them, – possessed many of them in a splendid degree; but it may perhaps be doubted whether even he himself did not sometimes give scope to his faculty of expression to the prejudice of a higher poetical duty. For we must never forget that Shakspeare is the great poet he is from his skill in discerning and firmly conceiving an excellent action, from his power of intensely feeling a situation, of intimately associating with a character; not from his gift of expression, which rather even leads him astray, degenerating sometimes into a fondness for curiosity of expression, into an irritability of fancy, which seems to make it impossible for him to say a thing plainly, even when the press of the action demands the very directest language, or its level character the very simplest. Mr Hallam,[21] than whom it is impossible to find a saner and more judicious critic, has had the courage (for at the present day it needs courage) to remark, how extremely and faultily difficult Shakspeare's language often is. It is so: you may find main scenes in some of his greatest tragedies, *King Lear* for instance, where the language is so artificial, so curiously tortured, and so difficult, that every speech has to be read two or three times before its meaning can be comprehended. This over-curiousness of expression is indeed but the excessive employment of a wonderful gift, – of the power of saying a thing in a happier way than any other man; nevertheless, it is carried so far that one understands what M. Guizot meant, when he said that Shakspeare appears in his language to have tried all styles except that of simplicity.[22] He has not the severe and scrupulous self-restraint of the ancients, partly, no doubt, because he had a far less cultivated and exacting audience. He has indeed a far wider range than they had, a far richer fertility of thought; in this respect he rises above them. In his strong conception of his subject, in the genuine way in which he is penetrated with it, he resembles them, and is unlike the moderns. But in the accurate limitation of it, the conscientious rejection of

superfluities, the simple and rigorous development of it from
the first line of his work to the last, he falls below them, and
comes nearer to the moderns. In his chief works, besides
what he has of his own, he has the elementary soundness of
the ancients; he has their important action and their large
and broad manner; but he has not their purity of method.
He is therefore a less safe model; for what he has of his own
is personal, and inseparable from his own rich nature; it may
be imitated and exaggerated, it cannot be learned or applied
as an art. He is above all suggestive; more valuable, therefore, to young writers as men than as artists. But clearness of
arrangement, rigour of development, simplicity of style, –
these may to a certain extent be learned; and these may, I
am convinced, be learned best from the ancients, who,
although infinitely less suggestive than Shakspeare, are thus,
to the artist, more instructive.

What then, it will be asked, are the ancients to be our sole
models? the ancients with their comparatively narrow range
of experience, and their widely different circumstances?
Not, certainly, that which is narrow in the ancients, nor that
in which we can no longer sympathise. An action like the
action of the *Antigone* of Sophocles, which turns upon the
conflict between the heroine's duty to her brother's corpse
and that to the laws of her country, is no longer one in which
it is possible that we should feel a deep interest. I am
speaking too, it will be remembered, not of the best sources
of intellectual stimulus for the general reader, but of the best
models of instruction for the individual writer. This last may
certainly learn of the ancients, better than anywhere else,
three things which it is vitally important for him to know: –
the all-importance of the choice of a subject; the necessity of
accurate construction; and the subordinate character of
expression. He will learn from them how unspeakably
superior is the effect of the one moral impression left by a
great action treated as a whole, to the effect produced by the
most striking single thought or by the happiest image As he
penetrates into the spirit of the great classical works, as he
becomes gradually aware of their intense significance, their

noble simplicity, and their calm pathos, he will be convinced that it is this effect, unity and profoundness of moral impression, at which the ancient poets aimed; that it is this which constitutes the grandeur of their works, and which makes them immortal. He will desire to direct his own efforts towards producing the same effect. Above all, he will deliver himself from the jargon of modern criticism, and escape the danger of producing poetical works conceived in the spirit of the passing time, and which partake of its transitoriness.

The present age makes great claims upon us: we owe it service, it will not be satisfied without our admiration. I know not how it is, but their commerce with the ancients appears to me to produce, in those who constantly practise it, a steadying and composing effect upon their judgment, not of literary works only, but of men and events in general. They are like persons who have had a very weighty and impressive experience: they are more truly than others under the empire of facts, and more independent of the language current among those with whom they live. They wish neither to applaud nor to revile their age; they wish to know what it is, what it can give them, and whether this is what they want. What they want, they know very well; they want to educe and cultivate what is best and noblest in themselves; they know, too, that this is no easy task – χαλεπὸν as Pittacus said,[23] χαλεπὸν ἐσθλὸν ἔμμεναι – and they ask themselves sincerely whether their age and its literature can assist them in the attempt. If they are endeavouring to practise any art, they remember the plain and simple proceedings of the old artists, who attained their grand results by penetrating themselves with some noble and significant action, not by inflating themselves with a belief in the pre-eminent importance and greatness of their own times. They do not talk of their mission, nor of interpreting their age, nor of the coming poet; all this, they know, is the mere delirium of vanity; their business is not to praise their age, but to afford to the men who live in it the highest pleasure which they are capable of feeling. If asked to afford this by means of subjects drawn from the age itself, they ask what special fitness the present age has for supplying them. They are told that it is an era of progress, an age commissioned to carry out the great ideas of industrial development and social amelioration. They reply that with all this they can do nothing; that the elements they need for the exercise of their art are great actions, calculated powerfully and delightfully to affect what is permanent in the human soul; that so far as the present age can supply such actions, they will gladly make use of them; but that an age wanting in moral grandeur can with difficulty supply such, and an age of spiritual discomfort with difficulty be powerfully and delightfully affected by them.

A host of voices will indignantly rejoin that the present age is inferior to the past neither in moral grandeur nor in spiritual health. He who possesses the discipline I speak of will content himself with remembering the judgments passed upon the present age, in this respect, by the men of strongest head and widest culture whom it has produced; by Goethe and by Niebuhr.[24] It will be sufficient for him that he knows the opinions held by these two great men respecting the present age and its literature; and that he feels assured in his own mind that their aims and demands upon life were such as he would wish, at any rate, his own to be; and their judgment as to what is impeding and disabling such as he may safely follow. He will not, however, maintain a hostile attitude towards the false pretensions of his age: he will content himself with not being overwhelmed by them. He will esteem himself fortunate if he can succeed in banishing from his mind all feelings of contradiction, and irritation, and impatience; in order to delight himself with the contemplation of some noble action of a heroic time, and to enable others, through his representation of it, to delight in it also.

I am far indeed from making any claim, for myself, that I possess this discipline; or for the following poems, that they breathe its spirit. But I say, that in the sincere endeavour to learn and practise, amid the bewildering confusion of our times, what is sound and true in poetical art, I seemed to myself to find the only sure guidance, the only solid footing, among the ancients. They, at any rate, knew what they wanted in art, and we do not. It is this uncertainty which is disheartening, and not hostile criticism. How often have I felt this when reading words of disparagement or of cavil: that it is the uncertainty as to what is really to be aimed at which makes our difficulty, not the dissatisfaction of the critic, who himself suffers from the same uncertainty! *Non me tua fervida terrent Dicta; ... Dii me terrent, et Jupiter hostis.*[25]

Two kinds of *dilettanti*, says Goethe,[26] there are in poetry: he who neglects the indispensable mechanical part, and thinks he has done enough if he shows spirituality and feeling; and he who seeks to arrive at poetry merely by mechanism, in which he can acquire an artisan's readiness, and is without soul and matter. And he adds, that the first does most harm to art, and the last to himself. If we must be *dilettanti*: if it is impossible for us, under the circumstances amidst which we live, to think clearly, to feel nobly, and to delineate firmly: if we cannot attain to the mastery of the great artists; – let us, at least, have so much respect for our art as to prefer it to ourselves. Let us not bewilder our successors; let us transmit to them the practice of poetry, with its boundaries and wholesome regulative laws, under which excellent works may again, perhaps, at some future time, be produced, not yet fallen into oblivion through our neglect, not yet condemned and cancelled by the influence of their eternal enemy, caprice.

1 *Empedocles on Etna.*
2 Legendary Greek poet, said to have been a pupil of Orpheus, the founder of the religious mysteries.
3 Greek thinkers attacked by Socrates, who taught rhetoric rather than wisdom.
4 *Poetics*, IV, 1–5.
5 *Theogony*, 55.
6 Preface to *Die Braut von Messina*, para. 4.
7 Arnold's note reads: 'In the *Spectator* of April 2, 1853. The words

quoted were not used with reference to poems of mine.' Arnold seems to have attributed the anonymous review to R. S. Rintoul, the editor of *The Spectator*.

8 See Aristotle, *Poetics*, VI, 9–10.

9 A phrase deriving from Wordsworth's Preface to *Lyrical Ballads* (1800), para. 6, where the poet is said to deal with 'the primary laws of our nature.'

10 Central characters in Homer's *Iliad*, Aeschylus's *Prometheus Bound*, Aeschylus's *Agamemnon* and Vergil's *Aeneid*.

11 Works by Goethe (1797), Byron (1812–18), Alphonse de Lamartine (1836) and Wordsworth (1814) respectively.

12 Aristotle refers to these in the *Poetics* as the subjects of tragedies, but only the Oresteia trilogy of Aeschylus survives; Arnold published his tragedy *Merope* in 1858.

13 *The Persians* dramatises the victory of the Greeks over the Persian invaders, which took place eight years before the production of the play.

14 Polybius was a Greek historian of the second century BC, who used the term pragmatic to define the writing of history.

15 The fourth-century BC Greek comic poet; the story is told by Plutarch in *Moralia* 347 e–f.

16 David Masson, anonymous reviewer of Alexander Smith's *A Life-Drama* in *North American Review* XIX (1853), 338.

17 J. P. Eckermann, *Conversations with Goethe*, 3 January 1830.

18 In 'Über den sogenannten Dilettantismus' (1799); in *Werke* (Stuttgart, 1833), XLIV, 262–3.

19 'He says all he wants to, but unfortunately he has nothing to say'; a summary of the argument of Alfred Crampon's review of Théophile Gautier's *Emaux et Camées* and other books in the *Revue des deux mondes*, N.S. XVI (1852), 582–97.

20 Boccaccio tells the story in the *Decameron*, IV, 5.

21 Henry Hallam, *Introduction to the Literature of Europe* (Second Edition, 1843), III, 91–2.

22 François Guizot, *Shakspeare et son temps* (Paris, 1852), p. 114.

23 'It is hard to be good': recorded by Plato in *Protagoras* 343c. Pittacus was a statesman of the seventh century BC, traditionally one of the Seven Sages of ancient Greece.

24 Eckermann, *Conversations with Goethe*, 29 January 1829; the historian Niebuhr in a letter of 19 February 1830: "How barren and dumb is our literature now!" (*Life and Letters of Barthold George Niebuhr* (New York, 1852), p. 519).

25 'Your fiery words do not scare me; ... the Gods scare me, and Jupiter if he is my enemy.' From Virgil, *Aeneid*, XII, 894–5.

26 See Note 18 above; XLIV, 281.

21 Preface to the Second Edition of Poems, 1854

I have allowed the Preface to the former edition of these Poems to stand almost without change, because I still believe it to be, in the main, true. I must not, however, be supposed insensible to the force of much that has been alleged against portions of it, or unaware that it contains many things incompletely stated, many things which need limitation. It leaves, too, untouched the question, how far and in what manner the opinions there expressed respecting the choice of subjects apply to lyric poetry, – that region of the poetical field which is chiefly cultivated at present. But neither do I propose at the present time to supply these deficiencies, nor, indeed, would this be the proper place for attempting it. On one or two points alone I wish to offer, in the briefest possible way, some explanation.

An objection has been warmly urged to the classing together, as subjects equally belonging to a past time, Oedipus and Macbeth.[1] And it is no doubt true that to Shakspeare, standing on the verge of the middle ages, the epoch of Macbeth was more familiar than that of Oedipus. But I was speaking of actions as they presented themselves to us moderns: and it will hardly be said that the European mind, in our day, has much more affinity with the times of Macbeth than with those of Oedipus. As moderns, it seems to me, we have no longer any direct affinity with the circumstances and feelings of either. As individuals, we are attracted towards this or that personage, we have a capacity for imagining him, irrespective of his times, solely according to a law of personal sympathy; and those subjects for which we feel this personal attraction most strongly, we may hope to treat successfully. Prometheus or Joan of Arc, Charlemagne or Agamemnon, – one of these is not really nearer to us now than another. Each can be made present only by an act of poetic imagination; but this man's imagination has an affinity for one of them, and that man's for another.

It has been said that I wish to limit the poet, in his choice of subjects, to the period of Greek and Roman antiquity,[2] but it is not so. I only counsel him to choose for his subjects great actions, without regarding to what time they belong. Nor do I deny that the poetic faculty can and does manifest itself in treating the most trifling action, the most hopeless subject. But it is a pity that power should be wasted; and that the poet should be compelled to impart interest and force to his subject, instead of receiving them from it, and thereby doubling his impressiveness. There is, it has been excellently said, an immortal strength in the stories of great actions; the most gifted poet, then, may well be glad to supplement with it that mortal weakness, which, in presence of the vast spectacle of life and the world, he must for ever feel to be his individual portion.

Again, with respect to the study of the classical writers of antiquity: it has been said that we should emulate rather than imitate them.[3] I make no objection; all I say is, let us study them. They can help to cure us of what is, it seems to me, the great vice of our intellect, manifesting itself in our incredible vagaries in literature, in art, in religion, in morals: namely, that it is *fantastic*, and wants *sanity*. Sanity, – that is the great virtue of the ancient literature; the want of that is the great defect of the modern, in spite of all its variety and power. It is impossible to read carefully the great ancients, without losing something of our caprice and eccentricity; and to emulate them we must at least read them.

1 In a review of Arnold's *Poems* in *The Spectator*, 3 December 1853, Supplement, p. 5.
2 In reviews by J. D. Coleridge, *Christian Remembrancer*, XXVII, 1854, 318–20 and J. A. Froude, *Westminster Review* LXI, 1854, 158–9.
3 G. H. Lewes, 'Schools of Poetry' in *The Leader* IV, 1853, 1147.

22 From 'Heine' in *Essays in Criticism*, 1865

We in England, in our great burst of literature during the first thirty years of the present century, had no manifestation of the modern spirit, as this spirit manifests itself in Goethe's works or Heine's.[1] And the reason is not far to seek. We had neither the German wealth of ideas, nor the French enthusiasm for applying ideas. There reigned in the mass of the nation that inveterate inaccessibility to ideas, that Philistinism – to use the German nickname – which reacts even on the individual genius that is exempt from it. In our greatest literary epoch, that of the Elizabethan age, English society at large was accessible to ideas, was permeated by them, was vivified by them, to a degree which has never been reached in England since. Hence the unique greatness in English literature of Shakspeare and his contemporaries. They were powerfully upheld by the intellectual life of their nation; they applied freely in literature the then modern ideas, – ideas of the Renascence and the Reformation. A few years afterwards the great English middle class, the kernel of the nation, the class whose intelligent sympathy had upheld a Shakspeare, entered the prison of Puritanism, and had the key turned on its spirit there for two hundred years. *He enlargeth a nation*, says Job, *and straiteneth it again.*[2]

In the literary movement of the beginning of the nineteenth century the signal attempt to apply freely the modern spirit was made in England by two members of the aristocratic class, Byron and Shelley. Aristocracies are, as such, naturally impenetrable by ideas; but their individual members have a high courage and a turn for breaking bounds; and a man of genius, who is the born child of the idea, happening to be born in the aristocratic ranks, chafes against the obstacles which prevent him from freely developing it. But Byron and Shelley did not succeed in their attempt freely to apply the modern spirit in English literature; they could not succeed in it; the resistance to baffle them, the want of intelligent sympathy to guide and uphold them, were too great. Their literary creation, compared with the literary creation of Shakspeare and Spenser, compared with the literary creation of Goethe and Heine, is a failure. The best literary creation of that time in England proceeded from men who did not make the same bold attempt as Byron and Shelley. What, in fact, was the career of the chief English men of letters, their contemporaries? The gravest of them, Wordsworth, retired (in Middle-Age phrase) into a monastery. I mean he plunged himself in the inward life, he voluntarily cut himself off from the modern spirit. Coleridge took to opium. Scott became the historiographer royal of feudalism. Keats passionately gave himself up to a sensuous genius, to his faculty for interpreting nature; and he died of consumption at twenty-five. Wordsworth, Scott, and Keats have left admirable works; far more solid and complete works than those which Byron and Shelley have left. But their works have this defect; – they do not belong to that which is the main current of the literature of modern epochs, they do not apply modern ideas to life; they constitute, therefore, *minor currents*, and all other literary work of our day, however popular, which has the same defect, also constitutes but a minor current. Byron and Shelley will long be remembered, long after the inadequacy of their actual work is clearly recognised, for their passionate, their Titanic effort to flow in the main stream of modern literature; their names will be greater than their writings; *stat magni nominis umbra.*[3]

Heine's literary good fortune was superior to that of Byron and Shelley. His theatre of operations was Germany, whose Philistinism does not consist in her want of ideas, or in her inaccessibility to ideas, for she teems with them and loves them, but, as I have said, in her feeble and hesitating application of modern ideas to life. Heine's intense modernism, his absolute freedom, his utter rejection of stock classicism and stock romanticism, his bringing all things under the point of view of the nineteenth century, were understood and laid to heart by Germany, through virtue of her immense, tolerant intellectualism, much as there was in all Heine said to affront and wound Germany. The wit and ardent modern spirit of France Heine joined to the culture, the sentiment, the thought of Germany. This is what makes him so remarkable; his wonderful clearness, lightness, and freedom, united with such power of feeling, and width of range . . . .

1 Heinrich Heine (1797–1856), German lyric poet and ironist.
2 Job, XII. 23.
3 'Here stands the shadow of a great name': Lucan, *Pharsalia*
   I, 135.

JOHN RUSKIN

Ruskin (1819–1900) wrote influentially on a huge range of topics from painting and architecture to politics and economics, taking a critical view of many aspects of his age.

23 On the 'Pathetic Fallacy', 1856

[In *Modern Painters* III, 1856, Ch. XII, Ruskin discusses the Romantic tendency to allow the artist's subjective state to colour his account of the external world. He describes this as the 'Pathetic Fallacy', and sees it as characteristic of much contemporary art.]

Now, therefore, putting these tiresome and absurd words quite out of our way, we may go on at our ease to examine the point in question, – namely, the difference between the ordinary, proper, and true appearances of things to us; and the extraordinary, or false appearances, when we are under the influence of emotion, or contemplative fancy; false appearances, I say, as being entirely unconnected with any real power or character in the object, and only imputed to it by us.

For instance –

> The spendthrift crocus, bursting through the mould
> Naked and shivering, with his cup of gold.[1]

This is very beautiful, and yet very untrue. The crocus is not a spendthrift, but a hardy plant; its yellow is not gold, but saffron. How is it that we enjoy so much the having it put into our heads that it is anything else than a plain crocus?

It is an important question. For, throughout our past reasonings about art, we have always found that nothing could be good or useful, or ultimately pleasurable, which was untrue. But here is something pleasurable in written poetry which is nevertheless *un*true. And what is more, if we think over our favourite poetry, we shall find it full of this kind of fallacy, and that we like it all the more for being so.

It will appear also, on consideration of the matter, that this fallacy is of two principal kinds. Either, as in this case of the crocus, it is the fallacy of wilful fancy, which involves no real expectation that it will be believed; or else it is a fallacy caused by an excited state of the feelings, making us, for the time, more or less irrational. Of the cheating of the fancy we shall have to speak presently; but, in this chapter, I want to examine the nature of the other error, that which the mind admits when affected strongly by emotion. Thus, for instance, in *Alton Locke*, – [2]

> They rowed her in across the rolling foam –
> The cruel, crawling foam.

The foam is not cruel, neither does it crawl. The state of mind which attributes to it these characters of a living creature is one in which the reason is unhinged by grief. All violent feelings have the same effect. They produce in us a falseness in all our impressions of external things, which I would generally characterize as the 'pathetic fallacy'.

Now we are in the habit of considering this fallacy as eminently a character of poetical description, and the temper of mind in which we allow it, as one eminently poetical, because passionate. But I believe, if we look well into the matter, that we shall find the greatest poets do not often admit this kind of falseness, – that it is only the second order of poets who much delight in it. [3]

Thus, when Dante describes the spirits falling from the bank of Acheron 'as dead leaves flutter from a bough' [4] he gives the most perfect image possible of their utter lightness, feebleness, passiveness, and scattering agony of despair, without, however, for an instant losing his own clear perception that *these* are souls, and *those* are leaves; he makes no confusion of one with the other. But when Coleridge speaks of

> The one red leaf, the last of its clan
> That dances as often as dance it can,[5]

he has a morbid, that is to say, a so far false, idea about the leaf; he fancies a life in it, and will, which there are not; confuses its powerlessness with choice, its fading death with merriment, and the wind that shakes it with music. Here, however, there is some beauty, even in the morbid passage; but take an instance in Homer and Pope. Without the knowledge of Ulysses, Elpenor, his youngest follower, has fallen from an upper chamber in the Circean palace, and has been left dead, unmissed by his leader or companions, in the haste of their departure. They cross the sea to the Cimmerian land; and Ulysses summons the shades from Tartarus. The first which appears is that of the lost Elpenor. Ulysses, amazed, and in exactly the spirit of bitter and terrified lightness which is seen in Hamlet,[6] addresses the spirit with the simple, startled words: –

> Elpenor? How camest thou under the shadowy darkness?
> Hast thou come faster on foot than I in my black ship?[7]

Which Pope renders thus: –

> O, say, what angry power Elpenor led
> To glide in shades, and wander with the dead?
> How could thy soul, by realms and seas disjoined,
> Outfly the nimble sail, and leave the lagging wind?[8]

I sincerely hope the reader finds no pleasure here, either in the nimbleness of the sail, or the laziness of the wind! And yet how is it that these conceits are so painful now, when they have been pleasant to us in the other instances?

For a very simple reason. They are not a *pathetic* fallacy at all, for they are put into the mouth of the wrong passion – a

passion which never could possibly have spoken them –
agonized curiosity. Ulysses wants to know the facts of the
matter; and the very last thing his mind could do at the
moment would be to pause, or suggest in anywise what was
not a fact. The delay in the first three lines, and conceit in
the last, jar upon us instantly like the most frightful discord
in music. No poet of true imaginative power could possibly
have written the passage.[9]

Therefore we see that the spirit of truth must guide us in
some sort, even in our enjoyment of fallacy. Coleridge's
fallacy has no discord in it, but Pope's has set our teeth on
edge. Without farther questioning, I will endeavour to state
the main bearings of this matter.

The temperament which admits the pathetic fallacy, is, as
I said above, that of a mind and body in some sort too weak
to deal fully with what is before them or upon them; borne
away, or over-clouded, or over-dazzled by emotion; and it is
a more or less noble state, according to the force of the
emotion which has induced it. For it is no credit to a man
that he is not morbid or inaccurate in his perceptions, when
he has no strength of feeling to warp them; and it is in
general a sign of higher capacity and stand in the ranks of
being, that the emotions should be strong enough to van-
quish, partly, the intellect, and make it believe what they
choose. But it is still a grander condition when the intellect
also rises, till it is strong enough to assert its rule against, or
together with, the utmost efforts of the passions; and the
whole man stands in an iron glow, white hot, perhaps, but
still strong, and in no wise evaporating; even if he melts,
losing none of his weight.

So, then, we have the three ranks: the man who perceives
rightly, because he does not feel, and to whom the primrose
is very accurately the primrose, because he does not love it.
Then, secondly, the man who perceives wrongly, because he
feels, and to whom the primrose is anything else than a
primrose: a star, or a sun, or a fairy's shield, or a forsaken
maiden. And then, lastly, there is the man who perceives
rightly in spite of his feelings, and to whom the primrose is

for ever nothing else than itself – a little flower apprehended in the very plain and leafy fact of it, whatever and how many soever the associations and passions may be, that crowd around it. And, in general, these three classes may be rated in comparative order, as the men who are not poets at all, and the poets of the second order, and the poets of the first; only however great a man may be, there are always some subjects which *ought* to throw him off his balance; some, by which his poor human capacity of thought should be conquered, and brought into the inaccurate and vague state of perception, so that the language of the highest inspiration becomes broken, obscure, and wild in metaphor, resembling that of the weaker man, overborne by weaker things.

And thus, in full, there are four classes: the men who feel nothing, and therefore see truly; the men who feel strongly, think weakly, and see untruly (second order of poets); the men who feel strongly, think strongly, and see truly (first order of poets); and the men who, strong as human creatures can be, are yet submitted to influences stronger than they, and see in a sort untruly, because what they see is inconceivably above them. This last is the usual condition of prophetic inspiration.

I separate these classes, in order that their character may be clearly understood; but of course they are united each to the other by imperceptible transitions, and the same mind, according to the influences to which it is subjected, passes at different times into the various states. Still, the difference between the great and less man is, on the whole, chiefly in this point of *alterability*. That is to say, the one knows too much, and perceives and feels too much of the past and future, and of all things beside and around that which immediately affects him, to be in anywise shaken by it. His mind is made up; his thoughts have an accustomed current; his ways are steadfast; it is not this or that new sight which will at once unbalance him. He is tender to impression at the surface, like a rock with deep moss upon it; but there is too much mass of him to be moved. The smaller man, with the same degree of sensibility, is at once carried off his feet; he wants to do something he did not want to do before; he views all the universe in a new light through his tears; he is gay or enthusiastic, melancholy or passionate, as things come and go to him. Therefore the high creative poet might even be thought, to a great extent, impassive (as shallow people think Dante stern), receiving indeed all feelings to the full, but having a great centre of reflection and knowledge in which he stands serene, and watches the feeling, as it were, from far off.

Dante, in his most intense moods, has entire command of himself, and can look around calmly, at all moments, for the image or the word that will best tell what he sees to the upper or lower world. But Keats and Tennyson, and the poets of the second order, are generally themselves subdued by the feelings under which they write, or, at least, write as choosing to be so; and therefore admit certain expressions and modes of thought which are in some sort diseased or false.

Now so long as we see that the *feeling* is true, we pardon, or are even pleased by, the confessed fallacy of sight which it induces: we are pleased, for instance, with those lines of Kingsley's, above quoted, not because they fallaciously describe foam, but because they faithfully describe sorrow. But the moment the mind of the speaker becomes cold, that moment every such expression becomes untrue, as being for ever untrue in the external facts. And there is no greater baseness in literature than the habit of using these metaphorical expressions in cold blood. An inspired writer, in full impetuosity of passion, may speak wisely and truly of 'raging waves of the sea foaming out their own shame';[10] but it is only the basest writer who cannot speak of the sea without talking of 'raging waves', 'remorseless floods', 'ravenous billows', etc.; and it is one of the signs of the highest power in a writer to check all such habits of thought, and to keep his eyes fixed firmly on the *pure fact*, out of which if any feeling comes to him or his reader, he knows it must be a true one.

1 From 'Astraea' by the American poet and essayist Oliver Wendell Holmes (1809–94).
2 The novel by Charles Kingsley (1819–75), published in 1850, telling the tragic story of a working-class poet.
3 Ruskin's note reads:

> 'I admit two orders of poets, but no third; and by these two orders I mean the Creative (Shakespeare, Homer, Dante), and Reflective or Perceptive (Wordsworth, Keats, Tennyson). But both of these must be first-rate in their range, though their range is different; and with poetry second-rate in quality no one ought to be allowed to trouble mankind.'

4 Dante, *Inferno*, Canto III, 112.
5 Coleridge, 'Christabl', Part I.
6 *Hamlet*, I. v: 'Well said, old mole! cans't work in' the ground so fast?'
7 *Odyssey*, XI, 56.
8 Pope's translation of Homer.
9 Ruskin's note reads:

> 'It is worth while comparing the way a similar question is put by the exquisite sincerity of Keats:–

> > He wept, and his bright tears
> > Went trickling down the golden bow he held.
> > Thus, with half-shut, suffused eyes, he stood;
> > While from beneath some cumb'rous boughs hard by,
> > With solemn step, an awful goddess came,
> > And there was purport in her looks for him,
> > Which he with eager guess began to read:
> > Perplexed the while, melodiously he said,
> > 'How cam'st thou over the unfooted sea?'

> > > > > > (*Hyperion*, III)

10 Jude, 13.

24 From a letter to Tennyson, 1859

[Here Ruskin responds to Tennyson's volume of poems on Arthurian themes, *Idylls of the King*, raising questions about the poet's choice of subject-matter which was a central Victorian concern.]

DEAR MR. TENNYSON, – I have had the *Idylls*[1] in my travelling desk ever since I could get them across the water, and have only not written about them because I could not quite make up my mind about that increased quietness of style. I thought you would like a little to know what I felt about it, but did not quite know myself what I did feel.

To a certain extent you yourself of course know better what the work is than any one else, as all great artists do.

If you are satisfied with it, I believe it to be right. Satisfied with bits of it you must be, and so must all of us, however much we expect from you.

The four songs[2] seem to me the jewels of the crown, and bits come every here and there – the fright of the maid, for instance, and the 'In the darkness o'er her fallen head'[3] – which seem to me finer than almost all you have done yet. Nevertheless I am not sure but I feel the art and finish in these poems a little more than I like to feel it. Yet I am not a fair judge quite, for I am so much of a realist as not by any possibility to interest myself much in an unreal subject to feel it as I should, and the very sweetness and stateliness of the words strike me all the more as *pure* workmanship.

As a description of various nobleness and tenderness the book is without price; but I shall always wish it had been nobleness independent of a romantic condition of externals in general.

'In Memoriam', 'Maud', 'The Miller's Daughter',[4] and such like will always be my own pet rhymes, but I am quite prepared to admit this to be as good as any, for its own peculiar audience. Treasures of wisdom there are in it, and word-painting such as never was yet for concentration; nevertheless it seems to me that so great power ought not to be spent on visions of things past, but on the living present. For one hearer capable of feeling the depth of this poem I believe ten would feel a depth quite as great if the stream flowed through things nearer the hearer. And merely in the facts of modern life – not drawing-room, formal life, but the far-away and quite unknown growth of souls in and through any form of misery or servitude – there is an infinity of what men should be told, and what none but a poet can tell. I cannot but think that the intense, masterful, and unerring transcript of an actuality, and the relation of a story of any real human life as a poet would watch and analyze it, would make all men feel more or less what poetry was, as they felt what Life and Fate were in their instant workings.

This seems to me the true task of the modern poet. And I think I have seen faces, and heard voices, by road and street side, which claimed or conferred as much as ever the loveliest or saddest of Camelot. As I watch them, the feeling continually weighs upon me, day by day, more and more, that not the grief of the world but the loss of it is the wonder of it. I see creatures so full of all power and beauty, with none to understand or teach or save them. The making in them of miracles, and all cast away, for ever lost as far as we can trace. And no 'in memoriam'.

1 The 1859 volume consisted of four poems, 'Enid', 'Vivien', 'Elaine', and 'Guinivere'.
2 Respectively, 'Turn, Fortune, turn thy wheel'; 'In Love, if Love be Love'; 'Sweet is true love tho' given in vain'; and 'Late, late, so late!'
3 From 'Guinivere'.
4 Earlier poems by Tennyson dealing with contemporary subject-matter.

MARY ANN EVANS (GEORGE ELIOT)

Evans (1819–60) was the leading Victorian woman intellectual. She translated Strauss's *Life of Jesus* (1846) and Feuerbach's *Essence of Christianity* (1854), and contributed regularly from 1850 onwards to the influential *Westminster Review*, from which the articles quoted in part here are both taken. These show her thoughtful commitment to Realism. This was encouraged by her partner George Henry Lewes (see No. 28) and bore fruit in the fiction she went on to publish under the name of George Eliot, from *Scenes of Clerical Life* (1857) to *Daniel Deronda* (1876). T. Pinney edited *Essays of George Eliot* in 1963.

25 From 'The Natural History of German Life', 1856

[This was a review, in the *Westminster Review* LX, July 1856, of two works by the German sociologist, W. H. Riehl: *Die Bürgerliche Gesellschaft* (1855) and *Land und Leute* (1856).]

It is an interesting branch of psychological observation to note the images that are habitually associated with abstract or collective terms – what may be called the picture-writing of the mind, which it carries on concurrently with the more subtle symbolism of language. Perhaps the fixity or variety of these associated images would furnish a tolerably fair test of the amount of concrete knowledge and experience which a given word represents, in the minds of two persons who use it with equal familiarity. The word *railways*, for example, will probably call up, in the mind of a man who is not highly locomotive, the image either of a 'Bradshaw',[1] or of the station with which he is most familiar, or of an indefinite length of tram-road; he will alternate between these three images, which represent his stock of concrete acquaintance with railways. But suppose a man to have had successively the experience of a 'navvy', an engineer, a traveller, a railway director and shareholder, and a landed proprietor in treaty with a railway company, and it is probable that the range of images which would by turns present themselves to his mind at the mention of the *word* 'railways', would include all the essential facts in the existence and relations of the *thing*. Now it is possible for the first-mentioned personage to entertain very expanded views as to the multiplication of railways in the abstract, and their ultimate function in civilisation. He may talk of a vast network of railways stretching over the globe, of future 'lines' in Madagascar, and elegant refreshment-rooms in the Sandwich Islands, with none the less glibness because his distinct conceptions on the subject do not extend beyond his one station and his indefinite length of tram-road. But it is evident that if we want a railway to be made, or its affairs to be managed, this man of wide views and narrow observation will not serve our purpose.

Probably, if we could ascertain the images called up by the terms 'the people', 'the masses', 'the proletariat', 'the peasantry', by many who theorise on those bodies with eloquence, or who legislate for them without eloquence, we should find that they indicate almost as small an amount of concrete knowledge – that they are as far from completely representing the complex facts summed up in the collective term, as the railway images of our non-locomotive gentleman. How little the real characteristics of the working classes are known to those who are outside them, how little their natural history has been studied, is sufficiently disclosed by our Art as well as by our political and social theories. Where, in our picture exhibitions, shall we find a group of true peasantry? What English artist even attempts to rival in truthfulness such studies of popular life as the pictures of

Teniers[2] or the ragged boys of Murillo?[3] Even one of the
greatest painters of the pre-eminently realistic school,[4] while,
in his picture of 'The Hireling Shepherd', he gave us a landscape of marvellous truthfulness, placed a pair of peasants in
the foreground who were not much more real than the idyllic
swains and damsels of our chimney ornaments. Only a total
absence of acquaintance and sympathy with our peasantry
could give a moment's popularity to such a picture as 'Cross
Purposes', where we have a peasant girl who looks as if she
knew L. E. L.'s[5] poems by heart, and English rustics, whose
costume seems to indicate that they are meant for ploughmen, with exotic features that remind us of a handsome
primo tenore. Rather than such Cockney sentimentality as
this, as an education for the taste and sympathies, we prefer
the most crapulous group of boors that Teniers ever painted.
But even those among our painters who aim at giving the
rustic type of features, who are far above the effeminate
feebleness of the 'Keepsake' style,[6] treat their subjects
under the influence of traditions and prepossessions rather
than of direct observation. The notion that peasants are
joyous, that the typical moment to represent a man in a
smock-frock is when he is cracking a joke and showing a row
of sound teeth, that cottage matrons are usually buxom, and
village children necessarily rosy and merry, are prejudices
difficult to dislodge from the artistic mind, which looks for
its subjects into literature instead of life. The painter is still
under the influence of idyllic literature, which has always
expressed the imagination of the cultivated and town-bred,
rather than the truth of rustic life. Idyllic ploughmen are
jocund when they drive their team afield; idyllic shepherds
make bashful love under hawthorn-bushes; idyllic villagers
dance in the chequered shade and refresh themselves, not
immoderately, with spicy nut-brown ale. But no one who
has seen much of actual ploughmen thinks them jocund; no
one who is well acquainted with the English peasantry can
pronounce them merry. The slow gaze, in which no sense of
beauty beams, no humour twinkles, – the slow utterance,
and the heavy slouching walk, remind one rather of that

melancholy animal the camel, than of the sturdy countryman, with striped stockings, red waistcoat, and hat aside,
who represents the traditional English peasant. Observe a
company of haymakers. When you see them at a distance,
tossing up the forkfuls of hay in the golden light, while the
waggon creeps slowly with its increasing burthen over the
meadow, and the bright green space which tells of work
done gets larger and larger, you pronounce the scene
'smiling', and you think these companions in labour must be
as bright and cheerful as the picture to which they give
animation. Approach nearer, and you will certainly find that
haymaking-time is a time for joking, especially if there are
women among the labourers; but the coarse laugh that
bursts out every now and then, and expresses the triumphant
taunt, is as far as possible from your conception of idyllic
merriment. That delicious effervescence of the mind which
we call fun has no equivalent for the northern peasant,
except tipsy revelry; the only realm of fancy and imagination
for the English clown exists at the bottom of the third
quart-pot.

The conventional countryman of the stage, who picks up
pocket-books and never looks into them, and who is too
simple even to know that honesty has its opposite, represents the still lingering mistake, that an unintelligible dialect
is a guarantee for ingenuousness, and that slouching shoul-
ders indicate an upright disposition. It is quite true that a
thresher is likely to be innocent of any adroit arithmetical
cheating, but he is not the less likely to carry home his
master's corn in his shoes and pocket; a reaper is not given
to writing begging-letters, but he is quite capable of cajoling
the dairymaid into filling his small-beer bottle with ale. The
selfish instincts are not subdued by the sight of buttercups,
nor is integrity in the least established by that classic rural
occupation, sheep-washing. To make men moral, something
more is requisite than to turn them out to grass.

Opera peasants, whose unreality excites Mr Ruskin's
indignation,[7] are surely too frank an idealisation to be
misleading; and since popular chorus is one of the most

effective elements of the opera, we can hardly object to lyric
rustics in elegant laced bodices and picturesque motley,
unless we are prepared to advocate a chorus of colliers in
their pit costume, or a ballet of charwomen and stocking-
weavers. But our social novels profess to represent the
people as they are, and the unreality of their representations
is a grave evil. The greatest benefit we owe to the artist,
whether painter, poet, or novelist, is the extension of our
sympathies. Appeals founded on generalisations and statis-
tics require a sympathy ready-made, a moral sentiment
already in activity; but a picture of human life such as a great
artist can give, surprises even the trivial and the selfish into
that attention to what is apart from themselves, which may
be called the raw material of moral sentiment. When Scott
takes us into Luckie Mucklebackit's cottage, or tells the
story of 'The Two Drovers',[8] – when Wordsworth sings to us
the reverie of 'Poor Susan',[9] – when Kingsley shows us
Alton Locke gazing yearningly over the gate which leads
from the highway into the first wood he ever saw,[10] – when
Hornung[11] paints a group of chimney-sweepers, – more is
done towards linking the higher classes with the lower,
towards obliterating the vulgarity of exclusiveness, than by
hundreds of sermons and philosophical dissertations. Art is
the nearest thing to life; it is a mode of amplifying experience and extending our contact with our fellow-men beyond
the bounds of our personal lot. All the more sacred is the
task of the artist when he undertakes to paint the life of the
People. Falsification here is far more pernicious than in the
more artificial aspects of life. It is not so very serious that we
should have false ideas about evanescent fashions – about
the manners and conversation of beaux and duchesses; but it
is serious that our sympathy with the perennial joys and
struggles, the toil, the tragedy, and the humour in the life of
our more heavily laden fellow-men, should be perverted,
and turned towards a false object instead of the true one.

This perversion is not the less fatal because the mis-
representation which gives rise to it has what the artist
considers a moral end. The thing for mankind to know is,

not what are the motives and influences which the moralist thinks *ought* to act on the labourer or the artisan, but what are the motives and influences which *do* act on him. We want to be taught to feel, not for the heroic artisan or the sentimental peasant, but for the peasant in all his coarse apathy, and the artisan in all his suspicious selfishness.

We have one great novelist[12] who is gifted with the utmost power of rendering the external traits of our town population; and if he could give us their psychological character – their conceptions of life, and their emotions – with the same truth as their idiom and manners, his books would be the greatest contribution Art has ever made to the awakening of social sympathies. But while he can copy Mrs Plornish's[13] colloquial style with the delicate accuracy of a sun-picture, while there is the same startling inspiration in his description of the gestures and phrases of 'Boots',[14] as in the speeches of Shakespeare's mobs or numskulls, he scarcely ever passes from the humorous and external to the emotional and tragic, without becoming as transcendent in his unreality as he was a moment before in his artistic truthfulness. But for the precious salt of his humour, which compels him to reproduce external traits that serve, in some degree, as a corrective to his frequently false psychology, his preternaturally virtuous poor children and artisans, his melodramatic boatmen and courtesans, would be as noxious as Eugène Sue's[15] idealised proletaires in encouraging the miserable fallacy that high morality and refined sentiment can grow out of harsh social relations, ignorance, and want; or that the working classes are in a condition to enter at once into a millennial state of *altruism*, wherein every one is caring for every one else, and no one for himself.

If we need a true conception of the popular character to guide our sympathies rightly, we need it equally to check our theories, and direct us in their application. The tendency created by the splendid conquests of modern generalisation, to believe that all social questions are merged in economical science, and that the relations of men to their neighbours may be settled by algebraic equations, – the dream that the uncultured classes are prepared for a condition which appeals principally to their moral sensibilities, – the aristocratic dilettanteism which attempts to restore the 'good old times' by a sort of idyllic masquerading, and to grow feudal fidelity and veneration as we grow prize turnips, by an artificial system of culture, – none of these diverging mistakes can coexist with a real knowledge of the People, with a thorough study of their habits, their ideas, their motives. The land-holder, the clergyman, the mill-owner, the mining-agent, have each an opportunity for making precious observations on different sections of the working classes; but unfortunately their experience is too often not registered at all, or its results are too scattered to be available as a source of information and stimulus to the public mind generally. If any man of sufficient moral and intellectual breadth, whose observations would not be vitiated by a foregone conclusion, or by a professional point of view, would devote himself to studying the natural history of our social classes, especially of the small shopkeepers, artisans, and peasantry, – the degree in which they are influenced by local conditions, their maxims and habits, the points of view from which they regard their religious teachers, and the degree in which they are influenced by religious doctrines, the interaction of the various classes on each other, and what are the tendencies in their position towards disintegration or towards development, – and if, after all this study, he would give us the result of his observations in a book well nourished with specific facts, his work would be a valuable aid to the social and political reformer.

1   The railway timetable.
2   David Teniers the Younger (1610–90), the Dutch painter of low-life scenes.
3   Bartolomé Esteban Murillo (1617–82), the Spanish painter of devotional subjects and street scenes.
4   William Holman Hunt (1827–1910), one of the Pre-Raphaelite Brotherhood of painters, produced 'The Hireling Shepherd' in 1851.
5   Letitia Elizabeth Landon (1802–38), a writer of sentimental verse often published in *Keepsake*.

6 A sentimental literary annual.
7 Ruskin wrote in *Modern Painters* IV (1856), Part V, Ch. 19, of the
   hard lives of the Savoyard peasants by contrast with the popular
   romantic pictures of them presented on the stage.
8 The Mucklebackits are characters in Scott's *The Antiquary* (1816);
   'The Two Drovers' is one of his *Chronicles of the Canongate* (1827).
9 Wordsworth, 'The Reverie of Poor Susan' (?1797).
10 Charles Kingsley, *Alton Locke. Taylor and Poet* (1850), Ch. 11.
11 Joseph Hornung (1792–1870), a Swiss-born painter of Victorian *genre*
   scenes.
12 Dickens.
13 A character in *Little Dorrit* (then appearing serially).
14 'Boots at the Holly-Tree Inn' was the Christmas Number of Dickens's
   Household Words in 1855.
15 Sue (1804–57), the novelist of Parisian low-life.

26 From 'Silly Novels by Lady Novelists', 1856

[In the *Westminster Review* LXVI, Oct. 1856, 442–61, Evans
wrote this acerbic review of a number of novels, all published in 1856: Lady Chatterton's *Compensation: a Story of
Real Life Sixty Years Ago*; the anonymous *Laura Gay*, *Rank
and Beauty* and *The Enigma*; Caroline Lucy Scott's *The Old
Grey Church*; and Jane Margaret Strickland's *Adonijah, a
Tale of the Jewish Dispersion*. Passages relating specifically
to the novels have been omitted.]

Silly novels by Lady Novelists are a genus with many
species, determined by the particular quality of silliness that
predominates in them – the frothy, the prosy, the pious, or
the pedantic. But it is a mixture of all these – a composite
order of feminine fatuity, that produces the largest class of
such novels, which we shall distinguish as the *mind-and-
millinery* species. The heroine is usually an heiress, probably
a peeress in her own right, with perhaps a vicious baronet,
an amiable duke, and an irresistible younger son of a
marquis as lovers in the foreground, a clergyman and a poet
sighing for her in the middle distance, and a crowd of
undefined adorers dimly indicated beyond. Her eyes and her
wit are both dazzling; her nose and her morals are alike free

from any tendency to irregularity; she has a superb *contralto* and a superb intellect; she is perfectly well-dressed and perfectly religious; she dances like a sylph, and reads the Bible in the original tongues. Or it may be that the heroine is not an heiress – that rank and wealth are the only things in which she is deficient; but she infallibly gets into high society, she has the triumph of refusing many matches and securing the best, and she wears some family jewels or other as a sort of crown of righteousness at the end. Rakish men either bite their lips in impotent confusion at her repartees, or are touched to penitence by her reproofs, which, on appropriate occasions, rise to a lofty strain of rhetoric; indeed, there is a general propensity in her to make speeches, and to rhapsodize at some length when she retires to her bedroom. In her recorded conversations she is amazingly eloquent, and in her unrecorded conversations, amazingly witty. She is understood to have a depth of insight that looks through and through the shallow theories of philosophers, and her superior instincts are a sort of dial by which men have only to set their clocks and watches, and all will go well. The men play a very subordinate part by her side. You are consoled now and then by a hint that they have affairs, which keeps you in mind that the working-day business of the world is somehow being carried on, but ostensibly the final cause of their existence is that they may accompany the heroine on her 'starring' expedition through life. They see her at a ball, and are dazzled; at a flower-show, and they are fascinated; on a riding excursion, and they are witched by her noble horsemanship; at church, and they are awed by the sweet solemnity of her demeanour. She is the ideal woman in feelings, faculties, and flounces. For all this, she as often as not marries the wrong person to begin with, and she suffers terribly from the plots and intrigues of the vicious baronet; but even death has a soft place in his heart for such a paragon, and remedies all mistakes for her just at the right moment. The vicious baronet is sure to be killed in a duel, and the tedious husband dies in his bed requesting his wife, as a particular favour to him, to marry the man she loves best, and having already dispatched a note to the lover informing him of the comfortable arrangement. Before matters arrive at this desirable issue our feelings are tried by seeing the noble, lovely, and gifted heroine pass through many *mauvais moments*, but we have the satisfaction of knowing that her sorrows are wept into embroidered pocket-handkerchiefs, that her fainting form reclines on the very best upholstery, and that whatever vicissitudes she may undergo, from being dashed out of her carriage to having her head shaved in a fever, she comes out of them all with a complexion more blooming and locks more redundant than ever.

We may remark, by the way, that we have been relieved from a serious scruple by discovering that silly novels by lady novelists rarely introduce us into any other than very lofty and fashionable society. We had imagined that destitute women turned novelists, as they turned governesses, because they had no other 'lady-like' means of getting their bread. On this supposition, vacillating syntax and improbable incident had a certain pathos for us, like the extremely super-erogatory pincushions and ill-devised nightcaps that are offered for sale by a blind man. We felt the commodity to be a nuisance, but we were glad to think that the money went to relieve the necessitous, and we pictured to ourselves lonely women struggling for a maintenance, or wives and daughters devoting themselves to the production of 'copy' out of pure heroism – perhaps to pay their husband's debts, or to purchase luxuries for a sick father. Under these impressions we shrank from criticising a lady's novel: her English might be faulty, but, we said to ourselves, her motives are ir-reproachable; her imagination may be uninventive, but her patience is untiring. Empty writing was excused by an empty stomach, and twaddle was consecrated by tears. But no! This theory of ours, like many other pretty theories, has had to give way before observation. Women's silly novels, we are now convinced, are written under totally different circumstances. The fair writers have evidently never talked to a tradesman except from a carriage window; they have no

notion of the working-classes except as 'dependents'; they
think five hundred a-year a miserable pittance; Belgravia
and 'baronial halls' are their primary truths; and they have
no idea of feeling interest in any man who is not at least a
great landed proprietor, if not a prime minister. It is clear
that they write in elegant boudoirs, with violet-coloured ink
and a ruby pen; that they must be entirely indifferent to
publishers' accounts, and inexperienced in every form of
poverty except poverty of brains. It is true that we are
constantly struck with the want of verisimilitude in their
representations of the high society in which they seem to
live; but then they betray no closer acquaintance with any
other form of life. If their peers and peeresses are improbable, their literary men, tradespeople, and cottagers are
impossible; and their intellect seems to have the peculiar
impartiality of reproducing both what they *have* seen and
heard, and what they have *not* seen and heard, with equal
unfaithfulness.

. . .

Writers of the mind-and-millinery school are remarkably
unanimous in their choice of diction. In their novels, there is
usually a lady or gentleman who is more or less of a upas
tree:[1] the lover has a manly breast; minds are redolent of
various things; hearts are hollow; events are utilized; friends
are consigned to the tomb; infancy is an engaging period; the
sun is a luminary that goes to his western couch, or gathers
the rain-drops into his refulgent bosom; life is a melancholy
boon; Albion and Scotia are conversational epithets.[2] There
is a striking resemblance, too, in the character of their moral
comments, such, for instance, as that 'It is a fact, no less true
than melancholy, that all people, more or less, richer or
poorer, are swayed by bad example'; that 'Books, however
trivial, contain some subjects from which useful information
may be drawn'; that 'Vice can too often borrow the language
of virtue'; that 'Merit and nobility of nature must exist, to be
accepted, for clamour and pretension cannot impose upon

those too well read in human nature to be easily deceived'; and that, 'In order to forgive, we must have been injured.' There is, doubtless, a class of readers to whom these remarks appear peculiarly pointed and pungent; for we often find them doubly and trebly scored with the pencil, and delicate hands giving in their determined adhesion to these hardy novelties by a distinct *très vrai*, emphasized by many notes of exclamation. The colloquial style of these novels is often marked by much ingenious inversion, and a careful avoidance of such cheap phraseology as can be heard every day. Angry young gentlemen exclaim – "Tis ever thus, methinks'; and in the half-hour before dinner a young lady informs her next neighbour that the first day she read Shakspeare she 'stole away into the park, and beneath the shadow of the greenwood tree, devoured with rapture the inspired page of the great magician'. But the most remarkable efforts of the mind-and-millinery writers lie in their philosophic reflections. The authoress of 'Laura Gay', for example, having married her hero and heroine, improves the event by observing that 'if those sceptics, whose eyes have so long gazed on matter that they can no longer see aught else in man, could once enter with heart and soul into such bliss as this, they would come to say that the soul of man and the polypus are not of common origin, or of the same texture'. Lady novelists, it appears, can see something else besides matter; they are not limited to phenomena, but can relieve their eyesight by occasional glimpses of the *noumenon*,[3] and are, therefore, naturally better able than any one else to confound sceptics, even of that remarkable, but to us unknown school, which maintains that the soul of man is of the same texture as the polypus.[4]

The most pitiable of all silly novels by lady novelists are what we may call the *oracular* species – novels intended to expound the writer's religious, philosophical, or moral theories. There seems to be a notion abroad among women, rather akin to the superstition that the speech and actions of idiots are inspired, and that the human being most entirely exhausted of common sense is the fittest vehicle of

revelation. To judge from their writings, there are certain
ladies who think that an amazing ignorance, both of science
and of life, is the best possible qualification for forming an
opinion on the knottiest moral and speculative questions.
Apparently, their recipe for solving all such difficulties is
something like this: Take a woman's head, stuff it with a
smattering of philosophy and literature chopped small, and
with false notions of society baked hard, let it hang over a
desk a few hours every day, and serve up hot in feeble
English, when not required. You will rarely meet with a lady
novelist of the oracular class who is diffident of her ability to
decide on theological questions, – who has any suspicion
that she is not capable of discriminating with the nicest
accuracy between the good and evil in all church parties, –
who does not see precisely how it is that men have gone
wrong hitherto, – and pity philosophers in general that
they have not had the opportunity of consulting her. Great
writers, who have modestly contented themselves with putting their experience into fiction, and have thought it quite a
sufficient task to exhibit men and things as they are, she
sighs over as deplorably deficient in the application of their
powers. 'They have solved no great questions' – and she is
ready to remedy their omission by setting before you a complete theory of life and manual of divinity, in a love story,
where ladies and gentlemen of good family go through genteel vicissitudes, to the utter confusion of Deists,[5] Puseyites,[6]
and ultra-Protestants, and to the perfect establishment of
that particular view of Christianity which either condenses
itself into a sentence of small caps, or explodes into a cluster
of stars on the three hundred and thirtieth page. It is true,
the ladies and gentlemen will probably seem to you remarkably little like any you have had the fortune or misfortune to
meet with, for, as a general rule, the ability of a lady novelist
to describe actual life and her fellow-men, is in inverse
proportion to her confident eloquence about God and the
other world, and the means by which she usually chooses to
conduct you to true ideas of the invisible is a totally false
picture of the visible.

. . .

The epithet 'silly' may seem impertinent, applied to a novel which indicates so much reading and intellectual activity as 'The Enigma'; but we use this epithet advisedly. If, as the world has long agreed, a very great amount of instruction will not make a wise man, still less will a very mediocre amount of instruction make a wise woman. And the most mischievous form of femminine silliness is the literary form, because it tends to confirm the popular prejudice against the more solid education of women. When men see girls wasting their time in consultations about bonnets and ball dresses, and in giggling or sentimental love-confidences, or middle-aged women mismanaging their children, and solacing themselves with acrid gossip, they can hardly help saying, 'For Heaven's sake, let girls be better educated; let them have some better objects of thought – some more solid occupations.' But after a few hours' conversation with an oracular literary woman, or a few hours' reading of her books, they are likely enough to say, 'After all, when a woman gets some knowledge, see what use she makes of it! Her knowledge remains acquisition, instead of passing into culture; instead of being subdued into modesty and simplicity by a larger acquaintance with thought and fact, she has a feverish consciousness of her attainments; she keeps a sort of mental pocket-mirror, and is continually looking in it at her own "intellectuality"; she spoils the taste of one's muffin by questions of metaphysics; "puts down" men at a dinner table with her superior information; and seizes the opportunity of a *soirée* to catechise us on the vital question of the relation between mind and matter. And then, look at her writings! She mistakes vagueness for depth, bombast for eloquence, and affectation for originality; she struts on one page, rolls her eyes on another, grimaces in a third, and is hysterical in a fourth. She may have read many writings of great men, and a few writings of great women; but she is as unable to discern the difference between her own style and theirs as a Yorkshireman is to discern the difference between his own English and a Londoner's: rhodomontade[7] is the native accent of her intellect. No – the average nature of women is too shallow and feeble a soil to bear much tillage; it is only fit for the very lightest crops.'

It is true that the men who come to such a decision on such very superficial and imperfect observation may not be among the wisest in the world; but we have not now to contest their opinion – we are only pointing out how it is unconsciously encouraged by many women who have volunteered themselves as representatives of the feminine intellect. We do not believe that a man was ever strengthened in such an opinion by associating with a woman of true culture, whose mind had absorbed her knowledge instead of being absorbed by it. A really cultured woman, like a really cultured man, is all the simpler and the less obtrusive for her knowledge; it has made her see herself and her opinions in something like just proportions; she does not make it a pedestal from which she flatters herself that she commands a complete view of men and things, but makes it a point of observation from which to form a right estimate of herself. She neither spouts poetry nor quotes Cicero on slight provocation; not because she thinks that a sacrifice must be made to the prejudices of men, but because that mode of exhibiting her memory and Latinity does not present itself to her as edifying or graceful. She does not write books to confound philosophers, perhaps because she is able to write books that delight them. In conversation she is the least formidable of women, because she understands you, without wanting to make you aware that you *can't* understand her. She does not give you information, which is the raw material of culture, – she gives you sympathy, which is it subtlest essence.

A more numerous class of silly novels than the oracular, (which are generally inspired by some form of High Church, or transcendental Christianity,) is what we may call the *white neck-cloth* species, which represent the tone of thought and feeling in the Evangelical party. This species is a kind of genteel tract on a large scale, intended as a sort of medicinal sweetmeat for Low Church young ladies; an Evangelical substitute for the fashionable novel, as the May Meetings[8] are a substitute for the Opera. Even Quaker children, one would think, can hardly have been denied the indulgence of a doll; but it must be a doll dressed in a drab gown and a coal-scuttle bonnet – not a worldly doll, in gauze and spangles. And there are no young ladies, we imagine, – unless they belong to the Church of the United Brethren, in which people are married without any love-making – who can dispense with love stories. Thus, for Evangelical young ladies there are Evangelical love stories, in which the vicissitudes of the tender passion are sanctified by saving views of Regeneration and the Atonement. These novels differ from the oracular ones, as a Low Churchwoman often differs from a High Churchwoman: they are a little less supercilious, and a great deal more ignorant, a little less correct in their syntax, and a great deal more vulgar.

The Orlando[9] of Evangelical literature is the young curate, looked at from the point of view of the middle class, where cambric bands are understood to have as thrilling an effect on the hearts of young ladies as epaulettes have in the classes above and below it. In the ordinary type of these novels, the hero is almost sure to be a young curate, frowned upon, perhaps, by worldly mammas, but carrying captive the hearts of their daughters, who can 'never forget *that* sermon'; tender glances are seized from the pulpit stairs instead of the opera-box; *tête-à-têtes* are seasoned with quotations from Scripture, instead of quotations from the poets; and questions as to the state of the heroine's affections are mingled with anxieties as to the state of her soul. The young curate always has a background of well-dressed and wealthy, if not fashionable society; – for Evangelical silliness is as snobbish as any other kind of silliness; and the Evangelical lady novelist, while she explains to you the type of the scapegoat on one page, is ambitious on another to represent the manners and conversation of aristocratic people. Her pictures of fashionable society are often curious studies considered as efforts of the Evangelical imagination; but in one particular the novels of the White Neck-cloth School are meritoriously realistic, – their favourite hero, the Evangelical young curate is always rather an insipid personage.

But, perhaps, the least readable of silly women's novels, are the *modern-antique* species, which unfold to us the domestic life of Jannes and Jambres,[10] the private love affairs of Sennacherib,[11] or the mental struggles and ultimate conversion of Demetrius the silversmith.[12] From most silly novels we can at least extract a laugh; but those of the modern antique school have a ponderous, a leaden kind of fatuity, under which we groan. What can be more demonstrative of the inability of literary women to measure their own powers, than their frequent assumption of a task which can only be justified by the rarest concurrence of acquirement with genius? The finest effort to reanimate the past is of course only approximative – is always more or less an infusion of the modern spirit into the ancient form,

> Was ihr den Geist der Zeiten heisst,
> Das ist im Grund der Herren eigner Geist,
> In dem die Zeiten sich bespiegeln.[13]

Admitting that genius which has familiarized itself with all the relics of an ancient period can sometimes, by the force of its sympathetic divination, restore the missing notes in the 'music of humanity,'[14] and reconstruct the fragments into a whole which will really bring the remote past nearer to us, and interpret it to our duller apprehension, – this form of imaginative power must always be among the very rarest, because it demands as much accurate and minute knowledge as creative vigour. Yet we find ladies constantly choosing to make their mental mediocrity more conspicuous, by clothing it in a masquerade of ancient names; by putting their feeble sentimentality into the mouths of Roman vestals or Egyptian princesses, and attributing their rhetorical arguments to Jewish high-priests and Greek philosophers.

. . .

'Be not a baker if your head be made of butter', says a homely proverb, which, being interpreted, may mean, let no woman rush into print who is not prepared for the consequences. We are aware that our remarks are in a very different tone from that of the reviewers who, with a perennial recurrence of precisely similar emotions, only paralleled, we imagine, in the experience of monthly nurses, tell one lady novelist after another that they 'hail' her productions 'with delight'. We are aware that the ladies at whom our criticism is pointed are accustomed to be told, in the choicest phraseology of puffery, that their pictures of life are brilliant, their characters well drawn, their style fascinating, and their sentiments lofty. But if they are inclined to resent our plainness of speech, we ask them to reflect for a moment on the chary praise, and often captious blame, which their panegyrists give to writers whose works are on the way to become classics. No sooner does a woman show that she has genius or effective talent, than she receives the tribute of being moderately praised and severely criticised. By a peculiar thermometric adjustment, when a woman's talent is at zero, journalistic approbation is at the boiling pitch; when she attains mediocrity, it is already at no more than summer heat; and if ever she reaches excellence, critical enthusiasm drops to the freezing point. Harriet Martineau,[15] Currer Bell,[16] and Mrs. Gaskell have been treated as cavalierly as if they had been men. And every critic who forms a high estimate of the share women may ultimately take in literature, will, on principle, abstain from any exceptional indulgence towards the productions of literary women. For it must be plain to every one who looks impartially and extensively into feminine literature, that its greatest deficiencies are due hardly more to the want of intellectual power than to the want of those moral qualities that contribute to literary excellence – patient diligence, a sense of the responsibility involved in publication, and an appreciation of the sacredness of the writer's art. In the majority of women's books you see that kind of facility which springs from the absence of any high standard; that fertility in imbecile combination or feeble imitation which a little self-criticism would check and reduce to barrenness;

just as with a total want of musical ear people will sing out of tune, while a degree more melodic sensibility would suffice to render them silent. The foolish vanity of wishing to appear in print, instead of being counter balanced by any consciousness of the intellectual or moral derogation implied in futile authorship, seems to be encouraged by the extremely false impression that to write at all is a proof of superiority in a woman. On this ground, we believe that the average intellect of women is unfairly represented by the mass of feminine literature, and that while the few women who write well are very far above the ordinary intellectual level of their sex, the many women who write ill are very far below it. So that, after all, the severer critics are fulfilling a chivalrous duty in depriving the mere fact of feminine authorship of any false prestige which may give it a delusive attraction, and in recommending women of mediocre faculties – as at least a negative service they can render their sex – to abstain from writing.

The standing apology for women who become writers without any special qualification is, that society shuts them out from other spheres of occupation. Society is a very culpable entity, and has to answer for the manufacture of many unwholesome commodities, from bad pickles to bad poetry. But society, like 'matter', and Her Majesty's Government, and other lofty abstractions, has its share of excessive blame as well as excessive praise. Where there is one woman who writes from necessity, we believe there are three women who write from vanity; and, besides, there is something so antiseptic in the mere healthy fact of working for one's bread, that the most trashy and rotten kind of feminine literature is not likely to have been produced under such circumstances. 'In all labour there is profit';[17] but ladies' silly novels, we imagine, are less the result of labour than of busy idleness.

Happily, we are not dependent on argument to prove that Fiction is a department of literature in which women can, after their kind, fully equal men. A cluster of great names, both living and dead, rush to our memories in evidence that women can produce novels not only fine, but among the very finest; – novels, too, that have a precious speciality, lying quite apart from masculine aptitudes and experience. No educational restrictions can shut women out from the materials of fiction, and there is no species of art which is so free from rigid requirements. Like crystalline masses, it may take any form and yet be beautiful; we have only to pour in the right elements – genuine observation, humour, and passion. But it is precisely this absence of rigid requirement which constitutes the fatal seduction of novel-writing to incompetent women. Ladies are not wont to be very grossly deceived as to their power of playing on the piano; here certain positive difficulties of execution have to be conquered, and incompetence inevitably breaks down. Every art which has its absolute *technique* is, to a certain extent, guarded from the intrusions of mere left-handed imbecility. But in novel-writing there are no barriers for incapacity to stumble against, no external criteria to prevent a writer from mistaking foolish facility for mastery. And so we have again and again the old story of La Fontaine's ass,[18] who puts his nose to the flute, and, finding that he elicits some sound, exclaims, 'Moi, aussi, je joue de la flute;' – a fable which we commend, at parting, to the consideration of any feminine reader who is in danger of adding to the number of 'silly novels by lady novelists'.

1 A tree which produces poisonous juice.
2 Poetic names for England and Scotland, which sound affected in prose.
3 That which really exists, in Platonic terms, as contrasted with 'phenomenon', that which is perceived. The passage is sardonic about the novelist's claim to philosophical insight.
4 An octopus or cuttle-fish.
5 Believer in natural, as distinct from revealed, religion.
6 Followers of the High Church leader in the Church of England, Edward Bouverie Pusey (1800–82).
7 Extravagant language.
8 The annual meetings of the Church of England's Missionary Society, held in May in Exeter Hall, London.
9 Romantic hero; the most famous of Charlemagne's knights.

10 St Paul's names for the magicians who opposed Moses at Pharoah's Court (2 Timothy, 3.iii. 8).

11 King of Assyria in the Old Testament.

12 Who formerly made shrines to the honour of Diana of the Ephesians (Acts, XIV. 24–7).

13 Goethe, *Faust*, Part I (1808), 'Nacht', 577–79:

> 'What you call the spirit of the ages
> Is nothing but the spirit of yourselves
> In which the ages are reflected.'

14 Wordsworth, 'Tintern Abbey' (1798), line 91.

15 (1802–76), a leading Victorian woman intellectual, who wrote on economics and translated Comte.

16 Charlotte Brontë's pseudonym.

17 Proverbs XIV. 23.

18 Jean de la Fontaine (1621–95), the great French fabulist; the donkey here says, 'I too play the flute.'

ELIZABETH BARRETT BROWNING

Elizabeth Barrett (1806–61), who married Robert Browning in 1846, was the best-known woman poet of her period; she published *Poems* (1844); *Sonnets from the Portuguese* (1850); *Casa Guidi Windows* (1851); *Aurora Leigh* (1857) and *Poems before Congress* (1860).

27 From *Aurora Leigh*, 1857

Aurora Leigh is a narrative poem in nine books telling the story of the heroine's life. Aurora is a poet, and the poem includes discussions of many literary issues. In the two extracts here, (i) is from Book II, lines 179–259, in which Aurora's cousin Romney expresses a male view of the limitations of women as artists, to which Aurora replies; (ii) is from Book V, lines 139–388, and in it Aurora argues for modern subject-matter in poetry (an issue raised also by Clough and Ruskin) and considers the limitations of the contemporary theatre.

There is a recent edition of *Aurora Leigh* by Cora Kaplan (1978).

(I) FROM BOOK II

Romney: "There it is! –
You play beside a death-bed like a child,   180
Yet measure to yourself a prophet's place
To teach the living. None of all these things

Can woman understand. You generalise
Oh, nothing, – not even grief! Your quick-breathed
        hearts,
So sympathetic to the personal pang,
Close on each separate knife-stroke, yielding up
A whole life at each wound, incapable
Of deepening, widening a large lap of life
To hold the world-full woe. The human race
To you means, such a child, or such a man,   190
You saw one morning waiting in the cold,
Beside that gate, perhaps. You gather up
A few such cases, and when strong sometimes
Will write of factories and slaves, as if
Your father were a negro, and your son
A spinner in the mills. All's yours and you,
All, coloured with your blood, or otherwise
Just nothing to you. Why, I call you hard
To general suffering. Here's the world half-blind
With intellectual light, half-brutalised   200
With civilisation, having caught the plague
In silks from Tarsus, shrieking east and west
Along a thousand railroads, mad with pain
And sin too! ... does one woman of you all
(You who weep easily) grow pale to see
This tiger shake his cage? – does one of you
Stand still from dancing, stop from stringing pearls,
And pine and die because of the great sum
Of universal anguish? – Show me a tear
Wet as Cordelia's, in eyes bright as yours,   210
Because the world is made. You cannot count,
That you should weep for this account, not you!
You weep for what you know. A red-haired child
Sick in a fever, if you touch him once,
Though but so little as with a finger-tip,
Will set you weeping; but a million sick ...
You could as soon weep for the rule of three
Or compound fractions. Therefore, this same world,
Uncomprehended by you, must remain
Uninfluenced by you. – Women as you are,   220
Mere women, personal and passionate,
You give us doating mothers, and perfect wives,

Sublime Madonnas, and enduring saints!
We get no Christ from you, – and verily
We shall not get a poet, in my mind."
"With which conclusion you conclude!" . . .
                              "But this,
That you, Aurora, with the large live brow
And steady eyelids, cannot condescend
To play at art, as children play at swords,
To show a pretty spirit, chiefly admired   230
Because true action is impossible.
You never can be satisfied with praise
Which men give women when they judge a book
Not as mere work but as mere woman's work,
Expressing the comparative respect
Which means the absolute scorn. 'Oh, excellent,[1]

'What grace, what facile turns, what fluent sweeps,
'What delicate discernment . . . almost thought!
'The book does honour to the sex, we hold.
'Among our female authors we make room   240
'For this fair writer, and congratulate
'The country that produces in these times
'Such women, competent to . . . spell'."
                              "Stop there,"
I answered, burning through his thread of talk
With a quick flame of emotion, – "You have read
My soul, if not my book, and argue well
I would not condescend . . . we will not say
To such a kind of praise (a worthless end
Is praise of all kinds), but to such a use
Of holy art and golden life. I am young,   250
And peradventure weak – you tell me so –
Through being a woman. And, for all the rest,
Take thanks for justice. I would rather dance
At fairs on tight-rope, till the babies dropped
Their gingerbread for joy, – than shift the types
For tolerable verse, intolerable
To men who act and suffer. Better far
Pursue a frivolous trade by serious means,
Than a sublime art frivolously."

(II) FROM BOOK V

The critics say that epics have died out
With Agamemnon[2] and the goat-nursed gods; 140
I'll not believe it. I could never deem,
As Payne Knights[3] did (the mythic mountaineer
Who travelled higher than he was born to live,
And showed sometimes the goitre in his throat
Discoursing of an image seen through fog),
That Homer's heroes measured twelve feet high.
They were but men: – his Helen's hair turned grey
Like any plain Miss Smith's who wears a front;
And Hector's infant whimpered at a plume[4]
As yours last Friday at a turkey-cock. 150
All actual heroes are essential men,
And all men possible heroes; every age,
Heroic in proportions, double-faced,
Looks backward and before, expects a morn
And claims an epos.
     Ay, but every age
Appears to souls who live in't (ask Carlyle)[5]
Most unheroic. Ours, for instance, ours:
The thinkers scout it, and the poets abound
Who scorn to touch it with a finger-tip:
A pewter age, – mixed metal, silver washed; 160
An age of scum, spooned off the richer past,
An age of patches for old gaberdines,
An age of mere transitions, meaning nought
Except that what succeeds must shame it quite
If God please. That's wrong thinking, to my mind,
And wrong thoughts make poor poems.
       Every age,
Through being beheld too close, is ill-discerned
By those who have not lived past it. We'll suppose
Mount Athos carved, as Alexander schemed,[6]
To some colossal statue of a man. 170
The peasants, gathering brushwood in his ear,
Had guessed as little as the browsing goats
Of form or feature of humanity
Up there, – in fact, had travelled five miles off
Or ere the giant image broke on them,
Full human profile, nose and chin distinct,

Mouth, muttering rhythms of silence up the sky
And fed at evening with the blood of suns;
Grand torso, – hand, that flung perpetually
The largesse of a silver river down　　　　　　　180
To all the country pastures. 'Tis even thus
With times we live in, – evermore too great
To be apprehended near.
　　　　　　　　　　　But poets should
Exert a double vision; should have eyes
To see near things as comprehensively
As if afar they took their point of sight,
And distant things as intimately deep
As if they touched them. Let us strive for this.
I do distrust the poet who discerns
No character or glory in his times,　　　　　　190
And trundles back his soul five hundred years,
Past moat and drawbridge, into a castle-court,
To sing – oh, not of lizard or of toad
Alive i' the ditch there, – 'twere excusable,
But of some black chief, half knight, half sheep-lifter,
Some beauteous dame, half chattel and half queen,
As dead as must be, for the greater part,
The poems made on their chivalric bones;
And that's no wonder: death inherits death.

Nay, if there's room for poets in this world　　　200
A little overgrown (I think there is),
Their sole work is to represent the age,
Their age, not Charlemagne's[7] – this live, throbbing age,
That brawls, cheats, maddens, calculates, aspires,
And spends more passion, more heroic heat,
Betwixt the mirrors of its drawing-rooms,
Than Roland with his knights at Roncesvalles.[8]
To flinch from modern varnish, coat or flounce,
Cry out for togas and the picturesque,
Is fatal, – foolish too. King Arthur's self　　　　210
Was commonplace to Lady Guenever;
And Camelot to minstrels seemed as flat
As Fleet Street to our poets.
　　　　　　　　　　　Never flinch,
But still unscrupulously epic, catch

Upon the burning lava of a song
The full-veined, heaving, double-breasted Age:
That, when the next shall come, the men of that
May touch the impress with reverent hand, and say
"Behold, – behold the paps we all have sucked!
This bosom seems to beat still, or at least   220
It sets ours beating: this is living art,
Which thus presents and thus records true life."

What form is best for poems? Let me think
Of forms less, and the external. Trust the spirit,
As sovran nature does, to make the form;
For otherwise we only imprison spirit
And not embody. Inward evermore
To outward, – so in life, and so in art
Which still is life.
                    Five acts to make a play.
And why not fifteen? why not ten? or seven?   230
What matter for the number of the leaves,
Supposing the tree lives and grows? exact
The literal unities of time and place,
When 'tis the essence of passion to ignore
Both time and place? Absurd. Keep up the fire,
And leave the generous flames to shape themselves.

'Tis true the stage requires obsequiousness
To this or that convention; "exit" here
And "enter" there; the points for clapping, fixed,
Like Jacob's white-peeled rods before the rams,[9]   240
And all the close-curled imagery clipped
In manner of their fleece at sheering time.
Forget to prick the galleries to the heart
Precisely at the fourth act, – culminate
Our five pyramidal acts with one act more,
We're lost so: Shakespeare's ghost could scarcely plead
Against our just damnation. Stand aside;
We'll muse for comfort that, last century,
On this same tragic stage on which we have failed,
A wigless Hamlet would have failed the same.   250

And whosoever writes good poetry,
Looks just to art. He does not write for you
Or me, – for London or for Edinburgh;
He will not suffer the best critic known
To step into his sunshine of free thought
And self-absorbed conception and exact
An inch-long swerving of the holy lines.
If virtue done for popularity
Defiles like vice, can art, for praise or hire,
Still keep its splendour and remain pure art?   260
Eschew such serfdom. What the poet writes,
He writes: mankind accepts it if it suits,
And that's success: if not, the poem's passed
From hand to hand, and yet from hand to hand
Until the unborn snatch it, crying out
In pity on their fathers' being so dull,
And that's success too.

               I will write no plays;
Because the drama, less sublime in this,
Makes lower appeals, submits more menially,
Adopts the standard of the public taste   270
To chalk its height on, wears a dog-chain round
Its regal neck, and learns to carry and fetch
The fashions of the day to please the day,
Fawns close on pit and boxes, who clap hands
Commending chiefly its docility
And humour in stage-tricks, – or else indeed
Gets hissed at, howled at, stamped at like a dog,
Or worse, we'll say. For dogs, unjustly kicked,
Yell, bite at need, but if your dramatist
(Being wronged by some five hundred nobodies   280
Because their grosser brains most naturally
Misjudge the fineness of his subtle wit)
Shows teeth an almond's breadth, protests the length
Of a modest phrase, – "My gentle countrymen,
"There's something in it haply of your fault," –
Why then, besides five hundred nobodies,
He'll have five thousand and five thousand more
Against him, – the whole public, – all the hoofs
Of King Saul's father's asses, in full drove,
And obviously deserve it. He appealed   290

To these, – and why say more if they condemn,
Than if they praise him? – Weep, my Æschylus,
But low and far, upon Sicilian shores!
For since 'twas Athens (so I read the myth)
Who gave commission to that fatal weight
The tortoise, cold and hard, to drop on thee
And crush thee, – better cover thy bald head;[10]
She'll hear the softest hum of Hyblan bee[11]
Before thy loudest protestation!
                                        Then
The risk's still worse upon the modern stage.   300
I could not, for so little, accept success,
Nor would I risk so much, in ease and calm,
For manifester gains: let those who prize,
Pursue them: I stand off. And yet, forbid
That any irreverent fancy or conceit
Should litter in the Drama's throne-room where
The rulers of our art, in whose full veins
Dynastic glories mingle, sit in strength
And do their kingly work, – conceive, command,
And, from the imagination's crucial heat,   310
Catch up their men and women all a-flame
For action, all alive and forced to prove
Their life by living out heart, brain, and nerve,
Until mankind makes witness, "These be men
As we are," and vouchsafes the greeting due
To Imogen and Juliet – sweetest kin
On art's side.
                    'Tis that, honouring to its worth
The drama, I would fear to keep it down
To the level of the footlights. Dies no more
The sacrificial goat, for Bacchus slain,[12]   320
His filmed eyes fluttered by the whirling white
Of choral vestures, – troubled in his blood,
While tragic voices that clanged keen as swords,
Leapt high together with the altar-flame
And made the blue air wink. The waxen mask,
Which set the grand still front of Themis' son[13]
Upon the puckered visage of a player, –
The buskin,[14] which he rose upon and moved,
As some tall ship first conscious of the wind   329

Sweeps slowly past the piers, – the mouthpiece, where
The mere man's voice with all its breaths and breaks
Went sheathed in brass, and clashed on even heights
Its phrasèd thunders, – these things are no more,
Which once were. And concluding, which is clear,
The growing drama has outgrown such toys
Of simulated stature, face, and speech,
It also peradventure may outgrow
The simulation of the painted scene,
Boards, actors, prompters, gaslight, and costume,
And take for a worthier stage the soul itself,   340
Its shifting fancies and celestial lights,
With all its grand orchestral silences
To keep the pauses of its rhythmic sounds.

Alas, I still see something to be done,
And what I do falls short of what I see,
Though I waste myself on doing. Long green days,
Worn bare of grass and sunshine, – long calm nights
From which the silken sleeps were fretted out,
Be witness for me, with no amateur's
Irreverent haste and busy idleness   350
I set myself to art! What then? what's done?
What's done, at last?
               Behold, at last, a book.
If life-blood's necessary, which it is, –
(By that blue vein athrob on Mahomet's brow,
Each prophet-poet's book must show man's blood!)
If life-blood's fertilising, I wrung mine
On every leaf of this, – unless the drops
Slid heavily on one side and left it dry.
That chances often: many a fervid man
Writes books as cold and flat as gravyard stones   360
From which the lichen's scraped; and if Saint Preux[15]
Had written his own letters, as he might,
We had never wept to think of the little mole
'Neath Julie's drooping eyelid. Passion is
But something suffered, after all.
                    While Art
Sets action on the top of suffering:
The artist's part is both to be and do,

Transfixing with a special, central power
The flat experience of the common man,
And turning outward, with a sudden wrench,   370
Half agony, half ecstasy, the thing
He feels the inmost, – never felt the less
Because he sings it. Does a torch less burn
For burning next reflectors of blue steel,
That *he* should be the colder for his place
'Twixt two incessant fires, – his personal life's
And that intense refraction which burns back
Perpetually against him from the round
Of crystal conscience he was born into
If artist-born? O sorrowful great gift   380
Conferred on poets, of a twofold life,
When one life has been fond enough for pain!
We, staggering 'neath our burden as mere men,
Being called to stand up straight as demigods,
Support the intolerable strain and stress
Of the universal, and send clearly up,
With voices broken by the human sob,
Our poems to find rhymes among the stars!

1   The words reported here (lines 236–43) are Romney's summary of
    the kinds of condescending judgments given by male reviewers to
    women's writing.
2   The commander of the Greek expedition to Troy, as recounted by
    Homer in *The Iliad*.
3   Richard Payne Knight (1750–1824), classical scholar.
4   *Iliad*, VI, 595–601.
5   See No. 6; Elizabeth Barrett Browning was an admirer of Carlyle.
6   Alexander the Great (356–323 BC), who was said to have planned to
    have Mount Athos in Greece carved into a statue to his greatness.
7   (742–814), King of the Franks and creator of the great medieval
    empire.
8   As celebrated in the medieval 'Chanson de Roland', in which Roland
    is killed heroically resisting a Saracen attack.
9   Genesis XXX. 37–43: the rods here represent the restrictions im-
    posed in writing for the stage.
10 According to the legend, the great Greek dramatist was killed in
    456 BC by the fall of a tortoise which an eagle let drop, mistaking his
    bald head for a rock.
11 Hybla in Sicily, famous for its honey.

12 Tragedy is believed to have developed from the religious sacrifices made to the gods.
13 Prometheus.
14 The high thick-soled boots worn by actors in Greek tragedy.
15 A character in love with Julie in Rousseau's *La Nouvelle Héloise* (1761).

GEORGE HENRY LEWES

Lewes (1817–78) wrote on numerous subjects: his books include *The Life and Works of Goethe* (1855), *Principles of Success in Literature* (1865) and *Problems of Life and Mind* (1874–9). He became the partner of Mary Ann Evans in 1854, and encouraged her to write fiction. His own principles, as expressed here in a contribution to the *Westminster Review* LXX, 1858, 493–496, on recent German fiction, are close to those of George Eliot.

28 From 'Realism in Art', 1858

... A distinction is drawn between Art and Reality, and an antithesis established between Realism and Idealism which would never have gained acceptance had not men in general lost sight of the fact that Art is a Representation of Reality – a Representation which, inasmuch as it is not the thing itself, but only represents it, must necessarily be limited by the nature of its medium; the canvas of the painter, the marble of the sculptor, the chords of the musician, and the language of the writer, each bring with them peculiar laws; but while thus limited, while thus regulated by the necessities imposed on it by each medium of expression, Art always aims at the representation of Reality, *i.e.* of Truth; and no departure from truth is permissible, except such as inevitably lies in the nature of the medium itself. Realism is thus the basis of all Art, and its antithesis is not Idealism, but *Falsism*. When our painters represent peasants with regular features and irreproachable linen; when their milkmaids have the air of Keepsake beauties, whose costume is picturesque, and never old or dirty; when Hodge[1] is made to speak refined sentiments in unexceptionable English, and children utter long speeches of religious and poetic enthusiasm; when the conversation of the parlour and drawing-room is a succession of philosophical remarks, expressed with great clearness and logic, an attempt is made to idealize, but the result is simple falsification and bad art. To misrepresent the forms of ordinary life is no less an offence than to misrepresent the forms of ideal life: a pug-nosed Apollo, or Jupiter in a greatcoat, would not be more truly shocking to an artistic mind than are those senseless falsifications of nature into which incompetence is led under the pretence of idealizing, of 'beautifying' nature. Either give us true peasants, or leave them untouched; either paint no drapery at all, or paint it with the utmost fidelity; either keep your people silent, or make them speak the idiom of their class.

Raphael's[2] marvellous picture, the 'Madonna di San Sisto', presents us with a perfect epitome of illustration. In the figures of the Pope and St. Barbara we have a real man and woman, one of them a portrait, and the other not elevated above sweet womanhood. Below, we have the two exquisite angel children, intensely childlike, yet something *more*, something which renders their wings congruous with our conception of them. In the never-to-be-forgotten divine babe, we have at once the intensest realism of presentation, with the highest idealism of conception: the attitude is at once grand, easy, and natural; the face is that of a child, but the child is divine: in those eyes, and on that brow, there is an indefinable something which, greater than the expression of the angels', grander than that of pope or saint, is, to all who see it, a perfect *truth*; we feel that humanity in its highest conceivable form is before us, and that to transcend such a form would be to lose sight of the *human* nature there represented. In the virgin mother, again, we have a real woman, such as the *campagna*[3] of Rome will furnish every day, yet with eyes subdued to a consciousness of her divine mission. Here is a picture which from the first has enchained the hearts of men, which is assuredly in the highest sense ideal, and which is so because it is also in the highest sense real – a real man, a real woman, real angel-children, and a real Divine Child; the last a striking contrast to the ineffectual attempts of other painters to spiritualize and idealize the babe – attempts which represent no babe at all. Titian's[4] unsurpassable head of Christ, in the famous 'Christo del Moneta', if compared with all other heads by other painters, will likewise be found to have its profound significance and idealism in the wonderful reality of the presentation: the head is more intensely human than that of any other representation of Christ, but the humanity is such as accords with our highest conceptions.

We may now come to an understanding on the significance of the phrase Idealism in Art. Suppose two men equally gifted with the perceptive powers and technical skill necessary to the accurate representation of a village group, but the one to be gifted, over and above these qualities, with an emotional sensibility which leads him to sympathize intensely with the emotions playing amid that village group. Both will delight in the forms of external nature, both will lovingly depict the scene and scenery; but the second will not be satisfied therewith: his sympathy will lead him to express something of the emotional life of the group; the mother in his picture will not only hold her child in a graceful attitude, she will look at it with a mother's tenderness; the lovers will be tender; the old people venerable. Without once departing from strict reality, he will have thrown a sentiment into his group which every spectator will recognize as poetry. Is he not more *real* than a Teniers, who, admirable in externals, had little or no sympathy with the internal life, which, however, is as real as the other? But observe, the sentiment must be real, truly expressed as a sentiment, and as the sentiment of the very people represented; the tenderness of *Hodge* must not be that of *Romeo*, otherwise we shall have such maudlin as the 'Last Appeal' ...[5]

The novelist ... expresses his mind in his novels, and

according as his emotional sympathy is keen and active, according to his poetic disposition, will the choice and treatment of his subject be poetical: but it must always be real – true. If he select the incidents and characters of ordinary life, he must be rigidly bound down to accuracy in the presentation. He is at liberty to avoid such subjects, if he thinks them prosaic and uninteresting (which will mean that he does not feel their poetry and interest), but having chosen, he is not at liberty to falsify, under pretense of beautifying them; every departure from truth in motive, idiom, or probability, is, to that extent, a defect. His dressmaker must be a young woman who makes dresses, and not a sentimental 'heroine', evangelical and consumptive; she may be consumptive, she may also be evangelical, for dressmakers are so sometimes, but she must be individually a dressmaker. So also the merchant must have an air of the counting-house, an ostler must smell of the stables. To *call* a man a merchant, and tell us of his counting-house, while for anything else we might suppose him to be a nobleman, or an uncle from India, is not Art, because it is not representation of reality. If the writer's knowledge or sympathies do not lead him in the direction of ordinary life, if he can neither paint town nor country, let him take to the wide fields of History or Fancy. Even there the demands of truth will pursue him; he must paint what he distinctly *sees* with his imagination; if he succeed, he will create characters which are true although ideal; and in this sense Puck, Ariel, Brutus, and Falstaff are as real as Dick Swiveller[6] or Tom Jones. . . .

1 Name for a country labourer.
2 Raphael (1483–1520), the great painter of the High Renaissance; he painted the 'Sistine Madonna', now at Dresden, in about 1514.
3 Countryside.
4 Titian (c.1487–1576), the great Venetian painter; his 'The Tribute Money', painted around 1518, is now at Dresden.
5 A sentimental painting of 1843 by Frank Stone (1800–59).
6 In Dickens's *The Old Curiosity Shop* (1841).

WILLIAM WILKIE COLLINS

Collins (1824–1889) was a popular novelist and friend of Dickens, whose novels – which often have a large element of sensationalism and intrigue – include *The Woman in White* (1860), *No Name* (1862) and *The Moonstone* (1868). In the Preface printed here he makes his contribution to the debate about the respective importance of plot and character, which he asserts to be complementary, as well as indicating his concern for accuracy of social detail.

29 Preface to the 1861 edition of *The Woman in White*

'The Woman in White' has been received with such marked favour by a very large circle of readers, that this volume scarcely stands in need of any prefatory introduction on my part. All that it is necessary for me to say on the subject of the present edition – the first issued in a portable and popular form – may be summed up in few words.

I have endeavoured, by careful correction and revision, to make my story as worthy as I could of a continuance of the public approval. Certain technical errors which had escaped me while I was writing the book are here rectified. None of these little blemishes in the slightest degree interfered with the interest of the narrative, but it was as well to remove them at the first opportunity, out of respect to my readers, and in this edition, accordingly, they exist no more.

Some doubts having been expressed, in certain captious quarters, about the correct presentation of the legal 'points' incidental to the story, I may be permitted to mention that I spared no pains, in this instance, as in all others, to preserve myself from unintentionally misleading my readers. A solicitor of great experience in his profession most kindly and carefully guided my steps, whenever the course of the narrative led me into the labyrinth of the Law. Every doubful question was submitted to this gentleman, before I ventured on putting pen to paper, and all the proof-sheets which referred to legal matters were corrected by his hand before the story was published. I can add, on high judicial authority, that these precautions were not taken in vain. The 'law' in this book has been discussed, since its publication, by more than one competent tribunal, and has been decided to be sound.

One word more, before I conclude, in acknowledgment of the heavy debt of gratitude which I owe to the reading public.

It is no affectation on my part to say that the success of this book has been especially welcome to me, because it implied the recognition of a literary principle which has guided me since I first addressed my readers in the character of a novelist.

I have always held the old-fashioned opinion that the primary object of a work of fiction should be to tell a story; and I have never believed that the novelist who properly performed this first condition of his art, was in danger, on that account, of neglecting the delineation of character – for this plain reason, that the effect produced by any narrative of events is essentially dependent, not on the events themselves, but on the human interest which is directly connected with them. It may be possible, in novel-writing, to present characters successfully without telling a story; but it is not possible to tell a story successfully without presenting characters: their existence, as recognisable realities, being the sole condition on which the story can be effectively told. The only narrative which can hope to lay a strong hold on the attention of readers is a narrative which interests them about men and women – for the perfectly-obvious reason that they are men and women themselves.

The reception accorded to 'The Woman in White' has practically confirmed these opinions, and has satisfied me that I may trust to them in the future. Here is a novel which has met with a very kind reception, because it is a Story; and here is a story, the interest of which – as I know by the testimony, voluntarily addressed to me, of the readers themselves – is never disconnected from the interest of character. 'Laura', 'Miss Halcombe', and 'Anne Catherick'; 'Count Fosco', 'Mr. Fairlie', and 'Walter Hartright'; have made friends for me wherever they have made themselves known. I hope the time is not far distant when I may meet those friends again, and when I may try, through the medium of new characters, to awaken their interest in another story.

WALTER BAGEHOT

Bagehot (1826–77) was a banker and writer on political and economic matters as well as on literature. The two articles here, both published in 1864, express central Victorian beliefs about fiction and poetry (see Introduction, page 16).

There is a recent edition of Bagehot's works by Norman St. John Stevas.

30 From 'Sterne and Thackeray', 1862

[In the *National Review* XVIII, April 1864, 523–53, Bagehot reviewed recent biographies of the two writers; the discussion of Sterne's fiction is reprinted here.]

One part of Crazy Castle[1] has had effects which will last as long as English literature. It had a library richly stored in old folio learning, and also in the amatory reading of other days. Every page of *Tristram Shandy* bears traces of both elements. Sterne, when he wrote it, had filled his head and his mind, not with the literature of his own age, but with the literature of past ages. He was thinking of Rabelais[2] rather than of Fielding; of forgotten romances rather than of Richardson. He wrote, indeed, of his own times and of men he had seen, because his sensitive vivid nature would only endure to write of present things. But the *mode* in which he wrote was largely coloured by literary habits and literary fashions that had long passed away. The oddity of the book was a kind of advertisement to its genius, and that oddity consisted in the use of old manners upon new things. No analysis or account

of *Tristram Shandy* could be given which would suit the
present generation; being, indeed, a book without plan or
order, it is in every generation unfit for analysis. This age
would not endure a statement of the most telling points, as
the writer thought them, and no age would like an elaborate
plan of a book in which there is no plan, in which the
detached remarks and separate scenes were really meant to
be the whole. The notion that 'a plot was to hang plums
upon' was Sterne's notion exactly.

The real excellence of Sterne is single and simple; the
defects are numberless and complicated. He excels, perhaps, all other writers in mere simple description of common
sensitive human action. He places before you in their
simplest form the elemental facts of human life; he does not
view them through the intellect, he scarcely views them
through the imagination; he does but reflect the unimpaired
impression which the facts of life, which does not change
from age to age, make on the deep basis of human feeling,
which changes as little though years go on. The example we
quoted just now[3] is as good as any other, though not better
than any other. Our readers should go back to it again, or
our praise may seem overcharged. It is the portrait-painting
of the heart. It is as pure a reflection of mere natural feeling
as literature has ever given, or will ever give. The delineation is nearly perfect. Sterne's feeling in his higher moments
so much overpowered his intellect, and so directed his
imagination, that no intrusive thought blemishes, no distort-
ing fancy mars, the perfection of the representation. The
disenchanting facts which deface, the low circumstances
which debase, the simpler feelings oftener than any other
feelings, his art excludes. The feeling which would probably
be coarse in the reality is refined in the picture. The
unconscious tact of the nice artist heightens and chastens
reality, but yet it is reality still. His mind was like a pure lake
of delicate water: it reflects the ordinary landscape, the
rugged hills, the loose pebbles, the knotted and the distorted
firs perfectly and as they are, yet with a charm and fascination that they have not in themselves. This is the highest

attainment of art: to be at the same time nature and something more than nature.

But here the great excellence of Sterne ends as well as begins. In *Tristram Shandy* especially there are several defects which, while we are reading it, tease and disgust so much that we are scarcely willing even to admire as we ought to admire the nice pictures of human emotion. The first of these, and perhaps the worst, is the fantastic disorder of the form. It is an imperative law of the writing art that a book should go straight on. A great writer should be able to tell a great meaning as coherently as a small writer tells a small meaning. The magnitude of the thought to be conveyed, the delicacy of the emotion to be painted, render the introductory touches of consummate art not of less importance, but of more importance. A great writer should train the mind of the reader for his greatest things; that is, by first strokes and fitting preliminaries he should form and prepare his mind for the due appreciation and the perfect enjoyment of high creations. He should not blunder upon a beauty, nor, after a great imaginative creation, should he at once fall back to bare prose. The high-wrought feeling which a poet excites should not be turned out at once and without warning into the discomposing world. It is one of the greatest merits of the greatest living writer of fiction – of the authoress of *Adam Bede* – that she never brings you to anything without preparing you for it; she has no loose lumps of beauty; she puts in nothing at random; after her greatest scenes, too, a natural sequence of subordinate realities again tones down the mind to this sublunary world. Her logical style – the most logical, probably, which a woman ever wrote – aids in this matter her natural sense of due proportion. There is not a space of incoherency – not a gap. It is not natural to begin with the point of a story, and she does not begin with it. When some great marvel has been told, we all wish to know what came of it, and she tells us. Her natural way, as it seems to those who do not know its rarity, of telling what happened produces the consummate effect of gradual enchantment and as gradual disenchantment.

But Sterne's style is *un*natural. He never begins at the beginning and goes straight through to the end. He shies in a beauty suddenly; and just when you are affected he turns round and grins at it. 'Ah', he says, 'is it not fine?' And then he makes jokes which at that place and that time are out of place, or passes away in scholastic or other irrelevant matter, which simply disgusts and disheartens those whom he has just delighted. People excuse all this irregularity of form by saying that it was imitated from Rabelais. But this is nonsense. Rabelais, perhaps, could not in his day venture to tell his meaning straight out; at any rate, he did not tell it. Sterne should not have chosen a model so monstrous. Incoherency is not less a defect because an imperfect foreign writer once made use of it. 'You may have, sir, a reason', said Dr. Johnson, 'for saying that two and two make five, but they will still make four.' Just so, a writer may have a reason for selecting the defect of incoherency, but it is a defect still. Sterne's best things read best out of his books – in Enfield's *Speaker*[4] and other places – and you can say no worse of any one as a continuous artist.

Another most palpable defect – especially palpable nowadays – in *Tristram Shandy* is its indecency. It is quite true that the customary conventions of writing are much altered during the last century, and much which would formerly have been deemed blameless would now be censured and disliked. The audience has changed; and decency is of course in part dependent on who is within hearing. A divorce case may be talked over across a club-table with a plainness of speech and development of expression which would be indecent in a mixed party, and scandalous before young ladies. Now, a large part of old novels may very fairly be called club-books; they speak out plainly and simply the notorious facts of the world, as men speak of them to men. Much excellent and proper masculine conversation is wholly unfit for repetition to young girls; and just in the same way books written – as was almost all old literature, – for men only, or nearly only, seem coarse enough when contrasted with novels written by young ladies upon the subjects and in the tone of the drawing-room. The change is inevitable; as soon as works of fiction are addressed to boys and girls, they must be fit for boys and girls; they must deal with a life which is real so far as it goes, but which is yet most limited; which deals with the most passionate part of life, and yet omits the errors of the passions; which aims at describing men in their relations to women, and yet omits an all but universal influence which more or less distorts and modifies all these relations.

As we have said, the change cannot be helped. A young ladies' literature must be a limited and truncated literature. The indiscriminate study of human life is not desirable for them, either in fiction or in reality. But the habitual formation of a scheme of thought and a code of morality upon incomplete materials is a very serious evil. The readers for whose sake the omissions are made cannot fancy what is left out. Many a girl of the present day reads novels, and nothing but novels; she forms her mind by them, as far as she forms it by reading at all; even if she reads a few dull books, she soon forgets all about them, and remembers the novels only; she is more influenced by them than by sermons. They form her idea of the world, they define her taste, and modify her morality; not so much in explicit thought and direct act as unconsciously and in her floating fancy. How is it possible to convince such a girl, especially if she is clever, that on most points she is all wrong? She has been reading most excellent descriptions of mere society; she comprehends those descriptions perfectly, for her own experience elucidates and confirms them. She has a vivid picture of a *patch* of life. Even if she admits in words that there is something beyond, something of which she has no idea, she will not admit it really and in practice. What she has mastered and realised will incurably and inevitably overpower the unknown something of which she knows nothing, can imagine nothing, and can make nothing. 'I am not sure,' said an old lady, 'but I think it's the novels that make my girls so *heady*.' It is the novels. A very intelligent acquaintance with limited life makes them think that the world is far simpler than it is, that men are easy to understand, 'that mamma is *so* foolish'.

The novels of the last age have certainly not this fault. They do not err on the side of reticence. A girl may learn from them more than it is desirable for her to know. But, as we have explained, they were meant for men and not for girls; and if *Tristram Shandy* had simply given a plain exposition of necessary facts – necessary, that is, to the development of the writer's view of the world, and to the telling of the story in hand – we should not have complained; we should have regarded it as the natural product of a now extinct society. But there are most unmistakable traces of 'Crazy Castle' in *Tristram Shandy*. There is indecency for indecency's sake. It is made a sort of recurring and even permeating joke to mention things which are not generally mentioned. Sterne himself made a sort of defence, or rather denial, of this. He once asked a lady if she had read *Tristram*. 'I have not, Mr. Sterne,' was the answer; 'and, to be plain with you, I am informed it is not proper for female perusal.' 'My dear good lady,' said Sterne, 'do not be gulled by such stories; the book is like your young heir there' (pointing to a child of three years old who was rolling on the carpet in white tunics): 'he shows at times a good deal that is usually concealed, but it is all in perfect innocence.' But a perusal of *Tristram* would not make good the plea. The unusual publicity of what is ordinarily imperceptible is not the thoughtless accident of amusing play; it is deliberately sought after as a nice joke; it is treated as a good in itself.

The indecency of *Tristram Shandy* – at least of the early part, which was written before Sterne had been to France – is especially an offence against taste, because of its ugliness. *Moral* indecency is always disgusting. There certainly is a sort of writing which cannot be called decent, and which describes a society to the core immoral, which nevertheless is no offence against art; it violates a higher code than that of taste, but it does not violate the code of taste. The *Mémoires de Grammont*[5] – hundreds of French memoirs about France – are of this kind, more or less. They describe the refined,

witty, elegant immorality of an idle aristocracy. They describe a life 'unsuitable to such a being as man in such a world
as the present one', in which there are no high aims, no
severe duties, where some precepts of morals seem not so
much to be sometimes broken as to be generally suspended
and forgotten; such a life, in short, as God had never
suffered men to lead on this earth long, which He has always
crushed out by calamity and revolution. This life, though an
offence in morals, was not an offence in taste. It was an
elegant, a *pretty* thing while it lasted. Especially in en-
hancing description, where the alloy of life may be omitted,
where nothing vulgar need be noticed, where everything
elegant may be neatly painted, – such a world is elegant
enough. Morals and policy must decide how far such deli-
neations are permissible or expedient; but the art of beauty –
art criticism, – has no objection to them. They are pretty
paintings of pretty objects, and that is all it has to say. They
may very easily do harm; if generally read among the young
of the middle class, they would be sure to do harm: they
would teach not a few to aim at a sort of refinement denied
them by circumstances, and to neglect the duties allotted
them; it would make shopmen 'bad imitations of polished
ungodliness', and also bad shopmen. But still, though it
would in such places be noxious literature, in itself it would
be pretty literature. The critic must praise it, though the
moralist must condemn it, and perhaps the politician forbid
it.

But *Tristram*'s indecency is the very opposite to this
refined sort. It consists in allusions to certain inseparable
accompaniments of actual life which are not beautiful, which
can never be made interesting, which would, *if* they were
decent, be dull and uninteresting. There is, it appears, a
certain excitement in putting such matters into a book: there
is a minor exhilaration even in petty crime. At first such
things look so odd in print that you go on reading them to
see what they look like; but you soon give up. What is
disenchanting or even disgusting in reality does not become
enchanting or endurable in delineation. You are more angry

at it in literature than in life; there is much which is barbarous and animal in reality that we could wish away; we endure it because we cannot help it, because we did not make it and cannot alter it, because it is an inseparable part of this inexplicable world. But why we should put this coarse alloy, this dross of life, into the *optional* world of literature, which we can make as we please, it is impossible to say. The needless introduction of accessory ugliness is always a sin in art, and is not at all less so when such ugliness is disgusting and improper. *Tristram Shandy* is incurably tainted with a pervading vice; it dwells at length on, it seeks after, it returns to, it gloats over, the most unattractive part of the world.

There is another defect in *Tristram Shandy* which would of itself remove it from the list of first-rate books, even if those which we have mentioned did not do so. It contains eccentric characters only. Some part of this defect may be perhaps explained by one peculiarity of its origin. Sterne was so sensitive to the picturesque parts of life, that he wished to paint the picturesque parts of the people he hated. Country-towns in those days abounded in odd character. They were out of the way of the great opinion of the world, and shaped themselves to little opinions of their own. They regarded the customs which the place had inherited as the customs which were proper for it, and which it would be foolish, if not wicked, to try to change. This gave English country-life a motley picturesqueness then, which it wants now, when London ideas shoot out every morning, and carry on the wings of the railway a uniform creed to each cranny of the kingdom, north and south, east and west. These little public opinions of little places wanted, too, the crushing power of the great public opinion of our own day; at the worst, a man could escape from them into some different place which had customs and doctrines that suited him better. We now may fly into another 'city', but it is all the same Roman empire; the same uniform justice, the one code of heavy laws, press us down and make us – the sensible part of us at least – as like other people as we can make ourselves. The public

opinion of country-towns yielded soon to individual exceptions; it had not the confidence in itself which the opinion of
each place now receives from the accordant and simul-
taneous echo of a hundred places. If a man chose to be
queer, he was bullied for a year or two, then it was settled
that he was 'queer'; that was the fact about him, and must be
accepted. In a year or so he became an 'institution' of the
place, and the local pride would have been grieved if he had
amended the oddity which suggested their legends and
added a flavour to their life. Of course, if a man was rich and
influential, he might soon disregard the mere opinion of the
petty locality. Every place has wonderful traditions of old
rich men who did exactly as they pleased, because they could
set at naught the opinions of the neighbours, by whom they
were feared; and who did not, as now, dread the unanimous
conscience which does not fear even a squire of £2000 a year,
or a banker of £800, because it is backed by the wealth of
London and the magnitude of all the country. There is little
oddity in country-towns now; they are detached scraps of
great places; but in Sterne's time there was much, and he
used it unsparingly.

Much of the delineation is of the highest merit. Sterne
knew how to describe eccentricity, for he showed its relation
to our common human nature: he showed how we were
related to it, how in some sort and in some circumstances we
might ourselves become it. He reduced the abnormal forma-
tion to the normal rules. Except upon this condition, eccentricity is no fit subject for literary art. Every one must have
known characters which, if they were put down in books,
barely and as he sees them, would seem monstrous and
disproportioned, which would disgust all readers, which
every critic would term unnatural. While characters are
monstrous, they should be kept out of books; they are ugly
unintelligibilities, foreign to the realm of true art. But as
soon as they can be explained to us, as soon as they are
shown in their union with, in their outgrowth from, common
human nature, they are the best subjects for great art – for
they are new subjects. They teach us, not the old lesson

which our fathers knew, but a new lesson which will please us and make us better than them. Hamlet is an eccentric character, one of the most eccentric in literature; but because, by the art of the poet, we are made to understand that he is a possible, a *vividly* possible man, he enlarges our conceptions of human nature; he takes us out of the bounds of commonplace. He 'instructs us by means of delight'. Sterne does this too. Mr. Shandy, Uncle Toby, Corporal Trim, Mrs. Shandy, – for in strictness she too is eccentric from her abnormal commonplaceness, – are beings of which the possibility is brought home to us, which we feel we could under circumstances and by influences become, which, though contorted and twisted, are yet spun out of the same elementary nature, the same thread, as we are. Considering how odd these characters are, the success of Sterne is marvellous, and his art in this respect consummate. But yet on a point most nearly allied it is very faulty. Though each individual character is shaded off into human nature, the whole is not shaded off into the world. This society of originals and oddities is left to stand by itself, as if it were a natural and ordinary society, – a society easily conceivable and needing no explanation. Such is not the manner of the great masters; in their best works a constant atmosphere of half commonplace personages surrounds and shades off, illustrates and explains, every central group of singular persons.

On the whole, therefore, the judgment of criticism on *Tristram Shandy* is concise and easy. It is immortal because of certain scenes suggested by Sterne's curious experience, detected by his singular sensibility, and heightened by his delineative and discriminative imagination. It is defective because its style is fantastic, its method illogical and provoking; because its indecency is of the worst sort, as far as in such matters an artistic judgment can speak of worst and best; because its world of characters forms an incongruous group of singular persons utterly dissimilar to, and irreconcilable with, the world in which we live. It is a great work of art, but of barbarous art. Its mirth is boisterous. It is *provincial*. It is redolent of an inferior society; for those who think crude animal spirits in themselves delightful, who do not know that, without wit to point them or humour to convey them, they are disagreeable to others; who like disturbing transitions, blank pages, and tricks of style; who do not know that a simple and logical form of expression is the most effective, if not the easiest, – the least laborious to readers, if not always the most easily attained by writers.

1   The nick-name given to Skelton Castle, the home of Sterne's friend John Hill-Stevenson.
2   François Rabelais (1494–1553), the author of *Gargantua and Pantagruel* (1552).
3   From *Tristram Shandy*, Vol VI, Chs. 8–10, describing the sickness of Le Fever.
4   The Rev. William Enfield (1741–97) produced a popular book for training in elocution entitled *The Speaker, or Miscellaneous Pieces selected from the best English Writers* in 1774.
5   *Mémoires de la Vie du Comte de Gramont* (1713), an anonymous work written by Anthony Hamilton (1646–1720).

31 From 'Wordsworth, Tennyson, and Browning; or, Pure, Ornate and Grotesque Art in English Poetry', 1864

[This review of Tennyson's *Enoch Arden* and Browning's *Dramatis Personae* appeared in the *National Review*, N.S.I., Nov. 1864, 27–66. Sections reprinted here develop the general argument.]

. . . The word '*literatesque*',[1] would mean, if we possessed it, that perfect combination in the *subject-matter* of literature, which suits the *art* of literature. We often meet people, and say of them, sometimes meaning well and sometimes ill, 'How well so-and-so would do in a book!' Such people are by no means the best people; but they are the most effective people – the most rememberable people. Frequently, when we first know them, we like them because they explain to us so much of our experience; we have known many people 'like that', in one way or another, but we did not seem to understand them; they were nothing to us, for their traits were indistinct; we forgot them, for they *hitched* on to nothing, and we could not classify them; but when we see the *type* of the genus, at once we seem to comprehend its character; the inferior specimens are explained by the perfect embodiment; the approximations are definable when we know the ideal to which they draw near. There are an infinite number of classes of human beings, but in each of these classes there is a distinctive type which, if we could expand it out in words, would define the class. We cannot expand it in formal terms any more than a landscape, or a species of landscapes; but we have an art, an art of words, which can draw it. Travellers and others often bring home, in addition to their long journals – which, though so living to them, are so dead, so inanimate, so undescriptive to all else – a pen-and-ink sketch, rudely done very likely, but which, perhaps, even the more for the blots and strokes, gives a distinct notion, an emphatic image, to all who see it. They say at once, *now* we know the sort of thing. The sketch has *hit* the mind. True literature does the same. It describes sorts, varieties, and permutations, by delineating the type of each sort, the ideal of each variety, the central, the marking trait of each permutation.

On this account, the greatest artists of the world have ever shown an enthusiasm for reality. To care for notions and abstractions; to philosophise; to reason out conclusions; to care for schemes of thought, are signs in the artistic mind of secondary excellence. A Schiller, an Euripides, a Ben Jonson cares for *ideas* – for the parings of the intellect, and the distillation of the mind; a Shakespeare, a Homer, a Goethe finds his mental occupation, the true home of his natural thoughts, in the real world – 'which is the world of all of us' – where the face of nature, the moving masses of men and women, are ever changing, ever multiplying, ever mixing one with the other. The reason is plain – the business of the poet, of the artist, is with *types*; and those types are mirrored in reality. As a painter must not only have a hand to execute, but an eye to distinguish – as he must go here and then there through the real world to catch the picturesque man, the picturesque scene, which are to live on his canvas – so the poet must find in that reality, the *literatesque* man, the *literatesque* scene which nature intends for him, and which will live in his page. Even in reality he will not find this type complete, or the characteristics perfect; but there, he will find at least *something*, some hint, some animation, some suggestion; whereas, in the stagnant home of his own thoughts he will find nothing pure, nothing *as it is*, nothing which does not bear his own mark, which is not somehow altered by a mixture with himself.

. . .

We are disposed to believe that no very sharp definition can be given – at least in the present state of the critical art – of the boundary line between poetry and other sorts of imaginative delineation. Between the undoubted dominions of the two kinds there is a debateable land; everybody is agreed that the *Œdipus at Colonus is* poetry: everyone is agreed that the wonderful appearance of Mrs. Veal[2] is *not* poetry. But the exact line which separates grave novels in verse, like *Aylmer's Field* or *Enoch Arden*,[3] from grave novels not in verse, like *Silas Marner* or *Adam Bede*, we own we cannot draw with any confidence. Nor, perhaps, is it very important; whether a narrative is thrown into verse or not certainly depends in part on the taste of the age, and in part on its mechanical helps. Verse is the only mechanical help to the memory in rude times, and there is little writing till a cheap something is found to write upon, and a cheap something to write with. Poetry – verse, at least – is the literature of *all work* in early ages; it is only later ages which write in what *they* think a natural and simple prose. There are other casual influences in the matter too; but they are not material now. We need only say here that poetry, because it has a more marked rhythm than prose, must be more intense in meaning and more concise in style than prose. People expect a 'marked rhythm' to imply something

Walter Bagehot

worth marking; if it fails to do so they are disappointed. They are displeased at the visible waste of a powerful instrument; they call it 'doggerel', and rightly call it, for the metrical expression of full thought and eager feeling – the burst of metre – incident to high imagination, should not be wasted on petty matters which prose does as well, – which it does better – which it suits by its very limpness and weakness, whose small changes it follows more easily, and to whose lowest details it can fully and without effort degrade itself. Verse, too, should be *more concise*, for long continued rhythm tends to jade the mind, just as brief rhythm tends to attract the attention. Poetry should be memorable and emphatic, intense, and *soon over*.

The great divisions of poetry, and of all other literary art, arise from the different modes in which these *types* – these characteristic men, these characteristic feelings – may be variously described. There are three principal modes which we shall attempt to describe – the *pure*, which is sometimes, but not very wisely, called the classical; the *ornate*, which is also unwisely called romantic; and the *grotesque*, which might be called the mediæval. We will describe the nature of these a little. Criticism, we know, must be brief – not, like poetry, because its charm is too intense to be sustained – but on the contrary, because its interest is too weak to be prolonged; but elementary criticism, if an evil, is a necessary evil; a little while spent among the simple principles of art is the first condition, the absolute pre-requisite, for surely apprehending and wisely judging the complete embodiments and miscellaneous forms of actual literature.

The definition of *pure* literature is that it describes the type in its simplicity; we mean, with the exact amount of accessory circumstance which is necessary to bring it before the mind in finished perfection, and *no more* than that amount. The *type* needs some accessories from its nature – a picturesque landscape does not consist wholly of picturesque features. There is a setting of surroundings – as the Americans would say, of *fixings* – without which the reality is not itself. By a traditional mode of speech, as soon as we see a picture in which a complete effect is produced by detail so rare and so harmonised as to escape us, we say how 'classical'. The whole which is to be seen appears at once and through the detail, but the detail itself is not seen: we do not think of that which gives us the idea; we are absorbed in the idea itself. Just so in literature, the pure art is that which works with the fewest strokes; the fewest, that is, for its purpose, for its aim is to call up and bring home to men an idea, a form, a character; and if that idea be twisted, that form be involved, that character perplexed, many strokes of literary art will be needful. Pure art does not mutilate its object: it represents it as fully as is possible with the slightest effort which is possible: it shrinks from no needful circumstances, as little as it inserts any which are needless. The precise peculiarity is not merely that no incidental circumstance is inserted which does not tell on the main design: – no art is fit to be called *art* which permits a stroke to be put in without an object; – but that only the minimum of such circumstance is inserted at all. The form is sometimes said to be bare, the accessories are sometimes said to be invisible, because the appendages are so choice that the shape only is perceived.

The English literature undoubtedly contains much impure literature; impure in its style, if not in its meaning: but it also contains one great, one nearly perfect, model of the pure style in the literary expression of typical *sentiment*; and one not perfect, but gigantic and close approximation to perfection, in the pure delineation of objective character. Wordsworth, perhaps, comes as near to choice purity of style in sentiment as is possible; Milton, with exceptions and conditions to be explained, approaches perfection by the strenuous purity with which he depicts character.

A wit once said that '*pretty* women had more features than *beautiful* women', and though the expression may be criticised, the meaning is correct. Pretty women seem to have a great number of attractive points, each of which attracts your attention, and each one of which you remember afterwards; yet these points have not *grown together*, their features have not linked themselves into a single inseparable whole. But a beautiful woman is a whole as she is; you no more take her to pieces than a Greek statue; she is not an aggregate of divisible charms, she is a charm in herself. Such ever is the dividing test of pure art; if you catch yourself admiring its details, it is defective; you ought to think of it as a single whole which you must remember, which you must admire, which somehow subdues you while you admire it, which is a 'possession' to you 'for ever'.

Of course, no individual poem embodies this ideal perfectly; of course, every human word and phrase has its imperfections, and if we choose an instance to illustrate that ideal, the instance has scarcely a fair chance. By contrasting it with the ideal we suggest its imperfections; by protruding it as an example, we turn on its defectiveness the microscope of criticism. Yet these two sonnets of Wordsworth[4] may be read in this place, not because they are quite without faults, or because they are the very best examples of their kind of style; but because they are *luminous* examples; the compactness of the sonnet and the gravity of the sentiment, hedging in the thoughts, restraining the fancy, and helping to maintain a singleness of expression.

. . .

It is not unremarkable that we should find in Milton and in *Paradise Lost* the best specimen of pure style. He was a schoolmaster in a pedantic age, and there is nothing so unclassical – nothing so impure in style – as pedantry. The out-of-door conversational life of Athens was as opposed to bookish scholasticism as a life can be. The most perfect books have been written not by those who thought much of books, but by those who thought little; by those who were under the restraint of a sensitive talking world, to which books had contributed something, and a various eager life the rest. Milton is generally unclassical in spirit where he is learned, and naturally, because the purest poets do not overlay their conceptions with book knowledge, and the classical poets, having in comparison no books, were under less temptation to impair the purity of their style by the accumulation of their research. Over and above this, there is in Milton, and a little in Wordsworth also, one defect which is in the highest degree faulty and unclassical, which mars the effect and impairs the perfection of the pure style. There is a want of *spontaneity*, and a sense of effort. It has been happily said that Plato's words must have *grown* into their places. No one would say so of Milton, or even of Wordsworth. About both of them there is a taint of duty; a vicious sense of the good man's task. Things seem right where they are, but they seem to be put where they are. *Flexibility* is essential to the consummate perfection of the pure style, because the sensation of the poet's efforts carries away our thoughts from his achievements. We are admiring his labours when we should be enjoying his words. But this is a defect in those two writers, not a defect in pure art. Of course it *is* more difficult to write in few words than to write in many; to take the best adjuncts, and those only, for what you have to say, instead of using all which comes to hand; it *is* an additional labour, if you write verses in a morning, to spend the rest of the day in *choosing*, or making those verses fewer. But a perfect artist in the pure style is as effortless and as natural as in any style, perhaps is more so. Take the well-known lines:–

> There was a little lawny islet
> By anemone and violet,
>   Like mosaic, paven:
> And its roof was flowers and leaves
> Which the summer's breath enweaves,
> Where nor sun, nor showers, nor breeze,
> Pierce the pines and tallest trees,
>   Each a gem engraven; –
> Girt by many an azure wave
> With which the clouds and mountains pave
>   A lake's blue chasm.[5]

Shelley had many merits and many defects. This is not the place for a complete, or indeed for *any*, estimate of him. But one excellence is most evident. His words are as flexible as any words; the rhythm of some modulating air seems to move them into their place without a struggle by the poet, and almost without his knowledge. This is the perfection of pure art: to embody typical conceptions in the choicest, the fewest, accidents, to embody them so that each of these accidents may produce its full effect, and so to embody them without effort.

The extreme opposite to this pure art is what may be called ornate art. This species of art aims also at giving a delineation of the typical idea in its perfection and its fulness, but it aims at so doing in a manner most different. It wishes to surround the type with the greatest number of circumstances which it will *bear*. It works not by choice and selection, but by accumulation and aggregation. The idea is not, as in the pure style, presented with the least clothing which it will endure, but with the richest and most involved clothing that it will admit.

We are fortunate in not having to hunt out of past literature an illustrative specimen of the ornate style. Mr. Tennyson has just given one, admirable in itself, and most characteristic of the defects and the merits of this style. The story of *Enoch Arden*, as he has enhanced and presented it, is a rich and splendid composite of imagery and illustration. Yet how simple that story is in itself. A sailor who sells fish, breaks his leg, gets dismal, gives up selling fish, goes to sea, is wrecked on a desert island, stays there some years, on his return finds his wife married to a miller, speaks to a landlady on the subject, and dies. Told in the pure and simple, the unadorned and classical style, this story would not have taken three pages, but Mr. Tennyson has been able to make it the principal, the largest, tale in his new volume. He has done so only by giving to every event and incident in the volume an accompanying commentary. He tells a great deal about the torrid zone which a rough sailor like Enoch Arden certainly would not have perceived; and he gives to the fishing village, to which all the characters belong, a softness and a fascination which such villages scarcely possess in reality.

. . .

The essence of ornate art is in this manner to accumulate round the typical object, everything which can be said about it, every associated thought that can be connected with it, without impairing the essence of the delineation.

The first defect which strikes a student of ornate art – the first which arrests the mere reader of it – is what is called a want of simplicity. Nothing is described as it is, everything has about it an atmosphere of *something else*. The combined and associated thoughts, though they set off and heighten particular ideas and aspects of the central and typical conception, yet complicate it: a simple thing – 'a daisy by the river's brim' – is never left by itself, something else is put with it; something not more connected with it than 'lion-whelp' and the 'peacock yew-tree' are with the 'fresh fish for sale' that Enoch carries past them. Even in the highest cases, ornate art leaves upon a cultured and delicate taste the conviction that it is not the highest art, that it is somehow excessive and overrich, that it is not chaste in itself or chastening to the mind that sees it – that it is in an unexplained manner unsatisfactory, 'a thing in which we feel there is some hidden want!'

That want is a want of 'definition'. We must all know landscapes, river landscapes especially, which are in the highest sense beautiful, which when we first see them give us a delicate pleasure; which in some – and these the best cases – give even a gentle sense of surprise that such things should be so beautiful, and yet when we come to live in them, to spend even a few hours in them, we seem stifled and oppressed. On the other hand, there are people to whom the sea-shore is a companion, an exhilaration; and not so much for the brawl of the shore as for the *limited* vastness, the finite infinite, of the ocean as they see it. Such people often come home braced and nerved, and if they spoke out the truth, would have only to say 'We have seen the horizon line'; if they were let alone, indeed, they would gaze on it hour after hour, so great to them is the fascination, so full the sustaining calm, which they gain from that union of form and greatness. To a very inferior extent, but still, perhaps, to an extent which most people understand better, a common arch will have the same effect. A bridge completes a river landscape; if of the old and many-arched sort, it regulates by a long series of defined forms the vague outline of wood and river which before had nothing to measure it; if of the new scientific sort, it introduces still more strictly a geometrical element; it stiffens the scenery which was before too soft, too delicate, too vegetable. Just such is the effect of pure style in literary art. It calms by conciseness; while the ornate style leaves on the mind a mist of beauty, an excess of fascination, a complication of charm, the pure style leaves behind it the simple, defined, measured idea, as it is, and by itself. That which is chaste chastens; there is a poised energy – a state half thrill, and half tranquillity – which pure art gives; which no other can give; a pleasure justified as well as felt; an ennobled satisfaction at what ought to satisfy us, and must ennoble us.

Ornate art is to pure art what a painted statue is to an unpainted. It is impossible to deny that a touch of colour *does* bring out certain parts, does convey certain expressions, does heighten certain features, but it leaves on the work as a whole, a want, as we say, 'of something'; a want of that inseparable chasteness which clings to simple sculpture, an impairing predominance of alluring details which impairs our satisfaction with our own satisfaction; which makes us doubt whether a higher being than ourselves will be satisfied even though we are so. In the same manner, though the *rouge* of ornate literature excites our eye, it also impairs our confidence.

Mr. Arnold has justly observed that this self-justifying, self-*proving* purity of style is commoner in ancient literature than in modern literature, and also that Shakespeare is not a great or an unmixed example of it.[6] No one can say that he is. His works are full of undergrowth, are full of complexity, are not models of style; except by a miracle nothing in the Elizabethan could be a model of style; the restraining taste of that age was feebler and more mistaken than that of any other equally great age. Shakespeare's mind so teemed with creation that he required the most just, most forcible, most constant restraint from without. Of poets he most needed to be guided, and he was the least and worst guided. As a whole, no one can call his works finished models of the pure style, or of any style. But he has many passages of the most pure style, passages which could be easily cited if space served. And we must remember that the task which Shakespeare undertook was the most difficult which any poet has ever attempted, and that it is a task in which after a million efforts every other poet has failed. The Elizabethan drama – as Shakespeare has immortalised it – undertakes to delineate in five acts, under stage restrictions, and in mere dialogue, a whole list of *dramatis personæ*, a set of characters enough for a modern novel, and with the distinctness of a modern novel. Shakespeare is not content to give two or three great characters in solitude and dignity, like the classical dramatists; he wishes to give a whole *party* of characters in the play of life, and according to the nature of each. He would 'hold the mirror up to nature,' not to catch a monarch in a tragic posture, but a whole group of characters engaged in many actions, intent on many purposes, thinking many thoughts. There is life enough, there is action enough, in single plays of Shakespeare to set up an ancient dramatist for a long career. And Shakespeare succeeded. His characters, taken *en masse*, and as a whole, are as well known as any novelist's characters; cultivated men know all about them, as young ladies know all about Mr. Trollope's novels. But no other dramatist has succeeded in such an aim. No one else's characters are staple people in English literature, hereditary people whom everyone knows all about in every generation. The contemporary dramatists, Beaumont and Fletcher, Ben Jonson, Marlowe, &c., had many merits, some of them were great men. But a critic must say of them the worst thing he has to say: 'They were men who failed in their characteristic aim'; they attempted to describe numerous sets of complicated characters, and they failed.

No one of such characters, or hardly one, lives in common memory; the 'Faustus' of Marlowe, a really great idea, is not remembered. They undertook to write what they could not write, five acts full of real characters, and in consequence, the fine individual things they conceived are forgotten by the mixed multitude, and known only to a few of the few. Of the Spanish theatre we cannot speak; but there are no such characters in any French tragedy: the whole aim of that tragedy forbad it. Goethe has added to literature a few great characters; he may be said almost to have added to literature the idea of 'intellectual creation', – the idea of describing great characters through the intellect; but he has not added to the common stock what Shakespeare added, a new *multitude* of men and women; and these not in simple attitudes, but amid the most complex parts of life, with all their various natures roused, mixed, and strained. The severest art must have allowed many details, much overflowing circumstance, to a poet who undertook to describe what almost defies description. Pure art would have *commanded* him to use details lavishly, for only by a multiplicity of such could the required effect have been at all produced. Shakespeare could accomplish it, for his mind was a *spring*, an inexhaustible fountain of human nature; and it is no wonder that being compelled by the task of his time to let the fulness of his nature overflow, he sometimes let it overflow too much, and covered with erroneous conceits and superfluous images characters and conceptions which would have been far more justly, far more effectually, delineated with conciseness and simplicity. But there is an infinity of pure art *in* Shakespeare although there is a great deal else also.

It will be said, if ornate art be, as you say, an inferior species of art, why should it ever be used? If pure art be the best sort of art, why should it not always be used?

The reason is this: literary art, as we just now explained, is concerned with literatesque characters in literatesque situations; and the best art is concerned with the *most* literatesque characters in the *most* literatesque situations. Such are the subjects of pure art; it embodies with the fewest touches, and under the most select and choice circumstances, the highest conceptions; but it does not follow that only the best subjects are to be treated by art, and then only in the very best way. Human nature could not endure such a critical commandment as that, and it would be an erroneous criticism which gave it. *Any* literatesque character may be described in literature under *any* circumstances which exhibit its literatesqueness.

The essence of pure art consists in its describing what is as it is, and that is very well for what can bear it; but there are many inferior things which will not bear it, and which nevertheless ought to be described in books. A certain kind of literature deals with illusions, and this kind of literature has given a colouring to the name romantic.

. . .

For these reasons ornate art is within the limits as legitimate as pure art. It does what pure art could not do. The very excellence of pure art confines its employment. Precisely because it gives the best things by themselves and exactly as they are, it fails when it is necessary to describe inferior things among other things, with a list of enhancements and a crowd of accompaniments that in reality do not belong to it. Illusion, half belief, unpleasant types, imperfect types, are as much the proper sphere of ornate art, as an inferior landscape is the proper sphere for the true efficacy of moonlight. A really great landscape needs sunlight and bears sunlight; but moonlight is an equaliser of beauties, it gives a romantic unreality to what will not stand the bare truth. And just so does romantic art.

There is, however, a third kind of art which differs from these on the point in which they most resemble one another. Ornate art and pure art have this in common, that they paint the types of literature in as good perfection as they can. Ornate art, indeed, uses undue disguises and unreal enhancements; it does not confine itself to the best types; on the contrary it is its office to make the best of imperfect types and lame approximations; but ornate art, as much as pure art, catches its subject in the best light it can, takes the most developed aspect of it which it can find, and throws upon it the most congruous colours it can use. But grotesque art does just the contrary. It takes the type, so to say, in *difficulties*. It gives a representation of it in its minimum development, amid the circumstances least favourable to it, just while it is struggling with obstacles, just where it is encumbered with incongruities. It deals, to use the language of science, not with normal types but with abnormal specimens; to use the language of old philosophy, not with what nature is striving to be, but with what by some lapse she has happened to become.

Thus art works by contrast. It enables you to see, it makes you see, the perfect type by painting the opposite deviation. It shows you what ought to be by what ought not to be; when complete, it reminds you of the perfect image by showing you the distorted and imperfect image. Of this art we possess in the present generation one prolific writer. Mr. Browning is an artist working by incongruity. Possibly hardly one of his most considerable efforts can be found which is not great because of its odd mixture. He puts together things which no one else would have put together, and produces on our minds a result which no one else would have produced, or tried to produce. His admirers may not like all we may have to say of him. But in our way we too are among his admirers. No one ever read him without seeing not only his great ability but his great *mind*. He not only possesses superficial useable talents, but the strong something, the inner secret something, which uses them and controls them; he is great, not in mere accomplishments, but in himself. He has applied a hard strong intellect to real life; he has applied the same intellect to the problems of his age. He has striven to know what *is*: he has endeavoured not to be cheated by counterfeits, to be infatuated with illusions. His heart is in what he says. He has battered his brain against his creed till he believes it.

. . .

Something more we had to say of Mr. Browning, but we must stop. It is singularly characteristic of this age that the poems which rise to the surface should be examples of ornate art and grotesque art, not of pure art. We live in the realm of the *half* educated. The number of readers grows daily, but the quality of readers does not improve rapidly. The middle class is scattered, headless; it is well-meaning, but aimless; wishing to be wise, but ignorant how to be wise. The aristocracy of England never was a literary aristocracy, never even in the days of its full power, of its unquestioned predominance, did it guide – did it even seriously try to guide – the taste of England. Without guidance young men, and tired men, are thrown amongst a mass of books; they have to choose which they like; many of them would much like to improve their culture, to chasten their taste, if they knew how. But left to themselves they take, not pure art, but showy art; not that which permanently relieves the eye and makes it happy whenever it looks, and as long as it looks, but *glaring* art which catches and arrests the eye for a moment, but which in the end fatigues it. But before the wholesome remedy of nature – the fatigue – arrives the hasty reader has passed on to some new excitement, which in its turn stimulates for an instant, and then is passed by for ever. These conditions are not favourable to the due appreciation of pure art – of that art which must be known before it is admired – which must have fastened irrevocably on the brain before you appreciate it – which you must love ere it will seem worthy of your love. Women, too, whose voice in literature counts as well as that of men – and in a light literature counts for more than that of men – women, such as we know them, such as they are likely to be, ever prefer a delicate unreality to a true or firm art. A dressy literature, an exaggerated literature, seem to be fated to us. These are our curses, as other times had theirs.

And yet
Think not the living times forget.
Ages of heroes fought and fell
That Homer in the end might tell;
O'er grovelling generations past
Upstood the Doric fane at last;
And countless hearts in countless years
Had wasted thoughts, and hopes, and fears,
Rude laughter and unmeaning tears,
Ere England Shakespeare saw, or Rome
The pure perfection of her dome.
Others, I doubt not, if not we,
The issue of our toils shall see;
And (they forgotten and unknown)
Young children gather as their own
The harvest that the dead had sown,
The dead forgotten and unknown.

1 Bagehot has been arguing for the usefulness of a term in relation to literature equivalent to picturesque in relation to painting.
2 Defoe's *True Relation of the Apparition of One Mrs Veal* (1714) is written in down-to-earth language to confirm the credibility of this account.
3 Poems by Tennyson, both based on stories of Suffolk life.
4 Bagehot quotes 'The Trossachs' and 'Composed upon Westminster Bridge, Sept. 3, 1802'.
5 An untitled lyric by Shelley, first published by Mary Shelley in *Posthumous Poems* (1824).
6 See No. 20 above.

ALGERNON CHARLES SWINBURNE

Swinburne (1837–1909) was the most flamboyant of the second generation of Victorian poets. His *Poems and Ballads* (1866) aroused a good deal of controversy because of its unconventional and subversive qualities. Swinburne also wrote criticism which defended the freedom of the poet to write on whatever subject-matter attracted him.

32 From a review of Baudelaire, 1862

[This extract is from 'Charles Baudelaire: *Les Fleurs du Mal*' in *The Spectator*, 6 Sept. 1862.]

It is now some time since France has turned out any new poet of very high note or importance; the graceful, slight, somewhat thin-spun classical work of M. Théodore de Banville[1] hardly carries weight enough to tell across the Channel; indeed, the best of this writer's books, in spite of exquisite humorous character and a most flexible and brilliant style, is too thoroughly Parisian to bear transplanting at all. French poetry of the present date, taken at its highest, is not less effectually hampered by tradition and the taste of the greater number of readers than our own is. A French poet is expected to believe in philanthropy, and break off on occasion in the middle of his proper work to lend a shove forward to some theory of progress. The critical students there, as well as here, judging by the books they praise and the advice they proffer, seem to have pretty well forgotten that a poet's business is presumably to write good verses, and by no means to redeem the age and remould society. No other form of art is so pestered with this impotent appetite for meddling in quite extraneous matters; but the mass of readers seem actually to think that a poem is the better for containing a moral lesson or assisting in a tangible and material good work. The courage and sense of a man who at such a time ventures to profess and act on the conviction that the art of poetry has absolutely nothing to do with didactic matter at all, are proof enough of the wise and serious manner in which he is likely to handle the materials of his art. From a critic who has put forward the just and sane view of this matter with a consistent eloquence, one may well expect to get as perfect and careful poetry as he can give.

To some English readers the name of M. Baudelaire[2] may be known rather through his admirable translations, and the criticisms on American and English writers appended to these, and framing them in fit and sufficient commentary, than by his volume of poems, which, perhaps, has hardly yet had time to make its way among us. That it will in the long run fail of its meed of admiration, whether here or in France, we do not believe. Impeded at starting by a foolish and shameless prosecution, the first edition was, it appears, withdrawn before anything like a fair hearing had been obtained for it. The book now comes before us with a few of the original poems cancelled, but with important additions. Such as it now is, to sum up the merit and meaning of it is not easy to do in a few sentences. Like all good books, and all work of any original savour and strength, it will be long a debated point of argument, vehemently impugned and eagerly upheld.

We believe that M. Baudelaire's first publications were his essays on the contemporary art of France, written now many years since.[3] In these early writings there is already such admirable judgment, vigour of thought and style, and appreciative devotion to the subject, that the worth of his own future work in art might have been foretold even then. He has more delicate power of verse than almost any man living, after Victor Hugo,[4] Browning, and (in his lyrics)

Tennyson. The sound of his metres suggests colour and perfume. His perfect workmanship makes every subject admirable and respectable. Throughout the chief part of this book, he has chosen to dwell mainly upon sad and strange things – the weariness of pain and the bitterness of pleasure – the perverse happiness and wayward sorrows of exceptional people. It has the languid lurid beauty of close and threatening weather – a heavy heated temperature, with dangerous hothouse scents in it; thick shadow of cloud about it, and fire of molten light. It is quite clear of all whining and windy lamentation; there is nothing of the blubbering and shrieking style long since exploded. The writer delights in problems, and has a natural leaning to obscure and sorrowful things. Failure and sorrow, next to physical beauty and pefection of sound or scent, seem to have an infinite attraction for him. In some points he resembles Keats, or still more his chosen favourite among modern poets, Edgar Poe,[5] at times, too, his manner of thought has a relish of Marlowe, and even the sincerer side of Byron. From Théophile Gautier,[6] to whom the book is dedicated, he has caught the habit of a faultless and studious simplicity; but, indeed, it seems merely natural to him always to use the right word and the right rhyme. How supremely musical and flexible a perfect artist in writing can make the French language, any chance page of the book is enough to prove; every description, the slightest and shortest even, has a special mark on it of the writer's keen and peculiar power. The style is sensuous and weighty; the sights seen are steeped most often in sad light and sullen colour.

. . .

M. Baudelaire's mastery of the sonnet form is worth remarking as a test of his natural bias towards such forms of verse as are most nearly capable of perfection. In a book of this sort, such a leaning of the writer's mind is almost necessary. The matters treated of will bear no rough or hasty handling. Only supreme excellence of words will suffice to grapple with and fitly render the effects of such material. Not the luxuries of pleasure in their simple first form, but the sharp and cruel enjoyments of pain, the acrid relish of suffering felt or inflicted, the sides on which nature looks unnatural, go to make up the stuff and substance of this poetry. Very good material they make, too; but evidently such things are unfit for rapid or careless treatment. The main charm of the book is, upon the whole, that nothing is wrongly given, nothing capable of being re-written or improved on its own ground. Concede the starting point, and you cannot have a better runner.

1   (1823–91), lyric poet, author of *Odes funambulesques* (1857).
2   Charles Baudelaire (1821–67), the great French poet, published *Les Fleurs du Mal* (Flowers of Evil) in 1857, when it was prosecuted for indecency. He had previously translated a number of English and American writers, including Edgar Allan Poe.
3   Though only published posthumously in book form as *L'Art romantique* (1868).
4   (1802–85), leading French Romantic poet, playwright and novelist.
5   Edgar Allan Poe (1804–49), the American writer.
6   (1811–72), French poet and critic, whose *Emaux et Camées* had appeared in 1852.

33 From *Notes on Poems and Reviews*, 1866

[In this short book Swinburne replied to the critics who had accused *Poems and Ballads* of indecency (see No. 34).]

To all this, however, there is a grave side. The question at issue is wider than any between a single writer and his critics, or it might well be allowed to drop. It is this: whether or not the first and last requisite of art is to give no offence, whether or not all that cannot be lisped in the nursery or fingered in the schoolroom is therefore to be cast out of the library; whether or not the domestic circle is to be for all men and writers the outer limit and extreme horizon of their world of work. For to this we have come; and all students of art must face the matter as it stands. Who has not heard it asked, in a final and triumphant tone, whether this book or that can be read aloud by her mother to a young girl? Whether such and such a picture can properly be exposed to the eyes of young persons? If you reply that this is nothing to the point, you fall at once into the ranks of the immoral. Never till now, and nowhere but in England, could so monstrous an absurdity rear for one moment its deformed and eyeless head. In no past century were artists ever bidden to work on these terms; nor are they now, except among us. The disease, of course, afflicts the meanest members of the body with most virulence. Nowhere is cant at once so foul-mouthed and so tight-laced as in the penny, twopenny, threepenny, or sixpenny press. Nothing is so favourable to the undergrowth of real indecency as this overshadowing foliage of fictions, this artificial network of proprieties. *L'Arioste rit au soleil, l'Aretin ricane a l'ombre.*[1] The whiter the sepulchre without, the ranker the rottenness within. Every touch of plaster is a sign of advancing decay. The virtue of our critical journals is a dowager of somewhat dubious antecedents: every day that thins and shrivels her cheek thickens and hardens the paint on it; she consumes more chalk and ceruse than would serve a whole courtful of crones. 'It is to be presumed', certainly, that in her case 'all is not sweet, all is not sound'.[2] The taint on her fly-blown reputation is hard to overcome by patches and perfumery. Literature, to be worthy of men, must be large, liberal, sincere; and cannot be chaste if it be prudish. Purity and prudery cannot keep house together. Where free speech and fair play are interdicted, foul hints and vile suggestions are hatched into fetid life. And if literature indeed is not to deal with the full life of man and the whole nature of things, let it be cast aside with the rods and rattles of childhood. Whether it affect to teach or to amuse, it is equally trivial and contemptible to us; only less so than the charge of immorality. Against how few really great names has not this small and dirt-encrusted pebble been thrown! A reputation seems imperfect without this tribute also: one jewel is wanting to the crown. It is good to be praised by those whom all men should praise; it is better to be reviled by those whom all men should scorn.

1 'Ariosto laughs in the sun; the Aretine sniggers in the shade.'
   Ludovico Ariosto (1474–1533) wrote the romantic epic *Orlando Furioso*; Pietro Aretino (1542–1566) wrote licentious comedies and satires.
2 Ben Jonson, *Epicoene, or The Silent Woman* (1609–10), I, i, 92.

JOHN MORLEY

Morley (1838–1923) was a Liberal writer and politician. He edited the *Fortnightly Review* from 1867 to 1882, and published books on Burke (1867), Voltaire (1872), Rousseau (1873) and, later, Gladstone (1903). His review of Swinburne's *Poems and Ballads*, 'Mr. Swinburne's New Poems', in the *Saturday Review*, 4 Aug. 1866, prompted the poet to reply (No. 33).

34 From 'Mr Swinburne's New Poems', 1866

It is a mere waste of time, and shows a curiously mistaken conception of human character, to blame an artist of any kind for working at a certain set of subjects rather than at some other set which the critic may happen to prefer. An artist, at all events an artist of such power and individuality as Mr Swinburne, works as his character compels him. If the character of his genius drives him pretty exclusively in the direction of libidinous song, we may be very sorry, but is of no use to advise him and to preach to him. What comes of discoursing to a fiery tropical flower of the pleasant fragrance of the rose or the fruitfulness of the fig-tree? Mr Swinburne is much too stoutly bent on taking his own course to pay any attention to critical monitions as to the duty of the poet, or any warnings of the worse than barrenness of the field in which he has chosen to labour. He is so firmly and avowedly fixed in an attitude of revolt against the current notions of decency and dignity and social

duty that to beg of him to become a little more decent, to fly
a little less persistently and gleefully to the animal side of
human nature, is simply to beg him to be something different from Mr Swinburne. It is a kind of protest which his
whole position makes it impossible for him to receive with
anything but laughter and contempt. A rebel of his calibre is
not to be brought to a better mind by solemn little sermons
on the loyalty which a man owes to virtue. His warmest
prayer to the gods is that they should

> Come down and redeem us from virtue.

His warmest hope for men is that they should change

> The lilies and languors of virtue
> For the raptures and roses of vice.[1]

It is of no use, therefore, to scold Mr Swinburne for
grovelling down among the nameless shameless abomina-
tions which inspire him with such frenzied delight. They
excite his imagination to its most vigorous efforts, they seem
to him the themes most proper for poetic treatment, and
they suggest ideas which, in his opinion, it is highly to be
wished that English men and women should brood upon and
make their own. He finds that these fleshly things are his
strong part, so he sticks to them. Is it wonderful that he
should? And at all events he deserves credit for the auda-
cious courage with which he has revealed to the world a
mind all aflame with the feverish carnality of a schoolboy
over the dirtiest passages in Lemprière.[2] It is not every poet
who would ask us all to go hear him tuning his lyre in a stye.
It is not everybody who would care to let the world know
that he found the most delicious food for poetic reflection in
the practices of the great island of the Ægean, in the habits
of Messalina,[3] of Faustina,[4] of Pasiphaë.[5] Yet these make up
Mr Swinburne's version of the dreams of fair women, and he
would scorn to throw any veil over pictures which kindle, as
these do, all the fires of his imagination in their intensest
heat and glow. It is not merely 'the noble, the nude, the
antique' which he strives to reproduce. If he were a rebel

against the fat-headed Philistines and poor-blooded Puritans who insist that all poetry should be such as may be wisely placed in the hands of girls of eighteen, and is fit for the use of Sunday schools, he would have all wise and enlarged readers on his side. But there is an enormous difference between an attempt to revivify among us the grand old pagan conceptions of Joy, and attempt to glorify all the bestial delights that the subtleness of Greek depravity was able to contrive. It is a good thing to vindicate passion, and the strong and large and rightful pleasure of sense, against the narrow and inhuman tyranny of shrivelled anchorities. It is a very bad and silly thing to try to set up the pleasures of sense in the seat of the reason they have dethroned. And no language is too strong to condemn the mixed vileness and childishness of depicting the spurious passion of a putrescent imagination, the unnamed lusts of sated wantons, as if they were the crown of character and their enjoyment the great glory of human life. The only comfort about the present volume is that such a piece as 'Anactoria' will be unintelligible to a great many people, and so will the fevered folly of 'Hermaphroditus', as well as much else that is nameless and abominable. Perhaps if Mr Swinburne can a second and third time find a respectable publisher willing to issue a volume of the same stamp, crammed with pieces which many a professional vendor of filthy prints might blush to sell if he only knew what they meant, English readers will gradually acquire a truly delightful familiarity with these unspeakable foulnesses; and a lover will be able to present to his mistress a copy of Mr Swinburne's latest verses with a happy confidence that she will have no difficulty in seeing the point of every allusion to Sappho[6] or the pleasing Hermaphroditus,[7] or the embodiment of anything else that is loathsome and horrible. It will be very charming to hear a drawing-room discussion on such verses as these, for example:

> Stray breaths of Sapphic song that blew
> Through Mitylene

> Shook the fierce quivering blood in you
>   By night, Faustine.
> The shameless nameless love that makes
>   Hell's iron gin
>
> Shut on you like a trap that breaks
>   The soul, Faustine.
> And when your veins were void and dead,
>   What ghosts unclean
> Swarmed round the straitened barren bed
>   That hid Faustine?
> What sterile growths of sexless root
>   Or epicene?
> What flower of kisses without fruit
>   Of love, Faustine?

We should be sorry to be guilty of anything so offensive to Mr Swinburne as we are quite sure an appeal to the morality of all the wisest and best men would be. The passionate votary of the goddess whom he hails as 'Daughter of Death and Priapus'[8] has got too high for this. But it may be presumed that common sense is not too insulting a standard by which to measure the worth and place of his new volume. Starting from this sufficiently modest point, we may ask him whether there is really nothing in woman worth singing about except 'quivering flanks' and 'splendid supple thighs', 'hot sweet throats' and 'hotter hands than fire', and their blood as 'hot wan wine of love'? Is purity to be expunged from the catalogue of desirable qualities? Does a poet show respect to his own genius by gloating, as Mr Swinburne does, page after page and poem after poem, upon a single subject, and that subject kept steadily in a single light? Are we to believe that having exhausted hot lustfulness, and wearied the reader with a luscious and nauseating iteration of the same fervid scenes and fervid ideas, he has got to the end of his tether?

1 From the poem 'Dolores'.
2 John Lemprière (d. 1824) produced the *Bibliotheca Classica* (1788), which became the standard Classical dictionary.

3 Messalina, wife of the Roman Emperor Claudius, was put to death in AD 48 for her profligate behaviour.

4 Faustina, wife of the Emperor Autoninus Pius, who died in AD 141, was noted for her immorality.

5 Pasiphaë, wife of Minos, who became enamoured of a bull and gave birth to the monster Minotaur.

6 Sappho, the Greek lyric poet of Lesbos in the seventh century BC, who was associated with the idea of Lesbian love.

7 Hermaphroditus, the son of Hermes and Aphrodite, was loved by the nymph Salmacis who was made one body with him by the gods.

8 Priapus, a fertility god, son of Dionysus and Aphrodite.

WALTER PATER

Pater (1839–94) was the critic responsible for promulgating the new aesthetic ideas of the later Victorian period. A Fellow of Brasenose College, Oxford, he began his critical career with an article on the German art historian, Winkelmann, in the *Westminster Review* in 1867. His review of Morris's *The Defence of Guenevere* (1858), *The Life and Death of Jason* (1867) and *The Earthly Paradise*, Part I (1868) appeared in the *Westminster Review*, XC, N.S. XXXIV, 1868, 300–12. The final section was used as the Conclusion to *The Renaissance* (1873), the book which made Pater's reputation as the exponent of new critical ideas; a revised version of the early part of the review appeared in the first (but no later) edition of *Appreciations* (1889) as 'Aesthetic Poetry'. In it Pater relates Morris's poetry to the general poetic developments of the period.

35 From 'Poems by William Morris', 1868

This poetry is neither a mere reproduction of Greek or mediaeval life or poetry, nor a disguised reflex of modern sentiment. The atmosphere on which its effect depends belongs to no actual form of life or simple form of poetry. Greek poetry, mediaeval or modern poetry, projects above the realities of its time a world in which the forms of things are transfigured. Of that world this new poetry takes possession, and sublimates beyond it another still fainter and more spectral, which is literally an artificial or 'earthly paradise'. It is a finer ideal, extracted from what in relation to any actual world is already an ideal. Like some strange second flowering after date, it renews on a more delicate type the poetry of a past age, but must not be confounded with it. The secret of the enjoyment of it is that inversion of home-sickness known to some, that incurable thirst for the sense of escape, which no actual form of life satisfies, no poetry even, if it be merely simple and spontaneous. It is this which in these poems defines the temperament or personality of the workman.

The writings of the romantic school mark a transition not so much from the pagan to the mediaeval ideal, as from a lower to a higher degree of passion in literature. The end of the eighteenth century, swept by vast disturbing currents, experienced an excitement of spirit of which one note was a reaction against an outworn classicalism severed not more from nature than from the genuine motives of ancient art; and a return to true Hellenism was as much a part of this reaction as the sudden pre-occupation with things mediaeval. The mediaeval tendency is in Goethe's *Goetz von Berlichingen*,[1] the Hellenic in his *Iphigenie*.[2] At first this mediaevalism was superficial. Adventure, romance in the poorest sense, grotesque individualism – that is one element in mediaeval poetry, and with it alone Scott and Goethe dealt. Beyond them were the two other elements of the mediaeval spirit; its mystic religion at its apex in Dante and Saint Louis, and its mystic passion, passing here and there into the great romantic loves of rebellious flesh, of Lancelot and Abelard. That stricter, imaginative mediaevalism which recreates the mind of the middle age, so that the form, the presentment grows outward from within, came later with Victor Hugo in France, with Heine in Germany.

The *Defence of Guenevere: and Other Poems*, published ten years ago, are a refinement upon this later, profounder mediaevalism. The poem which gives its name to the volume is a thing tormented and awry with passion, like the body of Guenevere defending herself from the charge of adultery, and the accent falls in strange, unwonted places with the

effect of a great cry. These Arthurian legends, pre-Christian
in their origin, yield all their sweeetness only in a Christian
atmosphere. What is characteristic in them is the strange
suggestion of a deliberate choice between Christ and a rival
lover. That religion shades into sensuous love, and sensuous
love into religion, has been often seen; it is the experience of
Rousseau as well as of the Christian mystics. The Christianity
of the middle age made way among a people whose loss was
in the life of the senses only by the possession of an idol, the
beautiful idol of the Latin hymn-writers, who for one moral
or spiritual sentiment have a hundred sensuous images. Only
by the inflaming influence of such idols can any religion
compete with the presence of the fleshly lover. And so in
these imaginative loves, in their highest expression the
Provençal poetry, it is a rival religion with a new rival cultus
that we see. Coloured through and through with Christian
sentiment, they are rebels against it. The rejection of one
idolatry for the other is never lost sight of. The jealousy of
that other lover, for whom these words and images and
strange ways of sentiment were first devised, is the secret
here of a triumphant colour and heat. It is the mood of the
cloister taking a new direction, and winning so a later space
of life it never anticipated. Who knows whether, when the
simple belief in them has faded away, the most cherished
sacred writings may not for the first time exercise their
highest influence as the most delicate amorous poetry in the
world?

. . .

One characteristic of the pagan spirit these new poems
have which is on their surface – the continual suggestion,
pensive or passionate, of the shortness of life; this is
contrasted with the bloom of the world and gives new
seduction to it; the sense of death and the desire of beauty;
the desire of beauty quickened by the sense of death.
'*Arrière!*' you say, 'here in a tangible form we have the
defect of all poetry like this. The modern world is in

possession of truths; what but a passing smile can it have for
a kind of poetry which, assuming artistic beauty of form
to be an end in itself, passes by those truths and the living
interests which are connected with them, to spend a thousand cares in telling once more these pagan fables as if it had
but to choose between a more and a less beautiful shadow?'
It is a strange transition from the earthly paradise to the sad-
coloured world of abstract philosophy. But let us accept the
challenge; let us see what modern philosophy, when it is
sincere, really does say about human life and the truth we
can attain in it, and the relation of this to the desire of
beauty.

To regard all things and principles of things as inconstant
modes or fashions has more and more become the tendency
of modern thought. Let us begin with that which is without,
– our physical life. Fix upon it in one of its more exquisite
intervals – the moment, for instance, of delicious recoil from
the flood of water in summer heat. What is the whole
physical life in that moment but a combination of natural
elements to which science gives their names? But those
elements, phosphorus and lime, and delicate fibres, are
present not in the human body alone; we detect them in
places most remote from it. Our physical life is a perpetual
motion of them – the passage of the blood, the wasting and
repairing of the lenses of the eye, the modification of the
tissues of the brain by every ray of light and sound –
processes which science reduces to simpler and more elementary forces. Like the elements of which we are composed, the action of these forces extends beyond us; it rusts
iron and ripens corn. Far out on every side of us these
elements are broadcast, driven by many forces; and birth
and gesture and death and the springing of violets from
the grave are but a few out of ten thousand resulting
combinations. That clear, perpetual outline of face and limb
is but an image of ours under which we group them – a
design in a web the actual threads of which pass out beyond
it. This at least of flame-like our life has, that it is but the

concurrence renewed from moment to moment of forces parting sooner or later on their ways.

Or if we begin with the inward world of thought and feeling, the whirlpool is still more rapid, the flame more eager and devouring. There is no longer the gradual darkening of the eye and fading of colour from the wall, the movement of the shore side, where the water flows down indeed, though in apparent rest, but the race of the midstream, a drift of momentary acts of sight and passion and thought. At first sight experience seems to bury us under a flood of external objects, pressing upon us with a sharp, importunate reality, calling us out of ourselves in a thousand forms of action. But when reflection begins to act upon those objects they are dissipated under its infuence, the cohesive force is suspended like a trick of magic, each object is loosed into a group of impressions, colour, odour, texture, in the mind of the observer. And if we continue to dwell on this world, not of objects in the solidity with which language invests them, but of impressions unstable, flickering, inconsistent, which burn, and are extinguished with our consciousness of them, it contracts still further, the whole scope of observation is dwarfed to the narrow chamber of the individual mind. Experience, already reduced to a swarm of impressions, is ringed round for each one of us by that thick wall of personality through which no real voice has ever pierced on its way to us, or from us to that, which we can only conjecture to be without. Every one of those impressions is the impression of an individual in his isolation, each mind keeping as a solitary prisoner its own dream of a world.

Analysis goes a step further still, and tells us that those impressions of the individual to which, for each one of us, experience dwindles down, are in perpetual flight; that each of them is limited by time, and that as time is infinitely divisible, each of them is infinitely divisible also, all that is actual in it being a single moment, gone while we try to apprehend it, of which it may ever be more truly said that it has ceased to be than it is. To such a tremulous wisp constantly reforming itself on the stream, to a single sharp impression, with a sense in it, a relic more or less fleeting, of such moments gone by, what is real in our life fines itself down. It is with the movement, the passage and dissolution of impressions, images, sensations, that analysis leaves off, that continual vanishing away, that strange perpetual weaving and unweaving of ourselves.

Such thoughts seem desolate at first; at times all the bitterness of life seems concentrated in them. They bring the image of one washed out beyond the bar in a sea at ebb, losing even his personality, as the elements of which he is composed pass into new combinations. Struggling, as he must, to save himself, it is himself that he loses at every moment.

Philosophiren, says Novalis, *ist dephlegmatisiren, vivificiren.*[3] The service of philosophy, and of religion and culture as well, to the human spirit, is to startle it into a sharp and eager observation. Every moment some form grows perfect in hand or face; some tone on the hills or sea is choicer than the rest; some mood of passion or insight or intellectual excitement is irresistibly real and attractive for us for that moment only. Not the fruit of experience but experience itself is the end. A counted number of pulses only is given to us of a variegated, dramatic life. How may we see in them all that is to be seen in them by the finest senses? How can we pass most swiftly from point to point, and be present always at the focus where the greatest number of vital forces unite in their purest energy?

To burn always with this hard gem-like flame, to maintain this ecstasy, is success in life. Failure is to form habits; for habit is relative to a stereotyped world; meantime it is only the roughness of the eye that makes any two things, persons, situations – seem alike. While all melts under our feet, we may well catch at any exquisite passion, or any contribution to knowledge that seems by a lifted horizon to set the spirit free for a moment, or any stirring of the senses, strange dyes, strange flowers and curious odours, or work of the artist's hands, or the face of one's friend. Not to discriminate every moment some passionate attitude in those about us

and in the brilliance of their gifts some tragic dividing of
forces on their ways, is on this short day of frost and sun to
sleep before evening. With this sense of the splendour of our
experience and of its awful brevity, gathering all we are into
one desperate effort to see and touch, we shall hardly have
time to make theories about the things we see and touch.
What we have to do is to be for ever curiously testing
opinion and courting new impressions, never acquiescing in
a facile orthodoxy of Comte or of Hegel or of our own.
Theories, religious or philosophical ideas, as points of view,
instruments of criticism, may help us to gather up what
might otherwise pass unregarded by us. '*La philosophie*,'
says Victor Hugo, '*c'est le microscope de la pensée*.'[4] The
theory or idea or system which requires of us the sacrifice of
any part of this experience, in consideration of some interest
into which we cannot enter, or some abstract morality we
have not identified with ourselves, or what is only conventional, has no real claim upon us.

One of the most beautiful places in the writings of
Rousseau is that in the sixth book of the *Confessions*, where
he describes the awakening in him of the literary sense. An
undefinable taint of death had always clung about him, and
now in early manhood he believed himself stricken by
mortal disease. He asked himself how he might make as
much as possible of the interval that remained; and he was
not biassed by anything in his previous life when he decided
that it must be by intellectual excitement, which he found in
the clear, fresh writings of Voltaire. Well, we are all
condamnés,[5] as Victor Hugo somewhere says: we have an
interval and then we cease to be. Some spend this interval in
listlessness, some in high passions, the wisest in art and song.
For our one chance is in expanding the interval, in getting as
many pulsations as possible into the given time. High
passions give one this quickened sense of life, ecstasy and
sorrow of love, political or religious enthusiasm, or the
'enthusiasm of humanity'. Only, be sure it is passion, that
it does yield you this fruit of a quickened, multiplied
consciousness. Of this wisdom, the poetic passion, the desire

of beauty, the love of art for art's sake, has most; for art comes to you professing frankly to give nothing but the highest quality to your moments as they pass, and simply for those moments' sake.

1 (1771), dealing with a sixteenth-century German knight.
2 *Iphigenie auf Tauris* (1787), an adaptation of the Greek play by Euripides.
3 'To philosophize is to get rid of apathy, to vivify.' Novalis was the pseudonym of the German Romantic poet and novelist Friedrich Leopold von Hardenberg (1772–1801).
4 'Philosophy is the microscope of thought.'
5 Condemned (to death).

FURTHER READING

Apart from works referred to in the headnotes to the material in this anthology, the following books contain much useful material:

Isobel Armstrong, *Victorian Scrutinies. Reviews of Poetry 1830–1870* (1972)

Joseph Bristow, *The Victorian Poet: Poetics and Personae* (1987)

E. M. Eigner and S. J. Worth, eds., *Victorian Criticism of the Novel* (1985)

Kenneth Graham, *English Criticism of the Novel 1865–1900* (1965)

Richard Stang, *The Theory of the Novel in England 1850–70* (1959)

Alba H. Warren, *English Poetic Theory 1825–65* (1950)

The appropriate volumes of the Routledge Critical Heritage series contain good selections of contemporary criticism:

Arnold: Poetry, ed. C. Dawson (1977)

Arnold: Prose Writings, eds. C. Dawson and J. Pfordresher (1979)

The Brontës, ed. Miriam Allott (1974)

Browning, eds. B. Litzenger and D. Smalley (1970)

Dickens, ed. P. Collins (1971)

George Eliot, ed. D. Carroll (1971)

Tennyson, ed. J. D. Jump (1967)

Thackeray, eds. G. Tillotson and D. Hawes (1968)

Trollope, ed. D. Smalley (1969)

INDEX

(**Bold type** indicates anthologized material)